On the Performance of Web Services

Zahir Tari • Ann Khoi Anh Phan • Malith
Jayasinghe • Vidura Gamini Abhaya

On the Performance
of Web Services

 Springer

Zahir Tari
School of Computer Science and
Information Technology
RMIT University
Melbourne Victoria
Australia
zahir.tari@rmit.edu.au

Ann Khoi Anh Phan
Macquarie University
North Ryde New South Wales
Australia
ann.phan@mq.edu.au

Malith Jayasinghe
School of Computer Science and IT
RMIT University
Melbourne Victoria
Australia
mjayasin@cs.rmit.edu.au

Vidura Gamini Abhaya
School of Computer Science and IT
RMIT University
Melbourne Victoria
Australia
vidura.abhaya@rmit.edu.au

ISBN 978-1-4614-1929-7   e-ISBN 978-1-4614-1930-3
DOI 10.1007/978-1-4614-1930-3
Springer New York Dordrecht Heidelberg London

Library of Congress Control Number: 2011940805

Printed on acid-free paper

Springer is part of Springer Science+Business Media (www.springer.com)

I dedicate this book to my lovely son Amazigh Tari who always keeps asking the question Why? and to my wife Astrid Blume-Tari who always was present during during difficult and good times of my life!
Zahir Tari

Contents

ix

Acronyms

BEEP: Blocks Extensible Exchange Protocol
BXSA: Binary XML for Scientific Applications
CBM: Content-based Multicast
CDR: Common Data Representation
CORBA: Common Object Request Broker Architecture
DCOM: Distributed Component Object Model
DDS: Differential Deserialization System
DR: Designated Router
DVMRP: Distance Vector Multicast Routing Protocol
FCFS: First Come First Serve
FTP: File Transfer Protocol
FB: Foreground-Background
FXI: Financial Information eXchange
HHFR: Handheld Flexible Representation
HTML: Hypertext Markup Language
QoS: Quality of Service
LCFS: Last Come First Serve
LLF: List Loaded First
LRW: Least Remaining Work
MEP: Message Exchange Pattern
MLTP: Multi-Level Time sharing Policy
MLMS: Multi-level Multi-server Load Distribution Policy
MLMS-M: Multi-level Multi-server Load Distribution Policy with Task Migration
MLMS-WC-M: Multi- Level-Multi-Server Task Assignment Policy with Work-Conserving Migration
MOSPF: Multicast Extension to OSPF
MQ-DMR: QoS-based Dynamic Multicast Routing
MTOM: Message Transmission Optimisation Mechanism
MTTMELL: Multi-Tier Task Assignment with Minimum Excess Load
OSPF: Open Shortest Path First

PIM: Protocol Inde- pendent Multicast
PIM-SM: PIM-Sparse Mode
RPC: Remote Procedure Call
RMI: Remote Method Invocation
RR: Round Robin
SITA-E: Size Interval Task Assignment with Equal load
SMP: Similarity-based Multicast Protocol
SMPT   Simple Mail Transfer Protocol
SOA: Service-Oriented Architecture
TAGS: Task Assignment by Guessing Size
TAGS-WC: TAGS with Work Conserving
TAPTF: Task Assignment based on Prioritising Traffic Flows
TAPTF-WC: TAPTF with Work Conserving
TCP: Transmission Control Protocol
tc-SMP: traffic-constrained SMP
UDDI: Universal Description, Discovery and Integration
UDP: User Datagram Protocol
WS: Web Services
WSDL: Web Service Description Language
WS-WRM: Web Service-Wireless Reliable Messaging
XOP: XML-binary Optimised Packaging
XML: eXtensible Markup Language

Chapter 1
Introduction

Over the past decade, we have seen phenomenal interest in the deployment of Web services in many enterprise applications. *Web services* are a new type of Web applications based on the *Simple Object Access Protocol* (SOAP) that allows interoperability between different platforms, systems and applications. There has been in the past such technologies, such as CORBA - Common Object Request Broker Architecture (139), which enabled interoperability, however they had quiet major limitations (e.g. the use of object model in the case of CORBA), which obvious have limited the scale of their use. Web services allows a text-based communication (i.e. Text based RPC), therefore not restricting communication and interoperability to specific models or patterns. Obviously there are much more advantages of Web services over other technologies, and these will be reviewed in the remaining parts of this book.

The development of Web services not only attracts interest from the research community but also from industry. Most large organisations in the software, information technology and telecommunication industries have been working closely with the World Wide Web consortium to develop Web service standards such as WS-Addressing, WS-Reliability, WS-Security and WS-Management. Many organisations have achieved some degree of success, such as generating new sources of revenue or streamlining their internal and external processes when deploying Web service technologies for their enterprise services (82, 83, 84, 146).

Web service technologies, such as SOAP, Web Services Description Language (WSDL) and Universal Description, Discovery and Integration (UDDI), promise to provide seamless integration of services provided by different vendors in different industries and written on various platforms and languages. Examples of such services include travel booking, real-time stock quotes, currency exchange rates, credit card verification, driving directions and yellow pages. A popular example used to illustrate Web services is the travel reservation application. A travel agent company offers a complete vacation package (in a form of a workflow), which includes airline/train/bus tickets, hotel reservation, car rental and tours. This service involves many service providers such as airlines, transport companies, hotels, tour organisers and credit card companies for payment. The back-end of service applications

1

offered by these service providers are likely to be written in different programming languages (e.g. C++, Java, .Net) and implemented on different platforms (e.g. Linux, Macintosh and Windows). But if all of these services are implemented using Web service technologies and are published on a public registry such as the UDDI (114), the travel agency can search all services from the one platform. Consumers who want to book vacation packages can come to the travel agency's website and specify some criteria such as location, means of transport and price range for their travel. The travel agency will act on behalf of the consumer and search for appropriate services registered on the UDDI and return results that satisfy the user's requests.

Obviously the application explained above can be implemented using traditional distributed computing technologies such as Distributed Component Object Model (DCOM) (69) and Common Object Request Broker Architecture (CORBA) (139). However, such traditional approaches do not provide the same high level of interoperability that Web services do. In particular, if an application were to be developed using DCOM, all participating nodes in the distributed application would have to be running on Windows platform (55). CORBA is based on the object-oriented model and a binary transport, Internet Inter-ORB Protocol (IIOP) (88), hence an Object Request Broker (ORB) node assumes a certain representation exists in other nodes to allow them understand each other. SOAP endpoints are, on the other hand, not dependent on any specific data representation or platform, since all data is already formatted in a "text"-based language (called XML - *eXtensible Markup Language*).

With the exciting prospects of what Web service technologies can bring come many difficult challenges. Web services' major problem is that they generate a *very large* amount of network traffic. This comes from the fact that a given call for an operation of a Web service (from the client side) is translated (more precisely "serialised") in XML, which could be a large document that is sent through the wire (as a SOAP call) to the sever side (which in turns "de-serialise" the XML-based call into a native call, such a C++ or Java operation call). Therefore SOAP provides the basic messaging infrastructure for Web services by exchanging XML messages. It is XML's textual representation and redundant characteristics that cause the major performance bottleneck. Tian et al. in (140) performed extensive performance tests showing the number of additional bytes Web services generate. There were 589 bytes in both request and response messages for a service requesting the details of a book given an ISBN in the parameter of the request. But more than 3900 bytes had to be sent when using SOAP, while only 1200 bytes were sent when traditional Web interaction with HTML was used.

SOAP's overhead stems mainly from the use of XML. Since both SOAP and WSDL are XML-based, XML messages have to be parsed on both the client and the server side. XML parsing occurs at run time, therefore the required additional processing time results in longer total response time. There has been so many evaluations of SOAP performance made in the last decade. Here we only list of them for illustration only. Some of the limitations of SOAP for scientific computing were investigated by Davis & Parashar in (40). Their experiments compared SOAP with Java RMI by sending large arrays of doubles; the results showed that SOAP was slower than Java RMI by a factor of *ten*. Another experimental evaluation of SOAP performance on business applications was done Kohlhoff & Steele in (73): SOAP was compared with Financial Information eXchange (FIX) protocol which also used a text based wire representation as SOAP, and with Common Data Representation (CDR), a common binary wire format. The results demonstrated that the text-based protocols (SOAP and FIX) have slightly lower performance than the binary protocol (CDR) due to the complexity of the XML syntax.

But the performance issues of Web services are not only related to SOAP! There are also major problems at the server side, when XML-requests are translated into native calls (C+/Java calls). Such problems have different nature and forms, depending on the configuration of the server. Simply, when the server receives a huge number of XML-requests (called *tasks*), this will not be able to process them as its queue/s will be full, and therefore the server will drop them. Overloaded servers are known problems in distributed systems and there has been a lot of research work done in the last two decades. *Load balancing* is a common approach used to improve performance: a server is replicated and tasks are dispatched to the "appropriate" server in a transparent way (i.e. the user is not aware of such replication). Load balancer, also called *dispatcher*, uses a specific policy, called *task assignment* policy, to decide how to allocate a given task to a given server so to make sure that this is processed in an efficient way (i.e. minimal waiting time in the server's queue). The earlier task assignment policies, called *static policies*, allocated tasks without relying on any specific information (e.g. load of a server, often measured as the # tasks in the queue). Random and Round Robin (RR) are typical static policies. It is well-known that such policies have serious limitations because of their static nature. More advanced policies were later proposed, called *dynamic policies*, which take into account dynamic information such as server load. LLF (Least Loaded First) is probably one of the well-known dynamic techniques, where tasks are allocated to the least loaded server. One may say ask the question about the way load is computed in a distributed environment like Web services. This is a good question though! Indeed measuring the load of a server, that is estimating the number of tasks in a queue, is well-known to be a very hard problem (i.e NP hard). Indeed, the computation of the *load index* can be complicated, as the load information computed at given time could be *stale*, meaning that they do not truly reflect the precise load at various queues, as tasks can arrive from different clients. Even though such a topic on the load index is important, this is not the focus of this book. The aim here is on the task assignment policies that can provide substantial performance improvement for Web services.

LLF is proven to be *optimal* under certain conditions. Indeed, if most of the tasks have similar size (i.e. the task size follows an exponential distribution), then a sensible way to measure the length of the queues (i.e. Load Index) is to count the *number of tasks* in each queue, as all the queues have similar type of tasks in terms of size. This obviously make a sense conceptually, and has been mathematically proven by Pollaczek & Khinchin in 1930s (94)(75). However such an assumption is problematic in Web services and, in general, for Internet traffic. Assuming an exponential distribution for task size does not stand anymore, as several recent studies (e.g. (13)) formally show the high variance of task size in the Internet traffic. In other words, the task size follows a different distribution, called *Pareto* distribution, where something like 1% of tasks could take up to 50% of the CPU time. Therefore a small number of tasks could be *very* large, which is problematic for the dispatcher attempting to equalise the load across different servers, as the number of tasks in a queue is not anymore the server's load. Indeed a very large task allocated to a given server (in the queue) can be much larger than thousands of small tasks in an another server. So the dispatcher needs to find the best way to allocate very large tasks and smaller tasks so the latter are not stuck in the queues behind very large tasks waiting for processing. This problem is known as *salvation*. Even more complicated, the high variance problem in the task size for Internet traffic is accentuated by the fact that the size of tasks at the dispatcher are not know beforehand (63, 64)(26, 97, 98), as SOAP requests are just XML calls and therefore there is not way to know how much CPU these will consume. They are known neither at compile nor at run time. Therefore the dispatcher will have a difficulties trying to figure out a way to *profile* tasks so it can efficiently allocate them to the right servers with less *waiting time* in the queues.

Dealing properly with two level performance problems of Web services, namely *system level* (i.e. those related to SOAP and XML) and *server level* (i.e. those related to the processing of SOAP requests at the server side), will definitely provide a more efficient and scalable infrastructure (in terms of performance) for deploying and running Web services. Despite the rapid growth in wired network bandwidth and steady increase in wireless bandwidth with new mobile technologies such as 3G networks, it is still not infinite. The available network bandwidth is often limited and expensive, especially in mobile and wireless environments. Enterprise IT systems need to process thousands of Web service requests in a short period of time. Considerable increased traffic represents high consumption of the network resources. Web services are promised to be a source of generating increased revenues for enterprises by exposing existing enterprise applications to a wide range of other applications on different platforms. High network traffic can hold up this potential for revenue generation and needs to be addressed. It is important to design Web services that have low communication overheads and make efficient use of available bandwidth.

What has been done so far in performance?

Several solutions have been proposed to improve SOAP performance, either using binary encoding (binary XML instead of textual XML), caching (at the client side by increasing the locality of objects), compression (by reducing the size of XML payload) or optimising the SOAP run-time implementation (by efficient optimisation of the kernel).

One type of solution attempts to reduce the size of SOAP messages by binary encoding (similar to CORBA encoding). It is transmissions of SOAP messages in binary instead of textual format. Generic SOAP engines support both textual and binary XML as the encoding scheme of messages. Scientific data could be directly transmitted as binary XML. (80) developed a binary XML encoding scheme called BXSA (Binary XML for Scientific Applications). BXSA supports the ability to convert a textual XML document to binary XML and vice versa. A SOAP message is modeled in the BXDM model (a scientific-data-friendly XML data model as an extension of XPath Data Model (51)) instead of the XML Infoset. To send a SOAP message, first a SOAP message is constructed in the BXDM model, then the encoding policy provider is invoked to serialise the message into an octet stream. Finally, the stream is transferred by calling the binding policy provider. The reverse procedure takes place when a message is received. Both SOAP over BXDM/TCP scheme and SOAP with HTTP data channel have similar performance. They can rebind the BXDM transport to multiple TCP streams, thus it can carry larger messages.

W3C XML Protocol Working Group recently released specifications for SOAP Message Transmission Optimisation Mechanism (MTOM) (59) and XML-binary Optimised Packaging (XOP) (60). These specifications are targeted to multimedia data (such as JPEG, GIF and MP3) and data that includes digital signatures. The specifications define an efficient means of XML Infoset serialisation. An XOP package is created by placing a serialisation of the XML Infoset inside an extensible packaging format such as MIME (60). MTOM describes how XOP is layered into the SOAP HTTP transport. However, XOP and MTOM still possess a parsing issue inherited from SOAP and XML.

Another example of work in binary SOAP encoding is a study by Oh & Fox in (89). They proposed a new mobile Web service architecture, called Handheld Flexible Representation (HHFR), that provides optimised SOAP communication using a binary message stream. HHFR architecture separates XML syntax of SOAP messages from SOAP message contents. This separation is negotiated at the beginning of a stream. An XML schema is used to characterise the syntax of the SOAP body. HHFR is most suited to Web service applications where two end-points exchange a stream of messages, because messages in a stream often share common structure and type information of the SOAP body and most parts of the SOAP headers. The message structure and type in form of XML schema are transmitted only once and the rest of the messages in the stream have only payloads. Oh and Fox compared HHFR prototype with a conventional SOAP and found the higher performance advantage of HHFR is achieved when there are multiple messages transmitted in a session. In particular, HHFR streaming communication outperforms conventional SOAP by 7 times in round trip time for a service adding float numbers.

Compression is a popular method to deal with large message sizes of Web services. Compression is particularly useful for poorly connected clients with resource-constrained devices or for clients that are charged by volume and not by connection time by their providers. However, compression decreases server performance due to the additional computation required. From experiments of XML compression in wireless networks, (140) found that in a low bandwidth network such as GPRS the service time was halved when compressing large SOAP responses. The response time during overload is however about 40% higher and the server throughput is about 50% lower when compression is used. Therefore, Tian et al. proposed that clients should decide whether they want their responses compressed. During low server demand, responses to all client requests except those that did not ask for compression are compressed. During high server demand, only responses to clients that asked for compressed responses are compressed. Despite high response time and low throughput, Tian et al. have shown that their dynamic compression approach is beneficial for both the server and for mobile clients with poor connectivity. It is also recommended that servers should only compress replies to clients that can benefit from compression.

Many studies have researched approaches to enhance SOAP performance through caching (41, 102, 137). Devaram & Andresen (41) implemented a partial caching strategy to cache SOAP payloads on the client side. In this method, the SOAP payload is cached when it is first generated. Every time the client makes a request, the payloads stored in the cache are reused to create a new payload by replacing some values of the XML tags with new parameter values. This technique is shown to provide better performance than non-caching for request messages with small number of tags. The performance of the partial caching technique degrades when there are many parameters defined in a SOAP request because the time spent on substituting the parameter values and accessing file I/O increases as the number of parameters increases, which in turn enlarges the size of the cache.

The advantage of Web services caching is mainly in supporting disconnected operations. Terry & Ramasubramanian (131) implemented an HTTP proxy server between a Web service provider and a Web service consumer to provide a simple cache for storing SOAP messages. Their study highlighted the benefits of employing a Web service cache to support disconnected operations. Specifically, in case of disconnection, SOAP response messages that are stored in the cache, will be returned to client requests. The SOAP requests are stored in a write back queue which is later played back to the server when the connection to the Web service is restored. However, there are still many issues with caching such as consistency and availability of offline access to Web services. Another difficulty with Web service caching is that a cache manager does not know which operation needs to be played back to the server. In addition, the effectiveness of a cache is often dependent on the similarity of future requests to past requests.

Liu & Deters (102) proposed a dual caching strategy for mobile Web services. In their method, one cache resides on the client side and the other on the server side to handle any problems due to loss of connectivity during the sending/receiving of request and response messages. The two caches are coordinated by a cache manager. An ontology Web language is used to describe meta-data used on the caches such as service description, client workflow description and connectivity description. This ensures interoperability with other Web service standards. Terry & Ramasubramanian (131) also emphasised the importance of understanding the cacheability of services in their work. Therefore, they propose to add annotations in the WSDL specification to support SOAP caching. The suggested annotations include semantic information such as cacheability, life time, play-back and default-response. This however leads to issues regarding standards and interoperability.

In cases when outgoing SOAP messages are very similar in content, it is advantageous to use differential encoding. With this technique, only the difference between a message and a previous one is sent over the wire. Documents containing only the differences can be more compact in size depending on content. Important studies in the differential encoding area are done as a differential serialisation (3), a differential deserialization (130), and differential compression (145).

After discussing the various techniques for system level optimisation (i.e. SOAP optimisation), the next step is to look at those techniques that optimise performance at the server side. As the reader may notice, one can use an optimised SOAP engine (to efficiently send requests to severs), but this does not guarantee overall performance improvement, as the server/s could be overloaded (and therefore delaying most of the executions of tasks). Carefully addressing the performance issues at the server is a key to the development of efficient and scalable Web service infrastructures. Both system and server considerations need to be addressed so substantial performance gain can be obtained. Unfortunately there is no **holistic** approach to **performance** in Web services (as well as in other systems). Both optimisation, system and sever optimisation, need to be done in combination so delays can be reduced both during the forwarding of requests as well as their processing at the server side. Obviously there exists a third dimension for Web Services performance optimisation, which relates to the application level (i.e. application programs). Applications can be badly written, which can induce additional overheads on the server side. A simple example of such bad design is when a given call (to return a given data structure - a large array) is repeated several times in a program. Therefore there will be a wastage in the usage of the network as well as CPU time in the server. Instead, a good design of an application program will store the retrieved data structure (in the cache) and later use for future processing. This book does not deal with such program design, as it has a different focus, namely a *system performance focus* for Web services. The design of "good" Web services as well as application programs is the area of software engineering. We advise the reader to look at the work by Perepletchikov & Ryan (92)(93), where they came up with a new design methodology as well as a set of (design) metrics for Web services.

In the context of server side performance, static-based approaches (like RR - Round Robin) definitely do not have a place in Web services, as they do not *properly* allocate tasks (i.e. XML-based requests) to the right servers. Indeed, RR will allocate tasks to an overloaded server (as it does not take into account the load during the task assignment process). As mentioned earlier, a more advanced policy, called LLF (Least Loaded First), does smartly assign task to the least loaded server (i.e. the server that has the least number of tasks in its queue). LLF is an optimal (task assignment) policy, under the condition that the task size does follow an exponential distribution. Of course, this can work when appropriate mechanisms to estimate the load at various servers are available. The computation of the load index is even harder when dealing with distributed environments (because of the network delays, and therefore making load information staler). Coming back to the assumption for the exponential distribution, this is not anymore true for a lot of cases of traffic, including for Internet traffic (13), and some mathematicians are even questioning the poison distribution (for arrival rate), as this many not be true for certain traffic. Here we will not go that far, but the research community do agree that task size follows a different distribution, namely Pareto distribution (or more Bounded Pareto distribution in the case of Web traffic). Such distributions are explained in details in the Background chapter. Those researchers, who are still considering the exponential distribution in their work, do it because this provides nice properties for a system (i.e. Markovian properties), and therefore they can easily derive essential information needed for task scheduling. This information includes: Waiting Time (WT) (i.e. time it takes for a task to wait in a queue before it gets processed by the server), Slow Down (SLD) (e.g. the ratio of WT by the task size), and Variance (i.e. the task variation in a queue). Such parameters are essential in the scheduling of tasks, and the overall objective is to minimise WT (so a task does not wait too much in a queue), SLD (so "fairness" can be enforced, meaning that all tasks will have the same SLD, where larger tasks will wait longer than small tasks), and Variance (where the scheduler will avoid to mix large tasks and small tasks in the same queue, otherwise this will increase the waiting time).

With the clear evidence about the heavy tail distribution for Internet traffic (13), a few researchers come up with a new class of task assignment policies, called *sized-based policies*. They basically take into account the specific nature of the traffic and try to assign tasks based on their size. Such policies assume that the size is known by the dispatcher before assigning them to specific queues. In SITA-E (65) (Size Interval Task Assignment with Equal load), a size range is associated with each server and a task is assigned to the appropriate server based on its size. The main idea is to a size for each sever in such a way the total load to each host will be the same. In that way the waiting time is minimised in the queues (because there is less variance, as most of the tasks in the same queue have the same size range). The LRW (Least Remaining Work) policy is an extension of LLF, and it assigns a task to the server that has the least remaining work in its queue. This is computed as the sum of the sizes of the tasks in the queue plus the work remaining on that task being served. LRW shows in order of 100 times better Random and RR (Round Robin) (65). With low variance (in task size), LRW keeps good performance. However with high variability in task size LRW has difficulties to maintain good performance. SITA-E in contrast does better with high variability in task size, as it does not mix large and small tasks in the same queues. Therefore it implements a sort of "fairness", where smaller tasks are processed quickly, because they are assigned to the same servers. Therefore smaller tasks avoid to get "stuck" behind larger tasks, which take time to get processed in dedicated servers.

Have the problems of performance then been all resolved and there is nothing to do?

As detailed earlier, there have been several key studies into the improvement of SOAP (for system performance) as well as load balancing (for server performance). Each of the proposed techniques has its own advantages in improving either SOAP performance or server side processing. However lots of problems remain and therefore requiring solutions that will cater to the specific requirements of Web services.

- Most of system solutions focus on the SOAP engine, compression and caching and fail to look at other aspects (like SOAP binding and networking). A little work has been done on the use of alternative binding options for SOAP to handle the inherent performance issues of wireless environments and on multicasting SOAP messages to reduce network traffic.

- Most of the load balancing techniques assume that the task size is known by the dispatcher. Size-based approaches assign tasks with such specific information. However in reality this cannot happen, as SOAP requests can come from anywhere (e.g. somebody making a booking from any place around the world) and therefore there is no way to know the size of requests at runtime. The dispatcher will have no information, and thus making size-based approaches not useful to be used in the context of Web services.

Let's look at each level and see what could be done to produce better performance for Web services.

The SOAP binding specifies which underlying protocol to be used to deliver a SOAP message (52). HTTP is the most widely used protocol for SOAP binding, however, there is high overhead associated with HTTP in wireless networks. Recently, the SOAP-over-UDP specification (18) has been proposed to provide basic guidelines on how to transmit SOAP messages over UDP; however, it does not cover the binding in wireless environments and for resource-constrained devices.

Multicasting is a well known technology for conserving network bandwidth. Multicast is often employed in applications where the same data is transmitted to a group of interested clients. Instead of sending replicated unicast packets of the same data to multiple clients, multicast reduces the number of packets sent over links, thus reduces the use of network resources. Existing work in IP, application and content-based multicasts (91, 113, 125, 154) have shown that the use of multicast utilises network bandwidth efficiently and can reduce delivery delay.

SOAP can benefit from the use of multicast as well because duplicate large SOAP messages can be avoided. This in turn reduces SOAP serialisation time on the server side and consumes less network resources. Previous studies on multicast were based on the assumption that multicast messages are identical. The work presented in this book is however not based on this assumption, but examines how similar (not necessarily identical) SOAP messages can be multicast together in an aggregated message represented in a special schema XML format. This will result in a further reduction in the total size of messages sent over a network because only one copy of matching parts within SOAP messages is sent. In particular, the feasibility of adapting a similarity-based multicast protocol for SOAP to reduce network traffic in low bandwidth environments is studied. This book also looks at the analytical and experimental analysis of some existing solutions and compare them to the suggested solutions. The similarity measurement of SOAP messages plays a key role in the proposed SOAP multicast protocol. In particular, the following problems are pursued:

- What are the performance limitations of current SOAP HTTP binding, particularly in supporting mobile Web services? What is an effective SOAP binding option for wireless environments? This book will deal with a performance benchmark which compares three implementations of SOAP binding options: SOAP-over-HTTP, SOAP-over-TCP and SOAP-over-UDP.

- What is a cost-effective method to reduce total traffic created by SOAP messages sent over a network? Techniques for reducing SOAP message size have widely been studied in the context of Web services (4, 137, 140, 145). However the results from these approaches are limited to reducing traffic at client or server side during caching or serialisation; and are dependent on the similarity of future requests to previous ones. Can multicasting SOAP messages lead to improved performance? Can multicast take advantage of SOAP's nature of having messages with similar data structure? What is an effective model to measure the similarity between SOAP messages?
- What are the most efficient routing algorithms that can be used to deliver similar SOAP messages so that the total traffic created over a network can be minimised? While routing algorithms (such as Dijkstra's and Bellman-Ford's algorithms) are widely used on the Internet, they consider only a simple cost metric (such as hop counts). Other Quality-of-Service (QoS) metrics (such as network bandwidth, network traffic and end-to-end delay) are not taken into consideration. Although there is a wide range of studies in the QoS routing area (33, 153, 158), little work has been done in developing appropriate QoS routing algorithms for SOAP traffic. What are approaches for QoS-based SOAP multicast routing? What are the trade-offs with the proposed algorithms?

With regards load balancing, two problems become the main hurdles for Web services performance: i) the heavy tail nature of the task size, and ii) the fact that tasks are not known by the dispatcher. The first problem is inherent to the nature of Internet traffic (as well as other traffic, including ftp etc.). The best way to address is to try to reduce the variance of task size in the queues of servers. When looking at the equation of the waiting time for a given task (see later chapters), this is depend on the variance[1]. Therefore reducing such a variance will bring down the value of the waiting time and therefore increasing the performance. SITA-E is a good example of task assignment that does that, where each server is assigned a specific range of task size. However SITA-E has the limitation of imposing the information about task size to be known by the dispatcher. Well if a dispatcher does not know the task size, the best way is to guess it! This was the nice idea behind TAGS (Task Assignment by Guessing Size) (63)(64): it behaves like SITA-E in the sense that it classifies servers based on the range of task they processing. Later works by associating a time limit with each server. A task will run until the designated limit with the host. If the task has been processed during the time limit, then there is nothing to do. However if this is not the case, the task is killed and started from scratch at the next server. This process continues till the task finds the "right" server where it finishes its processing during its time limit. This way of assigning tasks by re-starting them at new servers (because they have not finished during the time limit) is a simulation of SITA-E by trying to allocated a task to the "appropriate" server without knowing the task size.

TAGS is probably one of the most innovative scheduling approaches. It has both good conceptual foundations as well as analytical ones. It properly addresses the

---

[1] According to Pollaczek-Kinchin old formula (94)(75), we have: $E\{\text{Waiting Time}\} = \lambda \, E\{X^2\}/2(1-\rho)$, where X denoting the service distribution, $E\{X^2\}$ the variance and ρ the load.

problem of scheduling for modern applications (by getting rid off the conventional assumptions). Therefore TAGS can be used as basis to improve server performance for Web services. However there are much problems to fix with TAGS to make it efficient and scalable.

- Restarting tasks every time they do not finish processing in a given server is a real "wastage" of resources. This is technically called *excess load*, modelling the additional load on the system after a task is restarted. The challenge is to reduce the restarting of tasks and therefore enabling saving more processing.
- Assigning tasks in "sequential" manner (i.e. a task goes through the various servers and later ended up at the "right" server) is not the right strategy. Even if the dispatcher randomly assigns tasks to severs and later allowing them to be restarted can substantially improve performance. Indeed tasks will be much less restarted.
- The other major problem is to mix the re-started tasks with ordinary tasks (i.e. tasks assigned by the dispatcher). This in fact increases the variance in the queues, as the restarted task have higher chance to be larger. Therefore the aim is to design a better mechanism with less variance in the queues, and therefore reducing the waiting time of tasks within the queues.

What does this book propose?

In addressing the above problems, this book makes a number of contributions to advance the current state of the art of research in SOAP performance and scheduling. Such contributions are summarised below.

- *SOAP Binding Benchmark.* A benchmark of different SOAP bindings in wireless environments is proposed and implemented. Its configuration and results can serve as a standard benchmark for other researchers who are also interested in the performance of SOAP bindings in wireless networks. Three sets of experiments were carried out: loopback mode, wireless network mode and mobile device mode. The experimental results show that HTTP binding inherits very high protocol overhead (30%–50% higher than UDP binding) from TCP due to the slow connection establishments and tear-down processes and the packet acknowledgement mechanism. UDP binding has the lower overhead because it does not require establishing connections before transmitting datagrams and does not address reliability. This results in a reduction in response time and an increase in total throughput.
- *Similarity-based SOAP Multicast Protocol.* A SOAP multicast technique, called SMP (Similarity-based Multicast Protocol) is described, which takes into account the similarity of SOAP messages. SMP exploits the feature of similar data structure among SOAP messages to group messages of similar content in one aggregated message (called SMP message) so that common data types or values are not repeated and are sent only once. A similarity measurement model for SOAP messages is proposed. The server must establish the similarity of outgoing messages in order to decide which messages can be aggregated to improve

the overall performance without incurring high communication costs. A SOAP message indexing technique is proposed to represent SOAP messages in a special XML format, so a more compact representation can be used to reduce more traffic. This indexing technique is based on the data type definitions contained in WSDL service description. Each XML node in an indexed version of a SOAP message is composed of the node's data type ID, which is referenced back to the WSDL document, the position of the node in breadth first search traversal, and the node value. The SOAP message index assists in fast merging of SOAP messages and splitting of SMP messages because it enables easy grouping of common and distinctive data in SMP messages.

- *Multicast Protocol to Minimize SOAP Network Traffic.* The original proposal of SMP uses the Open Shortest Path First (OSPF) routing protocol (37) to send SMP messages. Under SMP, the more similar SOAP messages can be aggregated over common links the more network bandwidth can be saved. However, when the OSPF protocol is used, some SOAP messages that are very similar in content will follow paths that may not share many common links. To deal with such a problem, an extension of SMP, which is the traffic-constrained similarity-based SOAP multicast protocol (tc-SMP) is proposed here. Two algorithms, greedy and incremental approaches, are described to address this problem. Both tc-SMP algorithms aim at minimising the total network traffic of the whole routing tree every time a new client is added to the tree. Two heuristic methods are also proposed for these algorithms to assist in choosing the order of clients being added to the tree. In general, the performance improvement of tc-SMP is about 30% higher network traffic reduction than SMP at a small expense of up to 10% rise in response time.

- *TAGS extension to deal with excess load.* As TAGS suffers from too much generated excess load, TAGS-WC (Work Conserving) is described as an extension to reduce excess load by work-conserving. Restarted tasks are just simply resumed at the next server. Both analytical and experimental results show important reduction in excess load in TAGS-WC and therefore better overall system performance. The extension of TAGS does not stop here, as TAGS-WC till suffers from the problems inherited from TAGS. TAPTF (Task Assignment based on Prioritising Traffic Flows) (26) is described where each server has two queues: priority queue (for restarted tasks) and ordinary queue (for dispatched tasks). TAPTF does show better performance than TAGS-WC, as it substantially reduces the variance of task size in the queue. TAPTF-WC (25) extends TAPTF to work conserving, thus borrowing the same ideas from TAGS-WS. All these extensions are compared both analytically and experimentally.

- *Multi-level Time Sharing* to properly use the CPU. Most of discussion on time sharing policies are based on the assumption that infinitely small quanta and infinite number of queueing levels. In this book we consider multi-level time sharing policy which have non-zero quanta and finite number of queueing levels because such a policy is more practical to implement on real computer systems.

Book Organisation

The rest of the book is organised as follows.

- Chapter 2 provides an overview of areas needed to understand the core chapters of this book. Important Web service concepts and standards, SOAP technologies, traditional multicast protocols and popular routing protocols on the Internet are discussed. Also basic queuing concepts needed to understand this book are also described.
- Chapter 3 details a benchmark suite of various SOAP binding options. Three extensive sets of experiments are described to highlight the advantages of using SOAP-over-UDP binding in mobile and wireless networks.
- Chapter 4 addresses the problem of high SOAP traffic in limited bandwidth environments by proposing a similarity-based SOAP multicast protocol (SMP). A model for measuring the similarity of SOAP messages is proposed. SMP routing algorithm is described in detail with its analytical model and experimental evaluation.
- An extension of SMP protocol, traffic-constrained SMP (tc-SMP), is described in Chapter 5. Two new source routing algorithms, greedy tc-SMP and incremental tc-SMP, are proposed to send SMP messages along paths that highly similar messages have more common routing links. The tc-SMP routing algorithms are used instead of the OSPF protocol to convey SMP messages. Both theoretical and experimental studies of tc-SMP are discussed.
- Chapter 6 describes the various extensions of TAGS, starting from TAGS-WC. Later TAPTF and TAPTF-WC are suggested as a way of resolving the various problems of TAGS. The analytical modelling of the various policies are given.
- Chapter 7 gives details of the process sharing policy with non-zero quanta and finite number of queueing levels. Both analytical and experimental results are given to demonstrate the efficiency of such policies.
- We conclude this book in Chapter 8 with final remarks.

Chapter 2
Background

"An intellectual is someone whose mind watches itself."

Albert Camus

This chapter describes some of the background information needed to facilitate the understanding of the research work described this book. There are several XML-based standards in the area of Web services. A brief survey of the most important standards needed to understand this book will be presented. In addition, some of the traditional protocols (e.g. multicast routing protocols) and network routing algorithms are reviewed to provide background knowledge for the chapters related to the network optimisation of Web Services to improve their overall performance.

This chapter is not meant to describe in details the concepts and the technology related to Web services, as these have been widely addressed by the community. A reader can refer to the two books written by Alonso et al. (7) and Papazoglou (90). This chapter provides only a brief overview of the Web services technology as well as those concepts needed in the rest of this book.

2.1 Web services

Web services have emerged as a key technology that enables interoperability between distributed applications. A *Web service* can be simply defined as a reusable piece of software that interacts with clients, possibly with other Web services by exchanging messages over a network which comply Extensible Markup Language (XML), SOAP (communication protocol) and other industry recognised standards. From a different perspective, a Web service is an interface that describes a collection of operations that are network-accessible through standardised XML messaging. A Web service is described using a standard and formal XML-based language (called WSDL - Web Service Description Language). A WSDL description covers all the details necessary to interact with the service, including message formats (that detail the operations), transport protocols and location. The interface hides the implementation details of the service, allowing it to be used independently of the hardware or software platform on which it is implemented, and also independently of the programming language in which it is written. This allows and encourages Web Services-based applications to be loosely coupled, component-oriented and be cross-technology implementations.

The most important ingredient of Web services is extensible Markup Language (XML), which organises information in a common format so that the information understood by a wide variety of computer systems. XML, which based on protocols established by leading software and computer vendors, enables Web services to be used in a wide range of application scenarios, from simple behind-the-firewall data sharing to large-scale, Internet-based retailing and B2B (Business to Business) commerce. A service may combine several applications that a user needs (e.g. different pieces of a supply chain architecture). For a client, however, the entire infrastructure will appear as a single application. Due to its potential of changing the Internet to a platform of application collaboration and integration, Web Services technology gains more and more attention in research and industry; products like IBM WebSphere, Microsoft .NET, or Sun ONE show this development.

Web Service Architecture

The Web Services architecture is defined using patterns. SOA is a component model that inter-relates different functional units of an application, called services, through well-defined interfaces and contracts between these services. The interface is defined in a neutral manner that should be independent of the hardware platform, the operating system, and the programming language the service is implemented in. SOA defines three roles: a service requestor, a service provider and a service registry. The three main roles and the interaction between the roles are depicted in Figure 2.1.

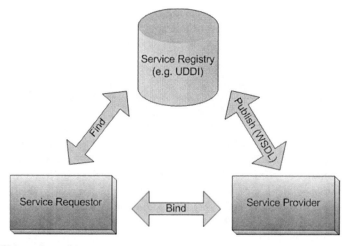

Fig. 2.1 Web service architecture

- A *Service Provider* is responsible for creating a service description, deploying that service in a runtime environment that makes it accessible by other entities

over the network, publishing that service description to one or more service registries, and receiving Web service invocation messages from one or more service
requestors.

- A *service requestor* (or service consumer) is responsible for finding a service
  description published to one or more service registries and is responsible for
  using service descriptions to bind to or invoke Web services hosted by service
  providers.
- A *service registry* (or service broker) is responsible for advertising Web service
  descriptions submitted to it by service providers. It also allows service requestors
  to search the collection of service descriptions contained within the service registry by replying to the queries from the service requestor on the availability of
  the service and the quality of service (QoS) provided by an available service.
  Universal Description, Discovery and Integration (UDDI) (114) is an example of
  the most popular service registry for Web services currently.

As shown in Figure 2.2, the Web service layer is placed between the transport
layer and the application layer in the Internet reference model. Within the Web
service layer, the network protocols such as HTTP (Hypertext Transfer Protocol),
SMPT (Simple Mail Transfer Protocol), FTP (File Transfer Protocol) and BEEP
(Blocks Extensible Exchange Protocol) are at the bottom. HTTP is the de-facto
transport protocol for Web services because if its ubiquity and ability to pass through
firewalls. However, any other transport protocols, such as TCP, UDP, SMTP and
FTP could be used instead. The XML-based SOAP forms the next layer. WSDL is
in the top layer.

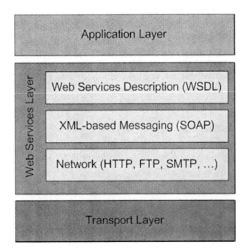

Fig. 2.2 Web service protocol stack

Web Service Description Language (WSDL)

Service description is a key feature within a service-oriented architecture (SOA). A service description is involved in each of the three operations of SOA: *publish*, *find* and *bind*. Referring back to Figure 2.1, the service provider publishes the service description to the service registry during the *publish* process. During the *find* operation, the service requestor searches available service descriptions in the service registry to identify a matching service. The service description also defines the message format expected by the service provider so that service requestor can send request messages that can be understood by the provider during the *bind* operation.

The service description of a Web service is defined by using Web Service Description Language (WSDL). WSDL is an XML-based language for describing the technical specifications of a Web service. It describes the operations offered by a Web service, the syntax of the input and output documents, the communication protocol to use for communication with the service and the location of the service. The structure of a WSDL document is complex, only a brief overview of the WSDL standard is presented here. A WSDL description has the following elements:

- PortType is a Web service's abstract interface definition where each child operation element defines an abstract method signature.
- Message defines the format of the message, or a set of parameters, referred to by the method signatures or operations. A message is composed of parts.
- Type defines the collection of all the data types used in the Web service as referenced by the various message part elements.
- Binding describes the implementation details of how the elements in a port-Type are converted into a concrete implementation in a particular combination of data formats and protocols.
- Port describes how a binding is deployed at a particular network endpoint.
- Service is a collection of concrete implementation endpoints of Web services.

In the appendix, an example of WSDL specification for the Stock Quote Service is given in Appendix.

2.2 Simple Object Access Protocol (SOAP)

This is *the* standard for Web services messaging (58). SOAP was designed to replace traditional remote communication methods such as DCOM, CORBA and RMI. The main benefit of SOAP is *interoperability*, enabling applications written in different languages and deployed on different platforms to communicate with each other over the network. SOAP uses XML technologies to define an extensible messaging framework, that provides a message construct that can be exchanged over a variety of underlying protocols (such as HTTP/HTTPS, TCP, UDP, BEEP and SMTP). Thus, the aim of SOAP is to provide a binding framework instead of a fixed binding (e.g. object-based for CORBA). Specifically, the SOAP binding framework specification provides a high level of flexibility in terms of how SOAP messages are transmitted.

SOAP is fundamentally a stateless, one-way message exchange paradigm, which can be used as a building block for creating more complex interaction patterns such as one-way, request/response, notification and notification/responses, by combining one-way exchanges with features provided by an underlying protocol or application-specific information. SOAP does not dictate the semantics of any application-specific data that it conveys, such as the routing of SOAP messages, reliable data transfer and firewall traversal. However, SOAP provides the framework by which application-specific information may be conveyed in an extensible manner. Also, SOAP provides a full description of the required actions to be taken by a SOAP processor node on receiving a SOAP message.

Figures 2.3 and 2.4 provide an example of a full HTTP SOAP request and response messages of a getTemperature service using Axis SOAP implementation (10).

```
POST /axis/servlet/AxisServlet HTTP/1.0
Content-Type" text/xml; charset=utf-8
Accept: application/soap+xml
User-Agent: Axis/1.2RC3
Host: http://www.weatherhost.com:8081
Cache-Control: no-cache
Pragma: no-cache
SOAPAction: ""
Content-Length: 438
Authorization: Basic dXN1cjE6cGFzczE=

<?xml version="1.0" encoding="UTF-8"?>
<soapenv:Envelope: xmlns:soapenv="..."
                   xmlns:xsd="..."
                   xmlns:xsi="...">
   <soapenv:Body>
     <ns1:getTemperature soapenv:encodingStyle="..."
                         xmlns:ns1="...">
        <symbol xsi:type="xsd:string">
           Melbourne
        </symbol>
     </ns1:getTemperature>
   </soapenv:Body>
</soapenv:Envelope>
```

Fig. 2.3 Sample SOAP request message

SOAP Message Structure

SOAP fellows response Message Exchange Pattern (MEP): a (SOAP) node sends a request message to a another node which receives and processes the request, and then returns a message in response. This is a simple, yet powerful messaging pattern which allows two applications to have a two-way conversation with one another over

```
HTTP/1.1 200 OK
Server: Apache-Coyote/1.1
Content-Type: text/xml;charset=utf-8
Date: Sat, 1 Jan 2005 00:00:00 GMT
Connection: close

<?xml version="1.0" encoding="UTF-8"?>
<soapenv:Envelope: xmlns:soapenv="..."
                    xmlns:xsd="..."
                    xmlns:xsi="...">
   <soapenv:Body>
     <ns1:getTemperatureResponse
         soapenv:encodingStyle="..."
         xmlns:ns1="...">
         <getTemperatureReturn href="#id0"/>
     </ns1:getTemperatureResponse>

     <multiRef id="id0" soapenc:root="0"
         soapenv:encodingStyle="..."
         xsi:type="xsd:float"
         xmlns:soapenc="...">
         23.5
     </multiRef>
   </soapenv:Body>
</soapenv:Envelope>
```

Fig. 2.4 Sample SOAP response message

a channel. There are exactly two SOAP messages in this MEP. This pattern can be implemented in a synchronous or asynchronously fashion in Web service calls.

Figure 2.5 shows the basic structure of a SOAP message consisting of three parts: an *envelope*, an optional *header*, and a mandatory *body*. The root element of a SOAP message is an envelope element containing an optional header element for SOAP extensions and a body element for payload. The header element of a SOAP message may include implementations of SOAP extensions such as Web Service Addressing (151), Web Service Security (104), Web Service Reliable Messaging (20). The body construct of a SOAP message acts as a container for the data being delivered by the SOAP message. SOAP offers a standard encoding style (serialisation mechanism) to convert arbitrary graphs of objects to an XML-based representation, but user-defined serialisation schemes can be used as well.

SOAP Extensions

SOAP extensions allow developers to augment the functionality of a Web service by altering the SOAP message sent to and from a Web service provider or consumer. For example, authentication, encryption or compression algorithms can be implemented to run with an existing Web service. The SOAP extension can be done during the `AfterSerialize` and `BeforeDeserialize` stages (58). For example, encrypting can be done in the `AfterSerialize` and decrypting can be

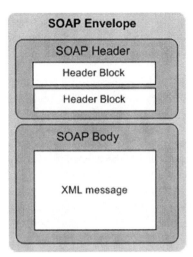

Fig. 2.5 SOAP envelope

done in the `BeforeDeserialize` stage. It is important to note that a SOAP extension that performs modification on a SOAP message must be done both on the client and the server.

SOAP Message Exchange Model

SOAP messages are primarily one-way transmissions. However, multiple messages can be combined to form message exchange patterns such as request/response pattern. A SOAP processing model includes an originator, one or more ultimate destinations, and none or more intermediaries. This model supports distributed message processing which is an advantage over the client-server messaging model.

Typically when a SOAP node receives a SOAP message, the following actions are performed:

- Identify all mandatory header blocks intended for the node.
- If there is any mandatory block identified in the preceding step that is not understood by the node, stop processing; otherwise process all the header blocks that are supported.
- If the current SOAP node is not the ultimate recipient of the message, remove all SOAP header blocks identified in the first step before forwarding it along the message path. At this stage, some new SOAP header blocks may be inserted into the SOAP message. If the node is the final destination, process the SOAP body.

A message exchange pattern (MEP) describes the sequence of messages exchanged between a service provider and a service consumer. SOAP supports two basic types of message pattern: single-message exchange and multiple-message exchange. The classification of each pattern is dependent on whether the provider or the consumer is the first party to initiate the message exchange and whether one side expects a response message to the initial message. There are two basic SOAP message exchange patterns defined in the SOAP Version 1.2 specification (150):

- Request-Response MEP: is a pattern for the exchange of two messages between two adjacent SOAP nodes along a SOAP message path. Typically, a request message is first transferred from a requesting SOAP node to a responding SOAP node. Upon successfully processing the request, the responding SOAP node sends a response message back to the requesting node.
- Response MEP: is a pattern for the exchange of a non-SOAP message acting as a request followed by a SOAP message acting as a response. A request that does not contain a SOAP envelope is transmitted to a receiving SOAP node. A response message which includes a SOAP envelope is then sent to respond back to the requesting node where the processing of the SOAP envelope occurs.

SOAP Messaging Styles

There are two SOAP messaging styles: Remote Procedure Call (RPC) style and document style. The RPC style is usually synchronous that is a client sends a message to a server and waits to get a response or a fault message back from the server. Under an RPC-style Web service implementation, a function on a remote machine is invoked as if it were a local function. The sender and receiver communicate with each other via an interface understood by both parties (45). Such an interface consists of a method name and a parameter list. The parameter list is composed of the variables passed to the called procedure and those returned as part of the response. All of the serialisation and deserialization of data is handled by SOAP standards. For example, part 2 of the SOAP version 1.2 specification defines the rules to encode RPC method calls and responses as XML elements (150). With document style messaging, it is up to developers to decide how the data is represented in XML. This gives developers flexibility in choosing the schema for validating the document's structure and the encoding scheme for interpreting data item values. Under a document-style Web service implementation, a client uses an XML parser to create an XML document and then inserts it into a SOAP message's body. The client serialises the message and sent to the server. A reverse process takes place on the server side.

RPC-style messaging's main strength is that it maps closely to an object-oriented model, hence it is a good option for creating new components and for creating interfaces between existing components and Web services. Secondly, it offers a standard-based and platform-independent component technology which allows clients and servers use different programming languages to implement their respective side of the interface. However, the messaging process in RPC-style is tightly coupled on the programmable interface. Changes on this interface would require changes on both sides of the interface. In contrast, with document-style messaging the rules are less strict and enhancements can be made to the XML schema without breaking the calling application (106). This advantage comes from the fact that in document-style an XML document is sent rather than a structured return value. Because of this nature, document-style messaging is also ideal for passing complex documents such as customer orders and invoices. Document-style messaging's drawback is that there is no standard service identification mechanism in place. The client and server must agree on a common way for determining which service needs to process a received document.

Both messaging styles suffer the same overhead in serialisation. Parsing XML documents is required on both client and server sides. In addition to the cost of XML parsing, there is the cost of carrying encoded data values, which can be much larger in size than its binary equivalent, across the network.

2.3 XML Similarity Measurements

Similarity is an important concept used to determine the syntactic relationship between two ore more SOAP messages. This concept is particularly important when dealing with improvement of Web services, as substantial eduction in number of SOAP messages can be obtained. In this section, existing tools and models for similarity measures are presented. Similarity measures for ontological structures, web data or XML documents have been widely researched in the software engineering, document management and database communities (44, 54).

APPROXML Tool

APPROXML (38) is a software tool for making XML pattern-based search queries to locate XML data items that are similar to a searched pattern. In this tool, XML documents are represented as graphs using the DOM model. Each edge of a document is weighted to express their importance. The weighting technique takes into account the various characteristics of each edge. Multiple weights on each edge are then aggregated in a single arc-weight.

A searched XML pattern is a partial subtree. APPROXML scans the graph data set searching for subgraphs matching the pattern supplied by the user. The tool uses the edge weights to compute the match value for each hit, and returns a list of results sorted according to the similarity level between the found subgraph and the searched pattern.

Subtree Matching in Approximate XML Joins

Another important work in XML matching is from Yiang & Yakota in (101). They proposed approximate XML join algorithms based on leaf-clustering for measuring the similarity between XML documents. The two XML documents to be joined are segmented into subtrees. The similarity degree between the two subtrees is determined by the percentage of the number of matched leaf nodes out of the number of leaf nodes in the base subtree.

However, with this solution the one-to-multiple matching problem may occur when there are more than one subtrees which have the same similarity degree with the base subtree. Liang & Yokota then extended their work and proposed a path-sequence based discrimination method (100) to determine the most similar one from several matched target subtrees. According to their definition, a path sequence of a pair of matched subtrees is the path from the root node to the matched leaf in either the base or target subtree. For a pair of matched leaves, the path-sequence similarity degree is the percentage of the number of nodes in the base path sequence that have the same labels or values with those in the target path sequence; and the total number of nodes in the base path sequence.

Jaccard's Coefficient

Different measurement methods have different ways to normalise the intersection values. One of the most popular measures is the *Jaccard's coefficient* (71), which is defined as follows. Given two sample sets X and Y, their *similarity* is defined as $sim_{Jacc}(X,Y) = \frac{|X \cap Y|}{|X \cup Y|}$, where

- $X \cap Y$ is the intersection of sets X and Y;
- $X \cup Y$ is the union of sets X and Y; and
- $|A|$ is the cardinality of set A.

Vector Space Model

Intersection-based measures do not accurately capture the similarities in certain domains, such as when the data is sparse or when there are known relationships between items within sets. The *Vector-Space* model is another popular model, especially in the information retrieval domain, where each element is modeled as a dimension in a vector space (54). A collection of elements is then represented by a vector, with components along the dimensions corresponding to the elements in the collection. The advantage of this technique is that weights can be assigned to the components of the vector.

2.4 Multicast Protocols

Some of the techniques suggested in later chapters of this book are at the level of the Web services engine (namely SOAP) to support multicast features. Such features are well-known to provide efficiency in various areas, including distributed systems (e.g. group multicast) and networking (e.g. IP multicast). Therefore it will be beneficial to give a reader an overview of different multicast solutions, and show they are suitable for Web services. Firstly, the characteristics of multicast applications are explained, followed by a discussion on the strengths and weaknesses of four various types of multicast protocols — IP multicast, application layer multicast, content-based multicast and explicit multicast protocols.

Theoretically, any application in which more than one participant shares some common data can be designed using multicast. Multicasting is suitable for the following types of applications: group type activities, file transfers, electronic distribution of software, video conferences, white-boards and live broadcasts (118). This section focuses on distribution-based type of multicast applications that are suitable for Web services deployment. Unlike broadcasting, where a message is sent to all clients, or replicated unicasting, in which messages are sent one by one to each client, multicasting involves sending messages to only a group of interested clients. Hence multicasting can be expected to reduce use of network resources.

IP Multicast Protocols

Traditionally, IP multicast routing protocols are used to perform multicast at the IP layer. IP multicast consists of a group of participants called multicast group, of which there is typically one source, many receivers, and a set of intermediate routers. The source sends the same information to all receivers by setting up a multicast tree. Each intermediate router in a multicast tree needs to support multicast in order to recognise a multicast packet, process and route it to its children nodes. Receivers use a group membership protocol to inform the network when they wish to join a group (121)(50). The network, in turn, runs a multicast routing protocol that is distinct from the unicast routing protocol. The former is used to build and maintain a distribution tree rooted at the source with branches that take the shortest, loop-free paths down to sub-networks where group members exist. A router on a multicast tree with two or more separate downstream links is responsible for copying the packet and transmitting it down each link. Figure 2.6 illustrates a typical multicast tree.

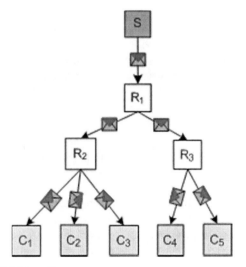

Fig. 2.6 A Simple IP Multicast Tree

Receivers C_1 to C_5 use a group membership protocol to inform the network when they wish to join a multicast group. This protocol is also used to build and maintain a distribution tree rooted at the source S. An intermediate router with two or more separate downstream links such as R_1 is responsible for copying the packet sent by the source and transmitting it down to R_2 and R_3. This process continues until all members of the multicast group receive the packet. With IP multicast, there are a total of 8 packets sent on 8 links; if unicast is used instead, 15 packets would be sent (the source needing to send a copy of the message to each client individually.) Thus, IP multicast significantly reduces the network traffic.

The most popular IP multicast protocols are Distance Vector Multicast Routing Protocol (DVMRP), Multicast Extension to OSPF (MOSPF), and Protocol Independent Multicast (PIM). DVMRP and MOSPF perform well if group members are densely packed. However, DVMRP periodically floods the network and MOSPF sends group membership information over the links (22), so these methods are not efficient in cases where group members are sparsely distributed among regions and the bandwidth is limited. Due to this scalability problem, most internet service providers rely on PIM-Sparse Mode (PIM-SM), which is adapted to groups where members are sparsely distributed (21).

One problem with IP multicast protocols is that routers have to keep a forwarding state for every multicast tree that passes through it (22). Thus these protocols suffer from scalability problems for high numbers of concurrently active multicast groups. However, the use of state maintenance contradicts the stateless philosophy of IP routing which requires network routers keep minimum possible state information for routing purposes.

Application Level Multicast Protocols

There are some applications, such as video conferences, multi-player games, private chat rooms and web cache replication, whose requirements are substantially different from the design point of IP multicast. Those applications contain small groups with few members and the groups are often terminated dynamically; the number of groups that are concurrently active may be large. For a large number of such small and sparse groups, the benefits in terms of bandwidth efficiency and scalability of IP multicast are often outweighed by the control cost and complexity associated with group set-up and maintenance (118). In these cases, there is a need for multi-sender multicast communication which scales well for a large number of communication groups with small number of members and does not depend on multicast support at routers.

Application layer multicast, a well-studied problem in the context of content distribution networks, provides multicast functionality at the application layer while assuming only unicast IP service at the network level. A range of research has addressed this area. Notably, an application level group multicast protocol, called ALMI (91), allows a simplified network configuration without need of network infrastructure support. ALMI takes a centralized approach to tree creation. Members of a multicast group perform network measurements between themselves as a measure of distance. A controller collects these measurements from all members, computes a minimum spanning tree based on measurements and then disseminates routing tables to all members.

In contrast to ALMI's centralized approach, Zhang et al. in (154) proposed a Host Multicast Tree Protocol (HMTP), which is a tree-based end-host multicast protocol. HMTP builds a group-shared tree instead of a source-specific tree. The deployment of the IP multicast protocol has been limited to "islands" of network domains under single administrative control. HMTP automates the interconnection of IP-multicast enabled islands and provides multicast delivery to end hosts where IP multicast is not available. With HMTP, end-hosts and proxy gateways of IP multicast-enabled islands can dynamically create shared multicast trees across different islands.

Each group member runs a daemon process (Host Multicast agent) in user space. The daemon program provides Host Multicast functionality at the end-host. An IP multicast island is a network of any size that supports IP multicast. Within an island, native IP multicast is used to send and receive data. One member host in an island is elected as the Designated Member (DM) for the island. Different islands are connected by UDP tunnels between DMs. Data encapsulated in UDP packets flow from one island to another through the tunnels. Upon reaching an island, the data packets are de-capsulated by the DM, and then multicast onto the island. Zhang et al.'s simulation results show that the host multicast tree has low cost and that data delivered over it experiences moderately low latency. HMTP supports the IP multicast service model and it automatically uses IP multicast where available. Thus, it takes advantages of the scalability of IP multicast, making HMTP itself more scalable.

Content-Based Multicast

A disadvantage of IP multicast is that IP multicast services do not consider the structure and semantics of the information being delivered. Especially for multicasting personalised information such as delivering country music but except some songs or artists to a recipient, traditional IP multicast does not utilize network bandwidth efficiently because full information is delivered to the recipient and filtering is done at the recipient end. Shahet et al. in (125) proposed the use of content-based multicast (CBM) in which extra content filtering is performed at the interior nodes of the IP multicast tree. If the filtering process is done at appropriate intermediary nodes, unnecessary information from each multicast group can be filtered out early, thus resulting in less total traffic.

Shah's, Ramzan's and Dendukur's objective is to minimise the total network bandwidth consumption. They describe an algorithm for an optimal filter placement in the IP multicast tree. CBM is different from application layer multicast in that IP multicast is enhanced by adding filters. The filters themselves might reside at the application or IP layer. The content filtering method will reduce network bandwidth usage and delivery delay, as well as the computation required at the sources and sinks. CBM reduces network bandwidth and recipient computation at the cost of increased computation in the network. The benefits of CBM depend critically upon how well filters are placed at interior nodes of the multicast tree.

2.5 Traditional Routing Algorithms

When dealing with Web services performance, one should not only deal with system's aspects (e.g. similarity, multicast). Network aspects must be looked at so to ensure that messages are transported (in efficient way) through various networks to destinations. This section provides an overview of existing routing algorithms.

Traditional IP networks generally employ shortest path routing algorithms. The most commonly used routing algorithms on the Internet are the Dijkstra and the Bellman-Ford shortest path algorithms.

The Bellman-Ford algorithm (19) solves the single-source shortest paths problem for a graph with both positive and negative edge weights. The algorithm maintains a distance value for each edge. At the beginning, it sets the source vertex distance to zero and all other vertices to a distance of infinity. It then loops through all edges in the graph and applies a relaxation operation to each edge. To guarantee that the distances between vertices have been reduced to the minimum, the relaxation process is repeated for n times where n is the number of vertices. The time complexity of the Bellman-Ford algorithm is $O(mn)$ where m is the number of edges.

Dijkstra's algorithm (37) is similar to the Bellman-Ford algorithm but has a lower execution time and requires non-negative edge weights. The cost of an edge can represent the distance between two associated vertices. For a given pair of vertices s and v, the algorithm finds the path from s to v with the lowest cost. The algorithm can also be used to build a shortest path tree from a source to multiple destinations by adding a new destination node with the minimum path cost from the source to the current tree at each step. Using the Fibonacci heap[1], Dijkstra's algorithm runs in $O(m+nlogn)$ time, where m is the number of edges and n is the number of vertices.

Another classical minimum spanning tree algorithm in graph theory is Prim's algorithm (95). Prim's algorithm finds a minimum-cost spanning tree of an edge-weighted, connected, and undirected graph. The algorithm begins with a tree that contains only one vertex, it then repeatedly adds the lowest-weight edge that would connect a new vertex to the tree without forming a cycle. The time complexity of Prim's algorithm is the same as Dijkstra's algorithm if it is implemented using the Fibonacci heap. Both Prim's and Dijkstra's algorithms implement the greedy-choice strategy for a minimum spanning tree; the difference between them is the cost function used to add a new node to a current tree. In Prim's algorithm, a new node that has the minimum edge cost to a node already in the tree will be added, while in Dijkstra's algorithm, a node that has the minimum total cost to the source is added.

The three routing algorithms described above (Dijkstra, Prim and Bellman-Ford algorithms) can find optimal paths according to their routing metrics in polynomial time. However, they cannot determine routing paths based on multiple QoS constraints such as delay, delay jitter and bandwidth constraints, constraints which are required by many applications (14).

---

[1] A Fibonacci heap is a heap data structure consisting of a collection of trees. Each tree satisfies the minimum-heap property, that is, the key of a child node is always greater than or equal to the key of the parent node (99).

2.6 Some Queueing Concepts

Queuing Theory

Throughout this book we utilise queueing theoretic principles to model the performance of various task task assignment policies. Queueing theory provides a stochastic and probabilistic approach to investigate the operation of queues. Figure 2.7 illustrates a basic queueing process.

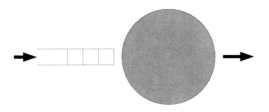

Fig. 2.7 A Cluster-based Distributed Computing System

Kendall's notation (72) is used to describe a queueing system. Kendall's notation represents a queueing system in a form of $(A/B/C/D/E/F)$ where

- A : The arrival pattern of tasks
- B : The service pattern of tasks
- C : The number of servers
- D : The system capacity
- E : The service discipline

The arrival pattern describes the distribution of arriving tasks while service pattern describes the distribution of services times of tasks. The arrival pattern to a queueing system is typically described in terms of average time between two successive arrivals or average number of arrivals per some unit of time. The capacity is the maximum number of customers allowed to enter the system this quantity is often referred as the buffer size and the buffer size could be either bounded or unbounded. Third parameter describes number of servers in a queueing system. Finally, the service discipline describes the manner by which the tasks are selected for service. First-Come-First-Serve (FCFS), Last-Come-First-Serve (LCFS) and shortest remaining processing time are a few examples of service disciplines, FCFS being the most common service discipline.

Poisson Process

Throughout this chapter we represent our arrivals using the Poisson arrival process. Poisson process typically appears in nature when we observe the aggregated effect of large number of arrivals into systems. Poisson process is typically used to model the task arrivals in web servers farms or super computing clusters (27, 147). Let us consider an arrival process $N(t), t \geq 0$, where $N(t)$ denotes the total number of tasks that arrive up to time t, then a Poisson process having rate λ is such that:

- $N(0) = 0$.
- The process has independent increments. This means that the numbers of arrivals in non-overlapping intervals are statistically independent.
- The number of arrivals in any interval of length t has a Poisson distribution with mean λt

$$P(N(t+x) - N(x)) = n) = \frac{\exp^{\lambda t}(\lambda t)^n}{n!} \quad n = 0, 1, \ldots \tag{2.1}$$

where $t \geq 0 \ \forall x$

If the arrival process is Poisson it can be shown that the inter-arrival time distribution is exponential. Let T_1, T_2,.. be the inter-arrival times of tasks then the distribution of inter-arrival times is given by;

$$P(t) = \lambda \exp^{\lambda t} \tag{2.2}$$

Alternatively, we can prove that if the inter-arrival time distribution exponential then the arrival process is Poisson.

Heavy-tailed workloads

The service time distribution of tasks (i.e. relates second parameter in Kendall's notation) plays an important role when designing a new task assignment policy. As mentioned earlier realistic computer workloads are highly variable and follow so called Heavy-tailed distributions. A distribution is said to be heavy-tailed if it has the following form:

$$P(X > x) \sim x^{-\alpha} \ 0 < \alpha < 2 \tag{2.3}$$

Heavy-tailed distributions possess *three* key properties, namely, the decreasing failure rate, infinite variance and the property that less than 1% of the tasks make up a 50% of the load. In equation 2.3, α represents the variability of tasks and it is related to the variance of the distribution. As α increases the variability of jobs in the distribution decreases and vice versa. A most widely used heavy-tailed distribution as the service time distribution is the Pareto Distribution. The probability density function of the Pareto distribution is given by

$$f(x) = \alpha k^{\alpha} x^{-\alpha - 1} \tag{2.4}$$

The Pareto distribution defined by Equation 2.4 does not have an upper bounded for the service time. If we assume that the service times have some maximum value, we obtain the Bounded Pareto distribution.

The probability density function of the Bounded Pareto distribution is depicted in equation 2.5.

$$f(x) = \frac{\alpha k^\alpha}{1 - (k/p)^\alpha} \; x^{-\alpha-1} \quad k < x < p \tag{2.5}$$

Note that

$$\int_k^p f(x) = \int_k^p \frac{\alpha k^\alpha}{1 - (k/p)^\alpha} \; x^{-\alpha-1} = 1, \quad k < x < p \tag{2.6}$$

A Bounded Pareto distribution is characterised by three parameters k, p and α, where, k and p are the smallest (shortest) and largest (longest) possible service times. α represents the job size variability and the lower the value of α the higher the variability of task sizes (variance) and vice versa. Figure 2.8, plots Bounded Pareto Distribution with an upper bound of 10^7 and a lower bounded of 100. We note Pr (service time = x) decreases rapidly with increasing task size. Also notice that as α increases, the tail of the distribution becomes thinner (in area) indicating that the variability of the distribution is decreasing as a result $P(X > x)$ increases.

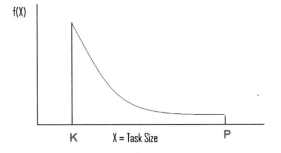

Fig. 2.8 Bounded Pareto Distribution

Many recent task assignment policies are based on Bounded Pareto Distribution (25, 26, 62, 98, 138) and in most cases it is possible to define an upper Bound for the workload distributions. For example, the upper bound of the service time distribution of files stored on a file sever is related to the largest file stored on the server.

Since, we consider task assignment in batch computing systems the expected waiting time of the policies we consider in this chapter are based on $M/G/1/FCFS$ queue. The expected waiting time of $M/G/1$ is given by the Pollaczek-Khinchin formula (74)

$$E[W]_{FCFS} = \frac{\lambda E[X^2]}{2(1 - \lambda E[X])} \tag{2.7}$$

In equation 2.7, $E[X^2]$, $E[X]$ and λ represent the second moment, the first moment (mean) and the average arrival rate into the system respectively. The jth, 1st

and 2nd moments of Bounded Pareto distribution are given by the following equations.

$$E[X^j] = \begin{cases} \frac{\alpha k^\alpha (k^{j-\alpha}-p^{j-\alpha})}{(\alpha-j)(1-(k/p)^\alpha)} & \text{if } \alpha \neq j, \\ \frac{k}{(1-(\frac{k}{p}))}(\ln p - \ln k) & \text{if } \alpha = j \end{cases} \qquad (2.8)$$

$$E[X] = \begin{cases} \frac{\alpha k^\alpha (k^{1-\alpha}-p^{1-\alpha})}{(\alpha-1)(1-(\frac{k}{p})^\alpha)} & \text{if } \alpha \neq j, \\ \frac{k}{(1-(\frac{k}{p}))}(\ln p - \ln k) & \text{if } \alpha = 1 \end{cases} \qquad (2.9)$$

$$E[X^2] = \begin{cases} \frac{\alpha k^\alpha (k^{2-\alpha}-p^{2-\alpha})}{(\alpha-2)(1-(\frac{k}{p})^\alpha)} & \text{if } \alpha \neq j, \\ \frac{k}{(1-(\frac{k}{p}))}(\ln p - \ln k) & \text{if } \alpha = 2 \end{cases} \qquad (2.10)$$

Task Migration

There are different types of migrations possible in cluster-based distributed systems. The types of systems that we consider are

- Systems that support no migration.
- Systems that support work-conserving migration: These type of systems allow tasks to migrated between two hosts during the execution of tasks. Work-conversing migration, migrates information such as process address space, register content from the source node to the destination hosts. The execution of the migrated task is resumed at the destination host.
- systems that supports non work-conserving migration: Non-work conserving migration is also called remote invocation. Remote invocation does not require the current status of running task to migrated from the source node to the destination node. Therefore, it is less expensive compared to work-conserving migration. The drawback is that this type of migration requires the migrated task to be restarted at the destination host.

The objective of task migration is to improve the overall performance of a given system. Whether to use migration and if so which type of migration to use depend on the workload characteristics such distribution of service times and system load.

2.7 Summary

In this chapter, the Web services architecture and its important standards were described. This architecture is important because it is the foundation of the work presented in this book. Traditional multicast protocols have also been explained to provide background for understanding the similarity-based multicast protocol for SOAP presented in the next chapters. In addition, common network routing algorithms such as Dijkstra's, Bellman-Ford's and Prim's algorithms have been reviewed. Finally we gave some basic concepts in queuing, which will be helpful to understand the chapters related to server side performance.

Part I
System Level Performance

Chapter 3
Benchmarking SOAP Binding

"Wisdom begins in Wonder."

Socrates

Wireless environments are the right ones where performance evaluation need to be done. Handheld devices with wireless capability are gaining popularity, and the future of Web Services will focus the large scale delivery of services on mobile devices. A lot of performance studies have been done on wired networks, and the aim of this chapter is to give another perspective to show the reader the major issues of SOAP when dealing with mobile applications.

SOAP is a text-based protocol for Web services, but it has high overhead, hence its suitability for resource-constrained devices over wireless networks needs to be reevaluated. Existing Web services often rely on HTTP — the most popular underlying transport protocol for SOAP messaging. While the HTTP protocol provides a number of benefits, including being able to pass through firewalls and being widely supported across different platforms, it was designed for wired networks with high bandwidth, low latency and low error rate transmissions. Due to the variability of wireless channels however, these assumptions do not hold in wireless environments. In this chapter, a benchmark of the performance of different underlying transport protocols for SOAP in wireless environments is reported. Through extensive testing, it is shown that SOAP-over-HTTP and SOAP-over-TCP are not well suited for wireless applications and lead to high latency and high transmission overhead. To overcome these limitations, the use of UDP as a binding protocol for SOAP is studied. The results obtained are promising and show that SOAP-over-UDP provides throughput that is up to six times higher than SOAP-over-HTTP in a wireless setting. Furthermore, using UDP to transport SOAP messages reduces transmission overhead by more than 30% compared to SOAP-over-HTTP. Finally, to illustrate where UDP binding can be useful, example applications are described.

3.1 Motivation

The mobile phone industry is enjoying an escalating growth all over the world. According to a recent market research (1), there are more than 300 million Java-enabled mobile handsets in use. In addition, there has been an explosive development of mobile telecommunications networks over the past few years. The expansion of 3G networks around the globe has changed the way people access services. Similarly, the sale of laptop and tablet type devices has also grown rapidly over the past ten years and these devices have become important tools for mobile workers who have to access and update data electronically.

Together with the expansion of mobile devices, their built-in capabilities are also being extended, especially towards programmable operating systems. This trend has led to the growth of new applications that can be built into these small devices. For example, the Compact .Net Framework (107) is supported on many Windows Mobile PDAs and smart phones, while J2ME (132) is supported on many Palm devices and Symbian operating system-based phones.

In parallel, Web service paradigm has experienced a great surge of interest in both industry and academia. Web services and mobile technology have together influenced the design aspect of mobile services. Web services enable mobile devices to consume and provide services. There has been a significant amount of research into adapting mobile computing to the Web services architecture. Recently, Sun Microsystems released JSR 172 (133), a specification that addresses the use of XML, SOA and Web service on J2ME devices.

However, SOAP was originally designed for wired networks; it is poor at dealing with the challenges of wireless communications and the resource limitations of mobile devices — slow CPU, low memory and limited battery life (29). Currently, SOAP performance is one of the critical integration issues attracting a lot of research in the area of mobile Web services. Other issues are context-awareness, adaptability and security (30).

Existing research on SOAP performance (39, 41, 111, 140) has found that current implementations of SOAP using HTTP as the transport protocol are slower than other middleware technologies such as Java RMI and CORBA. In particular, (35) investigated the limitations of SOAP for scientific computing. Their experiments compared SOAP to Java RMI by sending large arrays of doubles; the results showed that SOAP is about ten times slower than Java RMI. (73) studied SOAP performance in business applications in the context of trading systems. Their study compared SOAP to a binary wire format, called Common Data Representation (CDR), which is used in CORBA communication. Their results showed that SOAP is 2–3 times slower than the Internet Inter-ORB Protocol (IIOP) (88) that uses CDR.

Despite SOAP performance issues, XML, SOAP and WSDL together provide a framework for data exchange across various computing platforms and environments. Thus, Web services are used in favour of other middleware technologies for interoperability between heterogeneous systems. The binding implementation of SOAP over HTTP is universally used on the Internet today, but this implementation has some drawbacks especially in mobile environments. The disadvantages of using SOAP over HTTP in mobile computing are mostly due to the nature of HTTP and TCP protocols themselves. When a SOAP message is sent over HTTP, the following overhead results from the connection-oriented property of TCP:

- TCP requires a connection to be established before any data can be transmitted. Moreover, as data is received, acknowledgement packets are sent. This leads to additional overhead which may not be justifiable where bandwidth and client power are limited and reliable transmission of packets is not required.

- SOAP messages that carry only a small amount of data can finish transmitting while the TCP connection is in its slow start phase. This results in poor utilisation of the available bandwidth. The problem is particularly severe in wireless environments due to high round trip time.
- The congestion avoidance mechanism in TCP assumes packet losses are always due to congestion. However, in a wireless network, packet losses are usually due to disconnections and transmission errors. This impacts on bandwidth utilisation.

This chapter aims to provide a detailed comparison between three different SOAP binding options, SOAP over HTTP (with TCP as transport protocol), SOAP over TCP and SOAP over UDP in wireless environments. These comparisons are important because the results obtained will highlight the strengths and weaknesses of each binding option. With this knowledge, the most suitable binding can be determined for different types of usage scenarios. The results from this study will be useful for other researchers to examine the effectiveness in performance of these transport protocols to the development of Web service in wireless networks. Experimental results show that SOAP-over-UDP provides performance benefits over the traditional SOAP-over-HTTP binding.

The rest of this chapter is organised as follows. The next section examines the limitations of mobile devices and wireless networks, different SOAP engines used in wireless environments and the SOAP binding framework. Related work on mobile Web service performance is presented in Section 3.3. This is followed by a section outlining the experimental results and analysis of the benchmark. Section 3.6 presents some sample applications that are suitable for different kinds of SOAP bindings. Finally, this chapter concludes by a summary section reviewing the advantages of UDP binding over HTTP and TCP bindings.

3.2 Background

In this section, background on concepts related to the work presented in this chapter is described. Firstly, an overview of mobile Web services are explained, followed by a discussion of limitations of mobile devices and wireless networks. Subsequently, some popular SOAP implementations for mobile devices are described. Finally, common SOAP bindings with HTTP, TCP and SMTP transport protocols are presented.

Mobile Web Services

With the advancement in wireless technologies in general, and mobile device capabilities in particular, ubiquitous access of mobile Web services continues to be an important research topic. Mobile Web services are the deployment of Web services in mobile environments. Web service clients are not limited to desktop computers but extended to mobile devices such as laptops, tablet PCs, PDAs, smart-phones and mobile phones. However, the evolution of mobile Web services is not only about requesting services from mobile clients but also providing services on mobile devices. In the general case, a mobile device can act as either a Web service requestor or provider or both.

Due to the nature of mobile wireless networks, existing middleware infrastructure cannot efficiently support Web services on mobile devices. Deploying a SOAP client on a mobile phone might reveal some performance costs related to slow transmission and processing of both HTTP commands and XML. The mobility of devices raises a number of issues, such as service discovery, networking and security that are different from those in the domain of fixed workstations. Additionally, the constraints on computational power and battery life on mobile devices add another dimension to the challenge.

Limitations of Mobile Devices and Wireless Networks

Mobile devices generally have much lower CPU power, storage capacity and smaller memory than servers and desktop computers. Therefore, Web service implementations on mobile devices should take computational time, memory and energy resources into careful consideration.

Mobile devices are often dependent on wireless communication protocols for connectivity. Some wireless connections such as 802.11 or Bluetooth are short in range. The users of mobile devices may also experience frequent disconnections due to being out of range of a network access point — services that are offered on mobile devices should be tolerant to such network failures because the services may not be accessible all the time. In addition, mobile devices' constrained energy supply places a restriction on the design of mobile Web services that services should not consume too much device energy.

A brief summary of issues that are inherent to wireless environments is provided below.

- *Intermittent connections*: Mobile devices do not have network connectivity everywhere at all times. Whether it is a cellular, 802.11 network or Bluetooth, wireless networks suffer from regular disconnections.
- *Limited bandwidth*: Even though the available bandwidth of wireless networks is increasing, many wireless networks have limited bandwidth of around 64–300 Kb/s.
- *Latency*: Wireless network connections are slow; thus high latencies not only affect applications but may frustrate users.
- *High cost*: In spite of the dropping trend, wireless rates are expensive.

SOAP Implementations for Mobile Devices

A number of SOAP implementations such as as gSOAP (9), kSOAP (66) and pocketSOAP (47) have been implemented on mobile devices. Among the three, kSOAP was chosen as the SOAP client implementation in the SOAP binding benchmark presented in this chapter, because of its popularity and ease of use. In addition, kSOAP is written in Java and designed to run in an MIDP (Mobile Information Device Profile) (134) environment which most mobile phones support. The SOAP API of kSOAP provides a small footprint implementation of XML aimed at developing applications for mobile devices using J2ME (132). The implementation of kSOAP is based on kXML (67), an open source API that provides an XML pull parser especially designed for constrained environments such as Applets, Personal Java and MIDP devices.

SOAP Bindings. A SOAP binding is the enveloping of a SOAP data payload within underlying protocols. Such bindings have to specify the rules for encapsulating or decapsulating SOAP data from the underlying protocol. This section introduces some popular SOAP bindings.

SOAP-over-HTTP. Over the Internet, HTTP is the protocol that is most widely used for SOAP binding. Because HTTP is one of the core protocols of the Internet and is widely supported by Web servers, SOAP-over-HTTP is the only concrete binding specification defined in the SOAP binding framework proposal (58). Because it is often allowed to pass through firewalls, it is a convenient candidate for transporting SOAP. The recommended version of HTTP for SOAP binding is HTTP/1.1 and all SOAP implementations provide this binding.

A SOAP message can be transported using HTTP by encapsulating the SOAP request into the message body of a HTTP GET or HTTP POST. Similarly, a SOAP response can be encapsulated into the body of a HTTP response (85). HTTP binding provides reliable message transport, flow and congestion control. However, SOAP-over-HTTP has some drawbacks, for instance it does not support peer-to-peer messaging exchange between SOAP nodes. The response time is generally higher when using HTTP as the transport protocol for SOAP because of the handshake process occurring at the TCP layer.

SOAP-over-TCP. In order to transport a SOAP message using TCP as a direct underlying protocol, a SOAP message is stored in the data octets part of a TCP packet (see Figure 3.1). There is not yet any official specification for SOAP binding with TCP, however, Apache Axis (10) and Microsoft Web Service Enhancement (WSE) 2.0 (108) include APIs that enable the sending of SOAP messages via TCP. Two types of TCP-based messaging (namely synchronous and asynchronous) are supported in the WSE 2.0. In synchronous TCP messaging, the request and response messages are exchanged over a common TCP connection as in the Request-Response MEP. With the asynchronous mode, the TCP connection is removed after a message has been sent, representing the one-way messaging pattern in SOAP.

SOAP-over-SMTP In addition to the HTTP binding, a SOAP-over-email binding is also present in the W3C specification (85). However, unlike the HTTP binding, which forms part of the SOAP standard, the SOAP-over-email binding is only presented in the specification as an example to demonstrate the realisation of the SOAP

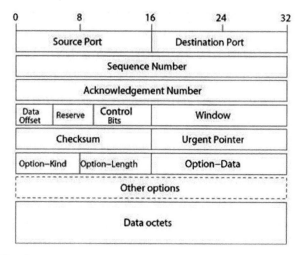

Fig. 3.1 A TCP packet

binding framework. In the SOAP-over-email binding, SOAP messages are piggy-backed on SMTP packets.

3.3 Related Work on SOAP Performance

Existing studies on improving SOAP performance in wired and wireless environments are discussed in this section.

SOAP performance has been the main focus of many research papers over the past few years. These studies have proposed several approaches for improving the overall performance of SOAP to make Web services technologies more viable in replacing traditional distributed object technologies such as CORBA and Java RMI. Gryazin and Seppala compared SOAP with CORBA for mobile devices and found that the performance of Web services does not depend on the implementation of SOAP (56). They also concluded that SOAP is more suitable for larger scale systems with non-critical architectures while CORBA is more robust and flexible for mobile applications.

(68) proposed a standard benchmark suite for different SOAP implementations. They reported on the performance of existing popular SOAP implementations including Axis Java (10), gSOAP (9) and bSOAP (5), from aspects of serialisation, deserialization, namespace and latency. Their results show that gSOAP is the best for latency critical applications. Axis Java does not perform well either in Windows or Linux environments. Protocol gSOAP also scales well with an increase in the size of complex data types, and can reduce the Web service overhead. In contrast, Axis Java does not provide good scalability. Protocol bSOAP is comparable to gSOAP when sending arrays of doubles, integers and strings.

The performance of Web services using J2ME and kSOAP clients measured on a PDA and an IBM Thinkpad laptop was reported by (15). These clients access a temperature service and a translation service which are available from the Internet. Bansal's and Dalton's results show that the main bottlenecks are low available bandwidth causing large transmission time and the high cost associated with XML parsing.

(57) proposed a framework to allow accessing Web services from J2ME mobile devices using WAP. Because of the high overhead of HTTP, the authors develop a Java Wireless Session Protocol (WSP) implementation to avoid the TCP three way handshake and to reduce header size. Their experiments show that the protocol header can be reduced by more than a third by choosing WSP instead of HTTP to transport SOAP messages. However, the memory footprint (the size of the MIDlet[1]) required when using WSP (89K) is higher than when using HTTP (54K). The time spent on parsing SOAP messages was similar for HTTP and WSP, however the transmission time of the SOAP messages was reduced by about a third by choosing WSP instead of HTTP.

Researchers at the DoCoMo USA labs proposed a set of SOAP optimisation techniques called Wireless SOAP (WSOAP) to transmit SOAP messages across wireless networks (12) with significant bandwidth reduction compared to generic SOAP. WSOAP's principles are based on adaptive encoding which relies on the underlying WSDL service description being known by both the sender and receiver. Their experiments demonstrate that WSOAP can reduce the size of SOAP messages by 3–12 times compared to generic SOAP. Their proposed optimisation techniques outperform the differential encoding technique proposed by (144) and WAP binary XML (148) by large factors.

(78) discussed issues and strategies to extend the reliability of Web services in wireless communication environments. A Web Service-Wireless Reliable Messaging (WS-WRM) framework is designed to interoperate with other reliability schemes such as WS-Reliability (115) and WS-ReliableMessaging (20) which are general specifications for Web service reliable messaging. WS-WRM uses negative acknowledgement messages to reduce the data communication overhead. The limited data storage capability on the mobile end-points is also taken into consideration. Not all three messaging patterns of HTTP binding (Request-Response, Callback and Polling) (115) are available on mobile devices. Due to this limitation, Lee and Fox implemented WS-WRM on top of their NaradaBrokering service (53) instead of binding WS-WRM directly to HTTP. NaradaBrokering service, which was built by the same authors, is a general purpose event brokering system designed to run a large network of cooperating broker nodes. The authors also propose a message integrity feature by offering multiple algorithms, and the services can specify the algorithm based on their requirements.

3.4 SOAP-over-UDP

UDP is a simple, low-overhead transport protocol, and Figure 3.2 shows a UDP datagram. Unlike TCP, it does not provide any flow-control mechanism and only

---

[1] A MIDlet is a Java program for embedded devices

guarantees best-effort delivery of packets. Packets delivered by UDP may be duplicated, arrive out of sequence or not even reach their destination at all. However, due to its simplicity, UDP provides a number of benefits over TCP:

- UDP does not require a connection to be established before sending a packet. Each UDP datagram carries its own destination address and is routed independently of other packets. This reduces the setup time associated with sending a message.
- UDP packets are smaller than TCP packets. The UDP header is only eight bytes in length, in comparison to the TCP header which is at least 20 bytes in length. For wireless environments where bandwidth availability is low and users are charged by the amount of data they transmit and receive, UDP provides a cheaper alternative to TCP.
- UDP supports multicasting. This opens up the opportunity to create push-based and publish/subscribe Web services, where SOAP messages or notifications are sent to multiple clients periodically or triggered by an event.

Because of these advantages, SOAP-over-UDP as an alternative binding for SOAP messaging is examined. UDP is light-weight, unreliable and connectionless. Due to its simplicity, UDP has little overhead and offers fast packet delivery. These characteristics may be desirable for applications where high transfer rate is valued over reliability, for example, real-time multimedia streaming. UDP is also suitable for quick exchange of information that is small in size. An example of this is the domain name service (DNS), which uses UDP datagrams to transmit domain name lookup requests (122).

The recently released SOAP-over-UDP specification (18) defines how a SOAP message can be encapsulated into the *data octets* part of a single UDP packet (see Figure 3.2). The SOAP message must be small enough to fit within a single datagram, less than 65,536 (2^{16}) bytes in size. The specification supports four message exchange patterns (MEP) as follows:

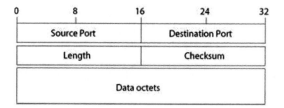

Fig. 3.2 A UDP datagram

- Unicast one-way: This is a pattern for the exchange of a non-SOAP message acting as a request followed by a SOAP message acting as a response.
- Multicast one-way: Only the request is sent out to a multicast or broadcast address.

- Unicast request, unicast response: The SOAP Request-Response MEP defines a pattern for the exchange of a SOAP message acting as a request followed by a message acting as a response.
- Multicast request, unicast response: The response must not be multicast. The sender of the request might receive multiple responses. The correlation between the request and response messages is realised by using Web Services Addressing properties.

A request message is first transferred from the requesting SOAP node to the responding SOAP node. Following the successful processing of the request message by the responding SOAP node, a response message is transferred from the responding SOAP node to the requesting SOAP node. In the absence of failure in the underlying protocol, this MEP consists of exactly two messages. Each message can be identified by a unique message identifier ($< wsa : MessageID >$) and a source and reply address can specify the message flow between the service requestor and provider. The Web Services Addressing information is stored within the SOAP header. The properties for the exchange of a SOAP message. In the absence of failure in the underlying protocol, this MEP consists of zero or more SOAP messages. The scope of a one-way MEP instance is limited to transmission of messages from one sending node to zero or more receiving SOAP node(s).

An abnormal operation during a Request-Response message exchange might be caused by a failure to transfer the request message, a failure at the responding SOAP node to process the request message, or a failure to transfer the response message. Such failures might be silent at either or both of the requesting and responding SOAP nodes involved, or might result in the generation of a SOAP or binding-specific fault. Also, during abnormal operation each SOAP node involved in the message exchange might differ in its determination of the successful completion of the message exchange.

The scope of a Request-Response MEP is limited to the exchange of a request message and a response message between one requesting and one responding SOAP node. This pattern does not mandate any correlation between multiple requests nor specific timing for multiple requests. Implementations may choose to support multiple ongoing requests (and associated response processing) at the same time.

The SOAP Response MEP defines a pattern for the exchange of a non-SOAP message acting as a request followed by a SOAP message acting as a response. In the absence of failure in the underlying protocol, this MEP consists of exactly two messages, only one of which is a SOAP message:

- A request transmitted in a binding-specific manner that does not include a SOAP envelope and hence does not involve any SOAP processing by the receiving SOAP node.
- The scope of a SOAP Response MEP is limited to the request for an exchange of a response message between one requesting and one responding SOAP node. This pattern does not mandate any correlation between multiple requests nor specific timing for multiple requests. Implementations MAY choose to support multiple ongoing requests (and associated response processing) at the same time.

- A response message which contains a SOAP envelope. The MEP is completed by the processing of the SOAP envelope following the rules of the SOAP processing model.

3.5 SOAP Binding Benchmark

This section presents the different experimental setups and results. The experiment was intended to identify the performance tradeoffs when selecting different transport protocols for SOAP. Three SOAP bindings (SOAP-over-HTTP, SOAP-over-TCP and SOAP-over-UDP) were tested and compared to each other. There are three sets of tests. In the first set, three transport protocols were tested in a loopback mode. In the second set, the tests were carried out between two computers under a WLAN mode. The last set of tests involved the deployment of SOAP clients on hand-held devices.

3.5.1 Experimental Setup

A test system was set up to measure the performance of the three transport protocols for SOAP communication. The test driver used for the benchmark is a modified version of the WSTest 1.0 (135) developed by Sun Microsystems. WSTest was specified as part of a benchmarking experiment comparing the performance of J2EE Web services and .Net Web services. Sun's WSTest has been revised to include the following Web service calls[2]:

- `echoVoid`: sends and receives an empty message, no deserialization or serialisation of payload is required. This service call examines the performance of the transport protocol infrastructure.
- `echoDouble`: sends and receives a message of type `Double`.
- `echoString`: sends and receives a message of type `String`.
- `echoStruct`: sends and receives an array of 10 elements, with each element consisting of a structure. The repeating structures within the array contain one element each of type `Integer`, `Float` and `String` data types. The longer the array size is; the more effort is required in deserializing and re-serialising the SOAP object to and from XML documents.
- `echoList`: sends and receives a linked list of 10 elements, each element consists of the same structure used in Struct as defined above. Within a test, the number of elements in a list is the same as in a struct.

These Web service calls were selected to separate message headers from payload and to create a test-bed with different message types and sizes.

The purpose of these tests is to examine SOAP performance with different data sizes and types. Each Web service method is an echo function in which a client sends a data message of a particular data structure to the server and the server responds with the same message. The test is highly configurable. The number of concurrent

---

[2] Web service calls: `echoDouble` and `echoString` were added from the original WSTest driver.

running clients, the startup (time allocated for warm up of the system, running (the interval when throughput is measured) and ramp-down (time allocated for completing operations) times can be specified. The size of the data payload in each service call can also be varied.

The WSTest service was hosted on a PC server while multiple clients were simulated on a PC client to request the service over a wireless network. The machines used for testing are two desktop PCs having similar hardware configurations: Pentium III, 966Mhz CPU with 256 Mb RAM, running Java 2 SDK 1.4.1 on a Redhat Linux 9 operating system. Both machines are equipped with an 802.11b wireless antenna each and connected via a Netgear WG602 wireless router. The experiments were performed using a wireless connection speed of 54Mbps. The SOAP frameworks used in the experiments were Apache Axis 1.2 (10) on the server and kSOAP 2.0 (66) on the client. Tomcat 5.0 (11) was used on the server to host the Web service. Both the client and the server were written in Java. The testing environment is depicted in Figure 3.3.

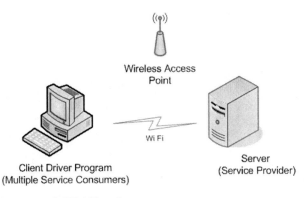

Wireless Access
Point

Wi Fi

Client Driver Program
(Multiple Service Consumers)

Server
(Service Provider)

Fig. 3.3 Experiment setup in WLAN mode

Performance was tested under three modes:

- *Loopback*: The server and the client both ran on the same computer. Connection was via the loopback (localhost) interface, therefore no packet loss or bandwidth limits apply to this mode.
- *WLAN*: Computer 1 hosted the server and computer 2 ran the client application that generated multiple concurrent requests to the Web service. The two computers were connected via a wireless router. They were the only machines connected to the router at the time of the test. A series of pings from computer 2 to computer 1 showed that the average round trip time was 27 ms.
- *Mobile device*: The Web service was hosted on the server. Client requests were made from mobile devices. The client tests were deployed on 2 PDAs: 1 HP iPAQ h6300 series and 1 Palm Treo 650. Two mobile clients accessed the service via a WLAN connection at the same time, and the response time of each request type

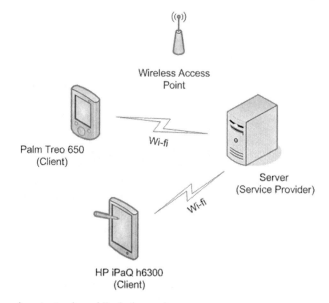

Fig. 3.4 Experiment setup in mobile device mode

was reported. The `echoDouble` call was not tested since the mobile devices did not support floating point. For the same reason, the Struct and the List data types do not include the float elements. Figure 3.4 illustrates the test environment for this mode.

The performance metrics used as part of the performance testing include:

- *Throughput*: The average number of Web service operations executed per second. A Web service operation here corresponds to a request/response cycle.
- *Average response time*: Average time taken to process a request at the server and send a response back to a client.

3.5.2 Experimental Results and Analysis

First, the protocol overhead of each binding is analysed. Then experimental results for loopback, WLAN and mobile device modes are presented. These experiments are designed to measure how many dynamic requests can be processed per second over a fixed amount of time (throughput), as well as the average response time for each client. Both measurements were calculated under varying user loads.

The number of concurrent users (user load) was steadily increased to see when each of the application server response times begins to degrade, and how long users have to wait for each page as the load increases (up to a maximum acceptable time of 3 seconds for each transaction).

Generally speaking, response times do not significantly increase as user load is added until a bottleneck is reached. In this testing, the network and database were scaled to ensure the tests accurately measured application tier capacity. Hence, once the application tier became saturated, response times would start to rapidly rise. The user load at which this change in slope was observed is the elbow in the performance curve, and was used to calculate the maximum number of users the application server can be expected to support. This elbow typically occurs at the point maximum throughput is observed.

Transmission Overhead

The metrics are used for packet overhead (which is the sum of the SOAP payload and the protocol header) and connection overhead (which is the sum of generated traffic as the result of connection establishment). Figure 3.5 shows the size of different messages created by different binding options. The messages shown here are request messages for different Web service operations. Since all service operations are echoing functions, the size of a response is similar to its request. It is shown that for an empty payload message, echoVoid, SOAP-over-HTTP transmits nearly twice the number of bytes compared to SOAP-over-UDP. With small size messages such as echoDouble and echoString, clients only need to send to the server a parameter of type Double or of type String (under 50 bytes), however the HTTP and TCP headers add significant overhead to the SOAP request for SOAP-over-HTTP messages. UDP has some header overhead, however this is only 8 bytes. Similar behaviours are seen for the echoStruct and echoList message types.

The size of echoStruct and echoList requests are significantly larger than the other message types because they contain an array of simple data types or a linked list of struct data types. With larger message types, SOAP-over-HTTP adds about 30% to the size of a SOAP message, compared to SOAP-over-UDP. In all cases, there is no significant difference in message size between TCP and UDP bindings because the TCP header is also small (24 bytes). For messages carrying only a few parameters (e.g. echoVoid, echoDouble and echoString), using UDP can reduce message size by about 50% compared to HTTP. This is significant for mobile clients that repeatedly send simple SOAP requests to a server, because such a reduction in message size leads to a huge saving in transmission cost and client energy consumption.

Figure 3.6 shows a breakdown of the message overhead in terms of packet overhead and connection overhead using HTTP, TCP and UDP bindings for the different message types. For example, SOAP-over-HTTP messages contains a HTTP header, a TCP header and the actual SOAP message. It can be seen that TCP and UDP have very similar packet overheads, however the connection overhead of using SOAP-over-TCP makes TCP more expensive than UDP. In the case of request messages, the connection overhead is a result of the connection establishment handshake consisting of three separate packets (SYN, SYN-ACK and ACK) (6). Once the server has responded to the requests, four more packets (FIN and ACK each from sender and receiver) are used to tear down the connection. The connection

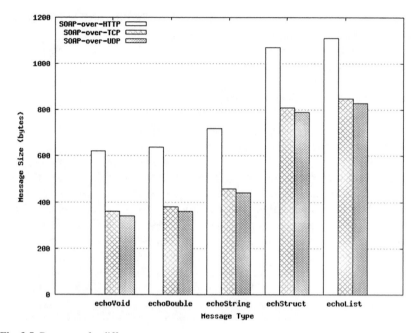

Fig. 3.5 Bytes sent for different message types

overheads of echoStruct and echoList are slightly increased further as the
SOAP responses for these requests do not fit into a single TCP packet. As a result,
a large response has to be segmented into multiple packets, which introduces TCP
acknowledgement packets with additional overheads into the message exchange.

Experiments performed over loopback connection

Next, the impacts of using different binding options on execution time and throughput are studied in loopback mode. Figure 3.7 shows the average time it takes for
each client to execute a request over the loopback connection when there were 50
simulated clients concurrently making requests. For various message types, SOAP-
over-UDP is significantly faster than SOAP-over-TCP and SOAP-over-HTTP. The
poor performance of TCP and HTTP is mainly due to the additional cost in encoding and decoding HTTP and TCP headers and also the time spent on connection establishment. SOAP-over-TCP is roughly 17% faster than SOAP-over-HTTP, while
SOAP-over-UDP is around 30% faster than SOAP-over-HTTP.

Another important performance metric is throughput, reflecting the scalability of
the binding options tested. Figure 3.8 plots the throughput (number of messages processed per second by the server) under the loopback connection scenario. With small
message types (echoVoid, echoDouble and echoString), it is found that the

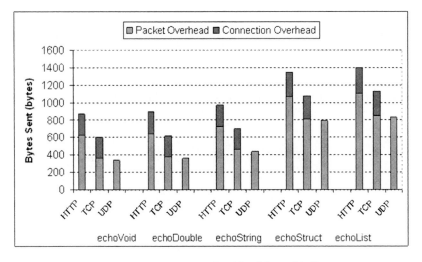

Fig. 3.6 Connection overhead versus Packet overhead for different bindings

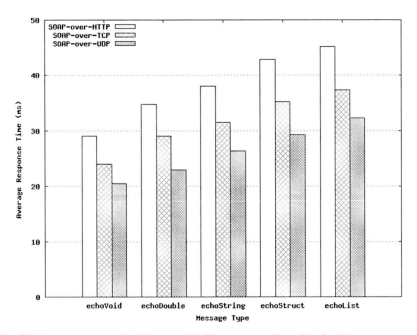

Fig. 3.7 Average response time for a test with 50 concurrent clients (loopback)

throughput of SOAP-over-HTTP (1800 transactions per second) is slightly smaller than that of SOAP-over-TCP (2000 transactions per second). The throughput of SOAP-over-UDP is significantly higher (over 2500 transactions per second) than both SOAP-over-HTTP and SOAP-over-TCP. Using the UDP binding, SOAP messages can be sent without setting up a connection, thus minimal system resources are used. Furthermore, the simplicity of the UDP protocol means the server can process UDP headers faster than TCP and HTTP headers.

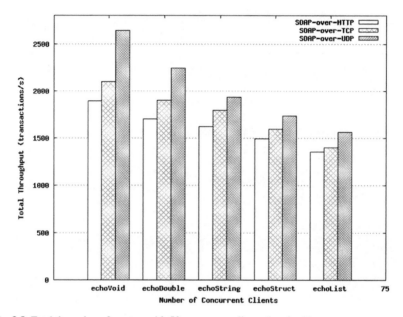

Fig. 3.8 Total throughput for a test with 50 concurrent clients (loopback)

With echoStruct and echoList message types, the sizes of the messages are much larger than the protocol headers; therefore, the advantage of light UDP messages does not produce a significant improvement in the total throughput. The total throughputs of HTTP, TCP and UDP bindings with echoList message type are 1350, 1400 and 1550 transactions per second respectively.

Experiments performed over Wi-Fi connections

The execution time and throughput experiments were repeated over a 802.11b Wi-Fi connection using Computer 1 and Computer 2. The computers were connected to a wireless router at 54Mbps. These experiments were carried out for various numbers of concurrent clients.

The average response times of different SOAP bindings for the echoVoid, echoString and echoDouble message types are plotted in Figure 3.9. The graphs show a significant difference between the result in Wi-Fi connection (see results for 50 clients) compared to those collected from the loopback experiments. For SOAP-over-HTTP and SOAP-over-TCP, the average response time over the wireless network is about 100 times higher than over loopback. The difference with the UDP results is less, average execution time over wireless is around 30 times higher than over loopback.

These results show that SOAP-over-UDP is much faster than HTTP and TCP, for a number of reasons. Firstly, in the HTTP and TCP bindings, connection establishment, packet acknowledgement, and connection tear-down require more packets. Due to the high round trip time in a wireless network, the higher number of packets exchanged leads to an increase in execution time. Secondly, unlike the loopback connection (which is reliable), the wireless link is susceptible to packet losses. When packet loss occurs, the retransmission mechanism in TCP is triggered, leading to an increase in execution time. Finally, when an acknowledgement packet is lost, the TCP client must wait for the TCP retransmission timeout (RTO), leading to a further increase in execution time. UDP does not spend any time in establishing and tearing down connections, therefore a large number of packets can be transmitted quickly.

Due to the unreliable nature of the wireless link, some packet loss occurred in the UDP binding case (below 1% for small messages and small number of concurrent clients, and around 3–5% for large messages and high number of simultaneous requests). However, for applications with high performance and low reliability requirements, SOAP-over-UDP provides significantly better performance than SOAP-over-HTTP and SOAP-over-TCP. The results show that for small to medium messages (echoVoid, echoDouble and echoString) and a large number of client requests (over 35 clients) SOAP-over-UDP is about 4–5 times faster than HTTP, and about 3–3.5 times faster than TCP. The results are less significant for smaller numbers of clients (under 35 clients). In particular, SOAP-over-UDP is only approximately 2–3 times faster than HTTP and TCP. SOAP-over-UDP scales quite well with a large number of concurrent clients. The results for SOAP-over-HTTP and SOAP-over-TCP are quite similar for small networks, however SOAP-over-TCP surpassed SOAP-over-HTTP by about 30% for larger networks.

The average response times for the echoStruct and echoList message types are shown in Figure 3.10. For larger messages (echoStruct and echoList), the difference in performance between SOAP-over-UDP and SOAP-over-HTTP is slightly less than in the experiments with smaller messages which are shown in Figure 3.9. Specifically, the UDP binding outperforms the HTTP binding by about only 2 times for a network of 10 clients and about 3 times for a network of 100 clients in the experiments with echoStruct and echoList message types. The performance differences between the HTTP binding and the TCP binding do not vary much for different sizes of messages (the TCP binding is still around 30% faster than the HTTP binding with echoStruct and echoList message types).

The total throughputs of different bindings over the Wi-Fi network for the scenario of 10 clients are shown in Figure 3.11(a). As expected from the average response time results, SOAP-over-HTTP and SOAP-over-TCP provide significantly

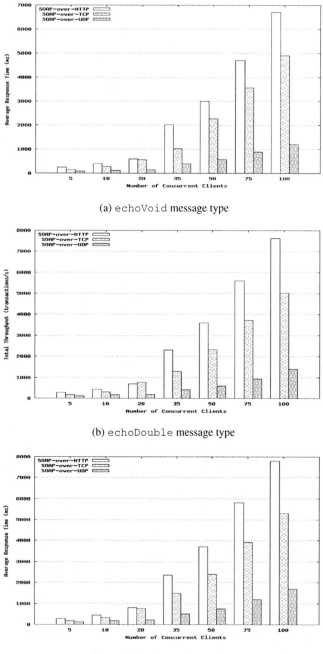

(a) echoVoid message type

(b) echoDouble message type

(c) echoString message type

Fig. 3.9 Average response times of different SOAP bindings for echoVoid, echoString and echoDouble message types under different numbers of concurrent clients

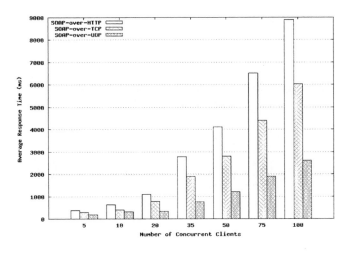

(a) echoStruct message type

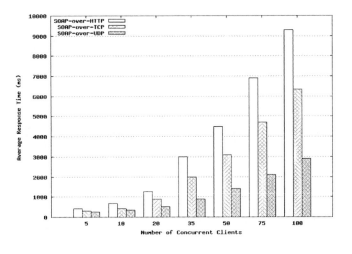

(b) echoList message type

Fig. 3.10 Average response times of different SOAP bindings for echoStruct and echoList message types under different numbers of concurrent clients.

lower throughput compared to SOAP-over-UDP. For small messages (echoVoid and echoDouble), SOAP-over-UDP achieves throughput nearly 3 times higher than SOAP-over-HTTP, while for large messages (echoString, echoStruct and echoList), the throughput under the UDP binding is 2 times higher. The performance difference is less for larger messages because TCP and HTTP perform better

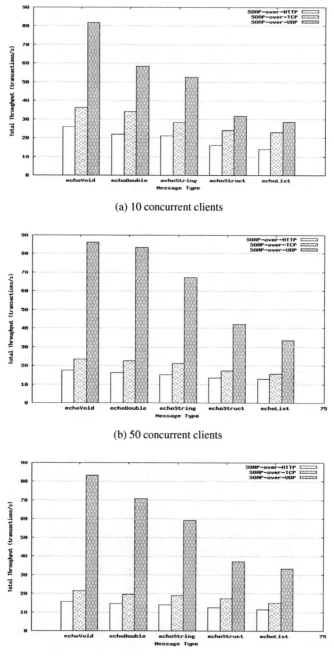

(a) 10 concurrent clients

(b) 50 concurrent clients

(c) 100 concurrent clients

Fig. 3.11 Total throughputs of different SOAP bindings under test scenarios of 10, 50 and 100 concurrent clients

when transmitting large amount of data because for large data transfers, the connection management overhead of TCP and HTTP becomes less significant compared to the transmission cost of the actual payload.

Figure 3.11(b) illustrates the throughput in the scenario of 50 clients. The performance differences between SOAP-over-HTTP and SOAP-over-UDP in this scenario are larger than the results in the case of 10 clients. Throughput achieved using the UDP binding is approximately 5–6 times higher than the HTTP and TCP bindings for small messages (echoVoid, echoString and echoDouble) and 2–3 times higher for large messages (echoStruct and echoList). There is no noticeable difference in the throughput performance between the HTTP and TCP binding options. Similar results were obtained for the experiments with 100 concurrent clients (see Figure 3.11(c)). The throughput performance of SOAP-over-UDP scales well as the number of clients in a network increases.

Experiments performed on mobile devices over Wi-Fi connections

This section reports the results obtained from the experiment carried out on mobile devices over the wireless network. The charts in Figures 3.12 and 3.13 show the average response time and the total throughput observed during this experiment.

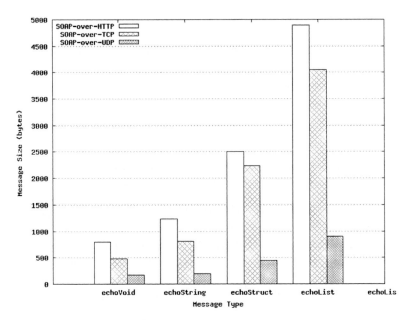

Fig. 3.12 Average Response time for 2 mobile clients

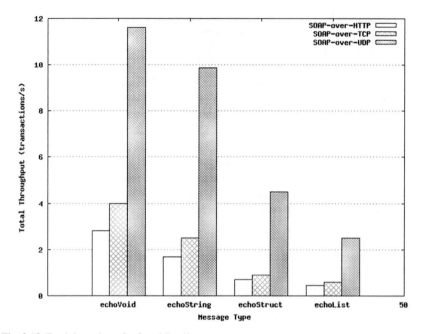

Fig. 3.13 Total throughput for 2 mobile clients

Although the performance of all three SOAP bindings under the mobile device tests is considerably lower than that under the desktop computer tests, the performance variances between the UDP binding and the HTTP binding are similar. Due to limited computational power of the mobile devices, the serialisation and the deserialisation of SOAP request and response messages took much longer. It took almost 5s for the devices to receive an `echoList` message using the HTTP binding but it only took 0.5s in the same test carried out on a computer. It is observed that the response time increases sharply as the size of the messages increases for all types of binding options. This indicates that mobile Web services do not cope well with large messages.

Similar trends were observed in the total throughput results. With the `echoList` message type, the throughput of the UDP binding decreases to nearly one fifth of that with the `echoVoid` message type (a reduction from 11.6 transactions/s to 2.5 transactions/s). However, the total throughput of the UDP binding is still significantly higher than that of the HTTP and TCP bindings. Specifically, with the `echoStruct` message call, SOAP-over-UDP achieves 4.5 transactions/s throughput while both SOAP-over-TCP and SOAP-over-UDP achieve less than 1 transaction/s throughput.

3.6 Application

This section gives examples of different applications that are suitable for the various SOAP bindings.

SOAP-over-HTTP

A significant advantage of the HTTP binding is that it allows SOAP messages to pass through firewalls and be processed by web servers. However, due to the size of the HTTP header and the use of TCP as the underlying transport protocol, SOAP-over-HTTP incurs relatively high overhead for small SOAP messages. HTTP binding is still a good choice for applications that require high level of reliability or high data payload. Some examples where SOAP-over-HTTP is suitable include:

- *Translation service* - where clients provide text in one language and the Web service performs translation to another language and sends it back to the client.
- *Payment service* - where the Web service collects sensitive credit card or banking information from clients, processes the transaction and replies with a receipt/confirmation. HTTPS can be used instead of HTTP to provide security.

SOAP-over-TCP

The experimental results show that SOAP-over-TCP does not provide significant benefit over SOAP-over-HTTP in terms of throughput and execution time. However, the packet size of a simple SOAP request using TCP is around 30% smaller than the equivalent request using the HTTP binding. As a result, TCP is suited to applications where clients send short requests to the server to request large amount of data, and the data needs to be transported reliably. An example of such an application may be:

- *Scientific data transfer* - where clients sent requests to retrieve large scientific data collections (e.g. planetary observations or genebank DNA sequences).

SOAP-over-UDP

The results obtained in Section 3.5 show that SOAP-over-UDP provides significantly higher throughput than SOAP-over-HTTP and SOAP-over-TCP. Additionally, it reduces the total message size required to deliver SOAP messages. As a result of this, SOAP-over-UDP is well suited to applications where short SOAP messages are sent frequently and reliability is of less concern. In this type of application, the small amount of data delivered does not justify the overhead of establishing a connection, so making the simple UDP transport appropriate. Secondly, as UDP supports multicasting and broadcasting, it can be used in push-based web services. Some example applications where SOAP-over-UDP is suitable include:

- *Postcode lookup* - where clients provide a location and the web service replies with the corresponding postcode or vice versa.

- *Stock quote push* - where the server broadcast stock prices to a large number of mobile clients. The frequency of such push could vary depending on the movement of stock value.

SOAP-over-UDP also shows certain performance improvement over SOAP-over-HTTP and SOAP-over-TCP for messages with large data payload. To transmit large amount of data using UDP binding, UDP datagram segmentation is used to split a SOAP message into multiple datagrams because a UDP datagram is limited to 65536 bytes. This can be achieved by assigning to all datagrams for the same SOAP message, the same unique Message ID. Each datagram has a Sequence Number to allow easy assembly of the SOAP message on the receiver's end.

3.7 Summary

Advances in wireless technologies and the increasing popularity of Web services have lead to the emergence of mobile Web services. As the main communication protocol for Web services, SOAP plays a very important role in this context. Existing work studied the performance of different SOAP implementations under different environments. However, the effects of using different SOAP bindings have not been extensively studied. The SOAP specification provides an open binding framework that allows SOAP messages to be transported using any underlying protocol. This chapter studied the performance of SOAP-over-HTTP, SOAP-over-TCP and SOAP-over-UDP in wireless networks. While HTTP and TCP have many benefits including the ability to pass through firewalls and reliability, these features may not be needed by all applications. HTTP and TCP perform poorly in wireless environments due to slow connection establishments and packet acknowledgements. Through an extensive set of experiments, it is shown that using the HTTP or TCP binding for SOAP leads to significantly higher overhead than using the UDP binding. Furthermore, the throughput of SOAP-over-UDP is approximately 6 times higher for small messages (around 500 bytes), and 3 times higher for large messages (greater than 1000 bytes), than SOAP-over-HTTP. The performance improvement of UDP scales with the size of the network. These results are attributed to the following:

- UDP does not require a connection to be established to transfer a datagram.
- UDP does not have a strict flow control mechanism as opposed to TCP.
- UDP does not assume packet loss is due to congestion.

SOAP messages that carry a small amount of data can benefit from being sent over wireless networks in UDP datagrams because of low UDP protocol overhead. Depending on the type of each application, a suitable transport protocol for SOAP binding should be selected allowing for efficiency and reliability. To illustrate where various bindings are useful, a number of applications suitable for each binding have been described. UDP binding is well suited to applications that need fast but not necessarily reliable exchange of small data payloads.

Chapter 4
The Use of Similarity & Multicast Protocols to Improve Performance

"Logic will get you from A to B. Imagination will take you everywhere."

Albert Einstein

SOAP technology is being used in many distributed systems nowadays, however its areas of application are limited by high latency and high protocol overheads. For messaging in environments with high-volume transactions (e.g. stock quote and multimedia applications or in mobile and wireless networks), bandwidth-efficient communication is imperative. When there are many transactions requesting similar service operations, using unicast to send SOAP response messages can potentially generate very large amount of traffic. To improve SOAP's performance, SOAP network traffic needs to be reduced. This chapter presents an approach to address this issue and to improve overall SOAP performance. A similarity-based SOAP multicast protocol (SMP), which reduces the network load by reducing the total generated traffic size, is described. In particular, SMP reuses common templates and payload values among the SOAP messages and only sends one copy of the common part to multiple clients. The results obtained from the experiments indicate that SMP can achieve up to 70% reduction in network traffic compared to traditional SOAP unicast.

4.1 Introduction

SOAP brings extensibility and interoperability to the communication and invocations of services among remote hosts. In contrast to its interoperability advantages, SOAP's major limitation is that its communication produces considerably more network traffic compared to its counterpart technologies such as CORBA and Java-RMI. This issue has drawn great interest from many studies to propose techniques enhancing SOAP's performance. SOAP's poor performance originates from the fact that SOAP is an XML-based communication protocol. Like other XML protocols, SOAP uses high network resources when transmitting messages over the wire. (145) implemented a simple Remote Procedure Call (RPC) server and client to compare the performance of different technologies including MS .Net SOAP, Apache Axis SOAP, CORBA, Java-RMI and RMI-IIOP. Their results showed that both Microsoft's and Apache Axis SOAP implementations typically generate over three times more network traffic than classical approaches like Java-RMI and CORBA.

In the previous chapter, one aspect of SOAP performance drawback in the underlying HTTP transport protocol of SOAP was examined. An alternative SOAP binding with UDP as the transport protocol was proposed to improve the response time and throughput in mobile Web service applications which are run on battery-powered devices and in low bandwidth mobile or wireless networks. SOAP-over-UDP binding performs well in environments with a high number of concurrent clients and small to medium payload messages, but reliability is not guaranteed in these applications. This chapter looks at methods to reduce SOAP traffic for messages with high data payload and without having to compromise for reliability.

Motivation

SOAP messages sent from the same server to multiple clients are generally have some similarity. It is important to emphasise that most SOAP messages have similar byte representations. SOAP messages created by the same implementation generally have the same message structure. Specifically, a SOAP message is surrounded by a large amount of non-domain-related XML data such as name space, encoding specifications and many other XML element names. The number of SOAP implementations is relatively small. Therefore, partial information in a SOAP messages is often known in advance by both receivers and senders. In addition, within business-to-business scenarios, message patterns are very limited and might be known by the server beforehand. Moreover, SOAP responses for the same SOAP request (with the same or different parameter values) will share the same XML document template. Even when the response messages are targeted for different operations of the same service, the response messages may have many similar data type structures.

Bandwidth is expensive in some environments such as mobile and wireless environments and sensors networks. At the current time, there is an increasing demand for the delivery of personalised information such as list of stock quotes, sports scores, weather forecasts and travel information to users, especially to mobile users. If the number of receivers for a service is large (at least several tens of requests) and there is sufficient commonality in their interests, multicast will be an efficient way of delivering information. This is because network resources are used more efficiently by multicasts than broadcasts or replicated unicasts.

In the past, approaches for improving the network bandwidth performance of SOAP Web services focused on the optimisation of differential SOAP compression (145) and differential SOAP deserialization (4, 130) techniques. The similarity-based SOAP multicast protocol (SMP) focuses on reducing duplications of common parts between messages.

The Problem

The main problem of SOAP that has been a focus for a large number of research is to reduce the size of SOAP messages; in turn decreasing the overall traffic caused by sending SOAP messages over a network. This can be done by reducing the size of each single SOAP message individually such as compression or by combining

SOAP messages to avoid sending unnecessary duplicate parts of the messages. The technique described in this chapter follows the latter approach. A number of issues need to be addressed to achieve the goal of sending aggregated messages to reduce the overall network traffic.

Firstly, the (performance) technique must be able to measure the similarity between messages to determine which messages are similar enough to be grouped together in one message. This becomes the problem of measuring the similarity between two and more structured XML documents whose schemas are known in advance. Secondly, a special SMP message structure based on the standard SOAP envelope must be defined to contain the data of multiple recipients in one message.

Thirdly, the SMP solution needs to deal with the processing of aggregated SOAP messages at intermediary SOAP nodes. Currently, when a normal SOAP message is received by a mid-way SOAP node (not the final destination of the SOAP message), the node only parses the SOAP header to carry out any actions required before forwarding the message to the next node. In the SMP solution, special information should be provided in the SMP message header so that SOAP nodes that are not final destinations of individual SOAP messages know how to process the data content before passing it to the following destination. Lastly, the drawback of the SMP approach needs to be realised and compared against with its advantage so that the improvement should outweigh the weakness.

An Overview of SMP

The approach to improving the performance of SOAP messaging is multicasting. The SOAP-based Multicast Protocol (SMP) is introduced, which is based on the *syntactic similarity of SOAP messages*. The nature of SOAP messages, having the same message structure if they are generated by the same service provider, has been utilised by different approaches to improving SOAP performance (3, 105, 130, 144). However, this feature of Web services has never been used in multicast before. This characteristic is applied to develop SMP.

The multicast technique presented here is built on top of SOAP unicast and does not rely on the low level multicast, so no complex network configuration is required at intermediate routers. In addition, SMP makes use of the commonly available WSDL description of a SOAP Web service when determining the similarity of response messages. For messages that are highly similar, instead of generating messages with duplicated similar parts for different clients, the duplicated parts are reused for multiple clients and are sent only once from the source. In this way, the network traffic can be reduced considerably.

Experiments have been carried out to evaluate the described protocol with different network topologies and are detailed in this chapter. Two metrics, response time and traffic load, are used to compare SMP performance with traditional SOAP unicast and multicast. Experiments have shown that a network traffic reduction of over 30% for small networks and up to 70% for large networks and large payload can be obtained using SMP instead of SOAP unicast. This improvement in total network traffic results in an increase in response time by 10% which is an acceptable level.

SOAP's poor performance has been investigated over the past few years. Many studies have proposed approaches for improving the overall performance without compromising interoperability. In particular, a study in (144) proposed a compression approach that only the difference between a message and a pre-defined template generated from the WSDL document is sent across the wire. SOAP templates are also utilised in (130) to develop a new deserialization method that reuses matching regions from the previously deserialized objects in earlier messages. However, to the best knowledge of the author, no previous study has utilised the similarity between SOAP messages to multicast them as an aggregated message in which the duplicated parts among individual messages appear only once.

In the next section, recent studies on Web services performance improvements utilising XML-based SOAP message structure are described. Subsequently, existing multicast and similarity measurement solutions will be studied in to provide a basis for describing the contribution of this chapter. SMP will be then comprehensively explained in Section 4.6. Section 4.7 presents the theoretical models of three communication schemes including unicast, multicast and SMP for SOAP as well as the analytical comparisons between these schemes. The performance evaluation and results will be subsequently presented in Section 4.8.

4.2 Related Work

This section discusses various approaches proposed in previous work on improving the performance of Web services based on the similarity of SOAP messages and describes how our method differs from them.

Many studies recognise the fundamental characteristics of Web services — SOAP messages are mostly generated by SOAP engines and there is a high level of similarity between processed messages. By making use of this feature and eliminating redundant processing, researchers have proposed approaches to improve the performance of Web services. Some areas that they have worked on are the XML parser, the serialization and deserialization processes, compression and Web service-Security. Serialization is the process of converting application data into XML messages, while deserialization is the opposite process where XML messages are converted into application objects to be passed to application logic.

(3) proposed a differential serialization technique on the server side in which the entire message is only serialised in the first time. The serialised form of the message is saved after the first dispatch. If subsequent requests ask for the same Web service, it only re-serialises just those elements that have changed and reuses parts of or all of the saved template instead of regenerating it from scratch.

Another research that also takes advantage of the similar structure of SOAP messages is the differential deserialization (130). They firstly proposed a new XML parser (136) which efficiently detects the differential regions between a new XML message and the past messages, and then partially parses only the differential portions. A state machine is used to store state transitions while parsing the XML message. They then extended on that concept to build a deserialization framework in the Web services architecture. Their version of differential deserialization optimises processing time by recycling in-memory objects on the receiver side of a SOAP communication pair, thereby eliminating the expensive step of creating these objects in memory, achieving substantial performance improvement.

A DDS (Differential Deserialization)-enabled processes the first SOAP message in a stream and computes the checksums for contiguous portions of the message. At the same time, it saves the corresponding full state of the XML parser. When subsequent messages arrive, before parsing them completely, the deserializer first calculates message portion checksums and compares them with saved corresponding checksums from previous messages. If the checksums match, there will be a high probability that the message contents will also match. Thus, the deserializer can avoid duplicating the work of parsing and converting the SOAP message contents in that region. However, if a coming message totally differs from the previous message, a DDS-enabled deserializer will perform more than a normal deserializer; because apart from parsing the message, a DDS-enabled deserializer needs to calculate checksums and creates parser checkpoints. Therefore, the effectiveness of the DDS optimisation depends largely on the contents similarity between consecutive incoming messages. In addition, this technique exposes high memory usage and processing time.

Makino et al.'s WS-Security approach focused on byte level similarities in WS-Security messages and implemented a template-based WS-Security processor (105). Templates consist of byte arrays and are stored in an automation. The automation matches the incoming messages against multiple templates in a merged form. If the incoming message matches a template, relevant values such as signatures and encrypted values are extracted from the template. WS-Security processing is subsequently performed by a traditional DOM-based processor and a new template corresponding to the unmatched message is generated. The new template will be then merged into the automation. Their evaluation performance shows that the template-based WS-Security processor performs 60% better than the stream-based processor at the server side and 44% faster than the Document Object Model (DOM)-based processor at the client side. The high performance of the proposed template-based processor is assisted by the elimination of costly XML parsing in either the DOM or SAX (Simple API for XML) fashion.

Another important contribution to reducing network traffic caused by SOAP is from (145). They come up with a differential SOAP compression technique that is based on the commonly available Web service's WSDL description document. In their method, the WSDL document of a Web service is used to generate SOAP messages' skeletons which contain only the markup, for all defined service operations. On the server-side, the skeletons are used to create SOAP difference documents which include only the differences between a SOAP message and its corresponding skeleton files. These difference documents are very small in size and are sent over the wire. On the client-side, the skeleton files are used with the difference files to reconstruct the original SOAP messages. They use two tools `diffxml` (87) and `XUpdate` (77) for creating difference documents. Their experiments show that their differential encoding technique is advantageous only when the the SOAP message' markup is predictable. When the payload amount increases, the structure of the SOAP messages cannot be predicted accurately, leading to minor improvement in the resulting message size of a compressed difference document compared to a compressed normal SOAP message.

4.3 Background

In this section, background of an existing multicast protocol that has similar approach as SMP and common XML similarity measurement methods are presented.

4.3.1 Explicit Multicast Protocols

Xcast (21) has been proposed to solve the problems with using IP multicast for small multicast groups. Xcast multicast scheme aims to support a very large number of small multicast groups by explicitly including the list of destinations in packets, instead of using a multicast address. The source stores a destination list in the Xcast header and then sends the packet to a router. Each downstream router parses the header, partitions the destinations based on each destination's next hop, and forwards a packet with an appropriate Xcast header along each of the next hops (see Figure 4.1).

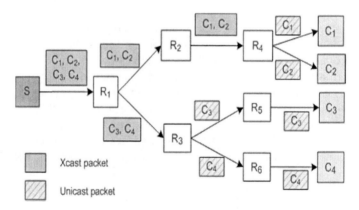

Fig. 4.1 Xcast Routing Mechanism

Each final router removes the Xcast encoding and forwards the data to its destination as a standard unicast packet. There is no need to maintain multicast states in the network because Xcast carries the state in each data packet and processes it in real time along the forwarding path.

Xcast performs well with small size multicast groups, but if the number of members in a group increases, the destination addresses cannot be sufficiently encoded in an Xcast packet header due to size limitation. Xcast+ (129) has been proposed to support a large number of medium size multicast groups. In Xcast+, every source or destination is associated with a Designated Router (DR). Instead of encoding the set of group members in the Xcast packet, Xcast+ encodes the set of their DRs. There are other variations and improved versions of Xcast, for example GXcast (22) and SEM (23).

In summary, IP multicast is a fast and efficient multicast communication mechanism, however it involves complex configuration at routers and does not scale well for a large number of concurrent multicast sessions. Xcast supports a large number of small group multicast sessions. Nevertheless, none of these multicast protocols are well suited for Web services because they were not designed with SOAP and XML in mind.

SMP differs from others in that it utilises the similar structure of SOAP messages to multicast messages in a more efficient way. Like Xcast, SMP uses unicast routing and encodes a list of clients inside the message, instead of using a multicast address. However, Xcast can only multicast identical messages, while SMP can also send slightly different ones together, as explained in Section 4.6.2.

4.3.2 Similarity Measurements

Two popular techniques for measuring document similarities are presented here.

Levenshtein's Edit Distance. The *edit distance* (79) is a well-established method for weighting the difference between two strings. It measures the minimum number of token insertions, deletions, and substitutions required to transform one string into another using a dynamic programming algorithm. For example, the edit distance, ed, between the two strings "3 − 1" and "3 − 0" equals 1, $ed(\text{"3 − 1"}, \text{"3 − 0"}) = 1$, because one substitution is required to change the string "3 − 1" into "3 − 0".

Syntactic Similarity Measures (96) proposed a syntactic similarity measure for strings which is based on Levenshtein's edit distance. It is defined as follows. Given two strings s_i and s_j, their syntactic similarity is defined as: $SM(s_i, s_j) = max(0, \frac{min(|s_i|, |s_j|) - ed(s_i - s_j)}{min(|s_i|, |s_j|)})$, where

- SM is the syntactic similarity measure, which has a value between 0 and 1;
- $|s_i|$ and $|s_j|$ are the lengths of two strings s_i and s_j respectively; and
- ed is the edit distance.

This formula has been widely used in many ontological studies. This measurement considers the number of changes that are required to change one string into the other and weighs the number of these changes against the length of the shortest string. In the previous example, $SM(\text{"3 − 1"}, \text{"3 − 0"}) = \frac{2}{3}$) is obtained.

4.4 Similarity Measurement Model for Clustering SOAP Messages

The goal of clustering is to group SOAP messages based on their syntactic similarities. By identifying the similarities in the message structures of the SOAP response messages, the source can determine which messages can be sent together using SMP multicast technique. The ability to measure the similarity between messages is paramount to determining if they have enough parts in common to justify the cost of extra processing time required at the source and routers. This section describes the similarity measurement model used in SMP.

The similarity between two messages is measured based on the XML schema of each SOAP message. The XML schema of a message is the WSDL document for a service, provided by a service provider to service consumers. The WSDL document defines a list of operations and their signatures. It also defines the complex data types that are used in operations. Response messages to any request for service operations are formed from these complex data type definitions.

A stock quote application will be used as examples throughout this chapter to explain the proposed similarity measurement and SMP routing methods. The stock quote application involves a large number of transactions requesting the latest stock prices. The responses for these requests would likely have similar message structures. Therefore, the chosen application satisfies our requirements for SMP's applicable services. The real-time stock quote Web service receives requests to retrieve stock prices, stock statistics over a day and general company information. The service provides a list of operations such as `getStockQuote()`, `getQuoteAndStatistic()`, `getCompanyInfo()`, `getFullQuote()` and `getMarketInfo()`. The inputs for these requests can be a string of more than one stock symbol.

Two SOAP messages, given in Figures 4.2 and 4.3, are used to illustrate how the similarity between two XML documents is measured. These are two response messages to operations `getQuote()` and `getQuoteAndStatistic()` respectively. For simplicity, the SOAP messages in this example are element-based and do not contain attributes. In reality, attributes can be considered by treating them as sub-elements.

4.4.1 Foundation Definitions

Basic concepts in a SOAP message document are presented here as the foundation for the proposed similarity measurement method. Since a SOAP message is based on XML, it is a hierarchical document with nested tags. As such, a SOAP message is best modeled as a rooted ordered tree.

Definition 4.1. [Message Tree] A SOAP message tree T is a rooted ordered tree, such that each node ε_T is a pair $\varepsilon_T = (\eta, \upsilon)$, where η is the node name and υ is the node value. υ can be of primitive type (Boolean, Float, Double and Date) or complex type (which may include one or more primitive types).

Elements of a SOAP message tree are defined as follows.

Definition 4.2. [*Element*] An element (Ele) represents a simple or complex node in a SOAP message. Each leaf element, also called simple element, represents one feature of a complex object. A non-leaf element is a set of features which describe one facet of the complex object.

```
<StockQuoteResponse>
<ArrayOfStockQuote>
 <StockQuote>
  <Symbol>NAB</Symbol>
  <QuoteInfo>
    <Price>28.56</Price>
    <LastUpdated>24/01/2007 10:15am</LastUpdated>
  </QuoteInfo>
 </StockQuote>
 <StockQuote>
  <Symbol>BHP</Symbol>
  <QuoteInfo>
    <Price>24.52</Price>
    <LastUpdated>24/01/2007 10:45am</LastUpdated>
  </QuoteInfo>
</StockQuote>
</ArrayOfStockQuote>
</StockQuoteResponse>
```

Fig. 4.2 $Soap_1$ message: A simple stock quote response message to the getStockQuote(''NAB, BHP") request.

```
<QuoteAndStatisticResponse>
<ArrayOfQuoteAndStatistic>
 <QuoteAndStatistic>
  <Symbol>BHP</Symbol>
  <QuoteInfo>
   <Price>24.52</Price>
   <LastUpdated>24/01/2007 10:45am</LastUpdated>
  </QuoteInfo>
  <Statistic>
   <Change>+0.50</Change>
   <OpenPrice>24.02</OpenPrice>
  </Statistic>
 </QuoteAndStatistic>
 <QuoteAndStatistic>
  <Symbol>NAB</Symbol>
  <QuoteInfo>
    <Price>28.56</Price>
    <LastUpdated>24/01/2007 10:15am</LastUpdated>
  <Statistic>
    <Change>-0.10</Change>
    <OpenPrice>28.66</OpenPrice>
  </Statistic>
 </QuoteAndStatistic>
 </ArrayOfQuoteAndStatistic>
 </QuoteAndStatisticResponse>
```

Fig. 4.3 $Soap_2$ message: A SOAP response message to the getQuoteAndStatistic(''BHP, NAB") request to get both stock quotes and their market statistics.

In our example of Soap₁ and Soap₂ messages, some complex elements are
StockQuote, QuoteInfo, QuoteAndStatistic and Statistic. Other
elements such as Symbol, Price, LastUpdated and Change are simple elements.

An instance of an element is defined as below.

Definition 4.3. [*Element instance*] An XML element instance (noted as *inst*) instan-
tiates an element of the schema.

For example, in the Soap₁ message, Figure 4.2, there are two instances of the
StockQuote element: one for NAB symbol and one for BHP.

An element is called a multi-instance element if there are more than one instance
of the element, and is called a single-instance element if there is only one instance
of the element in an XML document. In Figure 4.2, ArrayOfStockQuote and
ArrayOfQuoteAndStatistic are single-instance elements while StockQuote,
QuoteAndStatistic, Symbol and Price are multi-instance elements. An instance of the Price element in the Soap₁ message is <Price>28.56<Price>
(for symbol NAB).

Definition 4.4. [*Value*] A value is the value (V) of a leaf element instance.

The value of the first instance of *Symbol* in the Soap₁ message in Figure 4.2 is
'NAB'. Next, the computation for the instance similarity of a simple element between two instances of the element is presented.

Definition 4.5. [*Instance similarity of simple element*] Simple element instance similarity, noted as Sim_{inst}^{E}, of two instances of the same simple element, namely E, is
the similarity of leaf instances' values.

For different data types of a value, different methods can be used to calculate
instance similarity of simple element. There are a number of built-in data types
supported in XML schema (149) such as String, Boolean, Float, Double
and Date. For each data type, different methods should be used to calculate the
instance similarity of simple element. The methods presented in (81) are adopted
to define the similarity in value of two nodes that have the same simple data type
because they are widely used by others.

The following definition gives the similarity between two numeric values. A data
type is said to be numeric if its values are conceptually quantities (149).

Definition 4.6. Given two numeric values NV_1 and NV_2, the similarity between them
is defined as $sim(NV_1, NV_2) = 1 - \frac{|NV_1 - NV_2|}{|NV_1| + |NV_2|}$, where $|A|$ is the absolute value of
numeric value A.

The similarity between two boolean values can be measured as follows.

Definition 4.7. Given two boolean values BV_1 and BV_2, their similarity is defined
$sim(BV_1, BV_2) = NOT(XOR(BV_1, BV_2))$.

The similarity between two strings is computed using the method proposed in (96), which was discussed in the Background section.

The syntactic similarity is the only measurement of interest here because the objective is to find common contents among SOAP messages to apply the SMP routing algorithm so that the total size of traffic can be reduced. By applying the method to calculate the similarity between two strings to Definition 4.5, similarities between different Symbol instances in the $Soap_1$ and $Soap_2$, given in Figures 4.2 and 4.3, can be computed as follows:

$$Sim_{inst}^{"Symbol"}(NAB^{Soap_1}, BHP^{Soap_2})$$
$$= max(0, \frac{min(|`NAB'|, |`BHP'|) - ed(`NAB' - `BHP')}{min(|`NAB'|, |`BHP'|)})$$
$$Sim_{inst}^{"Symbol"}(NAB^{Soap_1}, NAB^{Soap_2})$$
$$= max(0, \frac{min(|`NAB'|, |`NAB'|) - ed(`NAB' - `NAB')}{min(|`NAB'|, |`NAB'|)})$$
$$Sim_{inst}^{"Symbol"}(BHP^{Soap_1}, BHP^{Soap_2}) = 1$$
$$Sim_{inst}^{"Symbol"}(BHP^{Soap_1}, NAB^{Soap_2}) = 0$$

The element similarity of a particular element in two SOAP messages is defined as the average of all instance similarities of all instances of E contained in the two messages.

Definition 4.8. The element similarity of an element, namely E, in two SOAP messages $Soap_1$ and $Soap_2$ is defined as:

$$Sim_{ele}^{E}(Soap_1, Soap_2) = \frac{\sum_{i=1}^{Nmax} Sim_{inst}^{E}(E_i^{Soap_1}, E^{Soap_2})}{N_{max}}$$

where

- $|E^{Soap_1}|$ and $|E^{Soap_2}|$ are the numbers of element E instances in $Soap_1$ and $Soap_2$ respectively;
- $N_{max} = Max(|E^{Soap_1}|, |E^{Soap_2}|)$; and
- $Sim_{inst}^{E}(E_i^{Soap_1}, E^{Soap_2}) = Max(Sim_{inst}^{E}(E_i^{Soap_1}, E_j^{Soap_2})), \forall E_j^{Soap_2} \in Soap_2$, which is the similarity of instance $E_i^{Soap_1}$ to all instances of E in $Soap_2$.

For single-instance elements, the element similarity is equal to its instance similarity. This definition applies to both simple and complex element types. In the example, the element similarity for the element Symbol between the $Soap_1$ and $Soap_2$ example messages can be computed as follows:

$$Sim_{ele}^{"Symbol"}(Soap_1, Soap_2) = \frac{\sum_{i=1}^{2} Sim_{inst}^{"Symbol"}("Symbol"_i^{Soap_1}, "Symbol"^{Soap_2})}{2}$$
$$= \frac{1}{2}(Sim_{inst}^{"Symbol"}(NAB^{Soap_1}, "Symbol"^{Soap_2}) + Sim_{inst}^{"Symbol"}(BHP^{Soap_1}, "Symbol"^{Soap_2}))$$
$$= \frac{1}{2}(Max(Sim_{inst}^{"Symbol"}(NAB^{Soap_1}, BHP^{Soap_2}), Sim_{inst}^{"Symbol"}(NAB^{Soap_1}, `NAB^{Soap_2}))$$
$$+ Max(Sim_{inst}^{"Symbol"}(BHP^{Soap_1}, BHP^{Soap_2}), Sim_{inst}^{"Symbol"}(BHP^{Soap_1}, `NAB^{Soap_2})))$$
$$= \frac{(1+1)}{2} = 1$$

The following definition gives a formula for computing the instance similarity between two instances of a complex element.

Definition 4.9. The instance similarity between two instances P_1 and P_2 of a complex element P is calculated based on the element similarities of all their sub-elements E_i, as defined as $Sim_{inst}^P(P_1,P_2) = \frac{\sum_{i=1}^N Sim_{ele}^{E_i}(P_1,P_2)}{N}$, where

- N is the number of sub-elements in the complex element P; and
- $Sim_{ele}^{E_i}(P_1,P_2)$ is the element similarity of element E_i in instance P_1 to E_i in instance P_2.

For example, the instance similarity of the complex element QuoteInfo between the first instances of QuoteInfo in the Soap$_1$ and Soap$_2$ messages can be computed as:

$$Sim_{inst}^{"QuoteInfo"}(\text{QuoteInfo}^{NAB},\text{QuoteInfo}^{BHP})$$

$$= \frac{1}{2}(Sim_{ele}^{"Price"}(\text{QuoteInfo}^{NAB},\text{QuoteInfo}^{BHP})$$

$$+Sim_{ele}^{"LastUpdated"}(\text{QuoteInfo}^{NAB},\text{QuoteInfo}^{BHP}))$$

$$= \frac{1}{2}(0.92+1) = 0.96.$$

4.4.2 Similarity between SOAP Messages

The method used to compute the overall similarity between two full SOAP messages is presented here. Most SOAP response messages, which are generated by the same service provider, will have a common message structure (or template). In particular, they will have similar information in the header and the same structure in the body, if they have been generated for the same operation. Based on this observation, the similarity between two SOAP messages Soap$_1$ and Soap$_2$, labeled as $sim(Soap_1,Soap_2)$, is defined as the product of the similarity between the two message templates and the similarity between the data values of the messages.

Definition 4.10. The similarity between two SOAP messages Soap$_1$ and Soap$_2$ is defined as $sim(Soap_1,Soap_2)= sim_{temp}(Soap_1,Soap_2) \times sim_{val}(Soap_1,Soap_2)$, where

- $sim(Soap_1,Soap_2) \in [0,1]$;
- $sim_{temp}(Soap_1,Soap_2)$ is the similarity between Soap$_1$'s and Soap$_2$'s templates; and
- $sim_{val}(Soap_1,Soap_2)$ is the similarity between $Soap_1's$ and $Soap_2's$ data values.

SOAP messages are based on XML templates which are formed by a set of elements. The similarity between two SOAP message templates is measured based on the common XML nodes between the two XML trees of the SOAP messages.

Definition 4.11. The similarity between Soap$_1$'s and Soap$_2$'s templates is defined as $sim_{temp}(Soap_1,Soap_2) = \frac{|N(Soap_1) \cap N(Soap_2)|}{|N(Soap_1) \cup N(Soap_2)|}$, where

- N(*xml_tree*) is the set of *distinctive* xml nodes in the *xml_tree* template; and
- $|S|$ is the cardinality of set S.

It is noteworthy to emphasise that only distinctive nodes (excluding closing tags) of a SOAP template are included in the above computation. In relation to the Stock-Quote example, the set of common nodes between Soap₁ and Soap₂ templates is:

$$N(Soap_1) \cap N(Soap_2) = \{Symbol, QuoteInfo, Price, LastUpdated\} \qquad (4.1)$$

The set of all distinctive nodes in both Soap₁'s and Soap₂'s templates is:

$$N(Soap_1) \cup N(Soap_2) = \{StockQuoteResponse, ArrayOfStockQuote, StockQuote, Symbol,$$
$$QuoteInfo, Price, LastUpdated, QuoteAndStatisticResponse,$$
$$ArrayOfQuoteAndStatistic, QuoteAndStatistic, Statistic,$$
$$Change, OpenPrice\}$$

Therefore, the similarity in *template* between the two example messages is:

$$Sim_{temp}(Soap_1, Soap_2) = \frac{|N(Soap_1) \cap N(Soap_2)|}{|N(Soap_1) \cup N(Soap_2)|} = \frac{4}{13} \qquad (4.2)$$

The following definition shows how the data values in two SOAP documents are compared.

Definition 4.12. The similarity between Soap₁'s and Soap₂'s data values is defined as $sim_{val}(Soap_1, Soap_2) = \frac{\sum_{i=1}^{|M|} sim_{ele}^{E_i}(Soap_1, Soap_2)}{|M|}$, where

- M is the set of common distinctive nodes but excluding sub-element nodes between Soap₁ and Soap₂ messages;
- E_i is an element in M;
- $|M|$ is the cardinality of set M; and
- $sim_{ele}^{E_i}(Soap_1, Soap_2)$ is the element similarity between two values of the common node E_i in both $Soap_1, Soap_2$.

It is important to note that only the values of the non-subelements nodes in the set $|N(Soap_1) \cap N(Soap_2)|$ are compared. Nodes that are not common between two messages are ignored in the value similarity computation because it is unlikely that two nodes of different data types have similar values. Sub-element nodes of a common node are not included in the computation either because their similarity is already considered during the similarity computation of their common parent node. Back to our example, among elements in the common node set between the Soap₁ and Soap₂ messages, the set M will include only Symbol and QuoteInfo. The similarity in value between the two SOAP messages Soap₁ and Soap₂ in our example can be computed as follows:

$$Sim_{val}(Soap_1, Soap_2) = \frac{1}{2}(Sim_{ele}^{"Symbol"}(Soap_1, Soap_2) + Sim_{ele}^{"QuoteInfo"}(Soap_1, Soap_2))$$

$$= \frac{1}{2}(1+1) = 1 \qquad\qquad (4.3)$$

Combining Equations 4.2 and 4.3 into Definition 4.10, the overall similarity between the two $Soap_1$ and $Soap_2$ messages is given by:

$$Sim(Soap_1, Soap_2) = \frac{4}{13} \times 1 = 0.3$$

Two SOAP messages are considered syntactically similar if their similarity degree is equal to or greater than a *similarity threshold*, denoted by ρ, which is dependent on the domain of each application.

Another example is given here to further illustrate the proposed similarity measurement model. $Soap_3$ (see Figure 4.4) is another sample SOAP response message to a $getStockQuote$ (``NAB, WIL, BHP") request. Since $Soap_1$ and $Soap_3$ have the same message structure, their similarity in template is 1: $Sim_{temp}(Soap_1, Soap_3)$ $= 1$.

```
<StockQuoteResponse>
<ArrayOfStockQuote>
 <StockQuote>
  <Symbol>NAB</Symbol>
  <QuoteInfo>
    <Price>28.56</Price>
    <LastUpdated>24/01/2007 10:15am</LastUpdated>
  </QuoteInfo>
 </StockQuote>
 <StockQuote>
  <Symbol>WIL</Symbol>
  <QuoteInfo>
    <Price>1.29</Price>
    <LastUpdated>24/01/2007 10:45am</LastUpdated>
  </QuoteInfo>
 </StockQuote>
  <StockQuote>
  <Symbol>BHP</Symbol>
  <QuoteInfo>
    <Price>24.52</Price>
    <LastUpdated>24/01/2007 10:45am</LastUpdated>
  </QuoteInfo>
 </StockQuote>
</ArrayOfStockQuote>
</StockQuoteResponse>
```

Fig. 4.4 $Soap_3$ message: A simple stock quote response message to the $getStockQuote$ (``NAB, WILL, BHP") request

For brevity, in the following equations SQR is used for StockQuoteResponse, AOSQ for ArrayOfStockQuote and SQ for StockQuote.

$$
\begin{aligned}
Sim_{val}(Soap_1, Soap_3) &= Sim_{ele}^{``SQR"}(Soap_1, Soap_3) = Sim_{inst}^{``AOSQ"}(Soap_1, Soap_3) \\
&= Sim_{ele}^{``SQ"}(Soap_1, Soap_3) \\
&= \frac{1}{3}(Sim_{inst}^{``SQ"}(SQ_{NAB}^{Soap_3}, SQ^{Soap_1}) + Sim_{inst}^{``SQ"}(SQ_{WIL}^{Soap_3}, SQ^{Soap_1}) \\
&\quad + Sim_{inst}^{``SQ"}(SQ_{BHP}^{Soap_3}, SQ^{Soap_1})) \\
&= \frac{1}{3}(1 + Sim_{inst}^{``SQ"}(SQ_{WIL}^{Soap_3}, SQ^{Soap_1}) + 1)
\end{aligned}
\tag{4.4}
$$

The instance similarity between the StockQuote instance that contains symbol WIL in the Soap$_3$ message and all instances of StockQuote in the Soap$_1$ message is computed as follows:

$$
\begin{aligned}
&Sim_{inst}^{``SQ"}(SQ_{WIL}^{Soap_3}, SQ^{Soap_1}) \\
&= Max(Sim_{inst}^{``SQ"}(SQ_{WIL}^{Soap_3}, SQ_{NAB}^{Soap_1}), Sim_{inst}^{``SQ"}(SQ_{WIL}^{Soap_3}, SQ_{BHP}^{Soap_1}))
\end{aligned}
\tag{4.5}
$$

First, the StockQuote instance that contains symbol WIL in the Soap$_3$ message is compared with the StockQuote instance that contains symbol NAB in the Soap$_1$ message.

$$
\begin{aligned}
Sim_{inst}^{``SQ"}(SQ_{WIL}^{Soap_3}, SQ_{NAB}^{Soap_1}) &= \frac{1}{2}(Sim_{ele}^{``Symbol"}(SQ_{WIL}^{Soap_3}, SQ_{NAB}^{Soap_1}) \\
&\quad + Sim_{ele}^{``QuoteInfo"}(SQ_{WIL}^{Soap_3}, SQ_{NAB}^{Soap_1})) \\
&= \frac{1}{2}(0 + Sim_{inst}^{QuoteInfo}(SQ_{WIL}^{Soap_3}, SQ_{NAB}^{Soap_1})) \\
&= \frac{1}{2}(0 + \frac{1}{2}(Sim_{inst}^{Price}(SQ_{WIL}^{Soap_3}, SQ_{NAB}^{Soap_1}) \\
&\quad + Sim_{inst}^{LastUpdated}(SQ_{WIL}^{Soap_3}, SQ_{NAB}^{Soap_1}))) \\
&= \frac{1}{4}(0.08 + 0.94) = 0.25
\end{aligned}
\tag{4.6}
$$

Next, the instance similarity between $SQ_{WIL}^{Soap_3}$ and $SQ_{BHP}^{Soap_1}$ is calculated.

$$
\begin{aligned}
Sim_{inst}^{"SQ"}(SQ_{WIL}^{Soap_3},SQ_{BHP}^{Soap_1}) &= \frac{1}{2}(Sim_{ele}^{"Symbol"}(SQ_{WIL}^{Soap_3},SQ_{BHP}^{Soap_1}) \\
&\quad + \; Sim_{ele}^{"QuoteInfo"}(SQ_{WIL}^{Soap_3},SQ_{BHP}^{Soap_1})) \\
&= \frac{1}{2}(0+Sim_{inst}^{QuoteInfo}(SQ_{WIL}^{Soap_3},SQ_{BHP}^{Soap_1})) \\
&= \frac{1}{2}(0+\frac{1}{2}(Sim_{inst}^{Price}(SQ_{WIL}^{Soap_3},SQ_{BHP}^{Soap_1}) \\
&\quad + \; Sim_{inst}^{LastUpdated}(SQ_{WIL}^{Soap_3},SQ_{NAB}^{Soap_1}))) \\
&= \frac{1}{4}(0.1+1) = 0.275 \qquad\qquad (4.7)
\end{aligned}
$$

From Equations 4.7 and 4.6, it can be drawn that $Sim_{inst}^{"SQ"}(SQ_{WIL}^{Soap_3},SQ^{Soap_1}) = 0.275$. Placing this value into Equation 4.4, a value for $Sim_{val}(Soap_1,Soap_3)$ of approximately 0.76 is obtained, which is also the overall similarity between the Soap₁ and Soap₃ messages.

4.5 SOAP Message Tree Indexing

An access method is described here to index SOAP element tags in messages, thus reducing message size. SOAP messages are generated based on a set of data types defined in a WSDL file, which is an XML-based document describing Web services and how they can be accessed. Both the server and clients generally have access to the WSDL document before the communication between them is initiated. Clients need to have the WSDL description for the service, so that they can send correctly formatted requests to the server and can de-serialise the server's responses to get the data they want to retrieve. In this thesis, it is assumed that clients have a copy of the WSDL document of the service they request. The WSDL specification for the Stock Quote service used in this chapter's examples is given in Appendix.

A WSDL document specifies names, structures, and types for all the data types that the SOAP service exposes. A SOAP response message typically consists of some of those data types and their values. Let us consider the Soap₁ message consisting of a complex data type <StockQuote> (which includes another complex data type <QuoteInfo> and a simple data type <Symbol>. The <StockQuote> element is a multiple instance element, which means that there may be multiple instances of <StockQuote> in SOAP messages. Since the clients have access to the XML structure definitions of all SOAP elements from the WSDL description, it is redundant to send the static data type templates over the network. Instead of sending full SOAP messages including templates and data, the indexed forms of the SOAP messages, which are more compact than standard SOAP messages, are sent to the clients. The indexed form of a SOAP message contains the identifiers (ID) of each element in the message template as well as the data values of the elements.

As given in Definition 4.1, a SOAP message is an ordered XML tree. In the context of this book, the term "SOAP messages" refers to SOAP response messages to clients' requests as response messages are typically much larger in size than request messages and generate high network traffic. The main objective of the algorithms presented in this thesis is to reduce the traffic generated by SOAP response messages.

Each data type definition specified in a WSDL document is indexed with a unique identifier (ID). The occurrences of a data type in SOAP messages are represented by its ID, which is much smaller than its full name. Nodes in a SOAP XML tree are labeled using a Dewey numbering system (42) that indicates the location of the nodes in the tree. Nodes are listed in the order that they are visited by the Breadth-First-Search (BFS) algorithm[1] (99). Dewey's notations are used to label XML documents in many research areas of pattern matching, searching and database (103, 155). Specifically, each node in a SOAP message tree is encoded in the format given in Definition 4.13 to become an element in the equivalent indexed SOAP message.

Definition 4.13. A node in a SOAP document is indexed in the following format: $<v\ pos =$ 'a position' $eRef =$ 'an ID' $val =$ 'a value'$>$, where

- The *pos* attribute is the position of the node in the SOAP message tree;
- The *eRef* attribute is the unique identifier of the data type at the node as defined in the WSDL document; and
- The *val* attribute is the value at the node. Depending on the node type, the data stored in *val* will be different. If the node is a:

    - Normal node: *val* stores the data value of the node;
    - Array node: *val* stores the number of elements in the array;
    - Complex node: *val* is empty.

Figures 4.5 and 4.6 show the tree representations of $Soap_1$ and $Soap_3$ messages with node labels. The labels are superscripted in these figures.

The full indexed version[2] of $Soap_1$ is given in Figure 4.7. The $<ArrayOf$ $StockQuote>$ node is encoded as $<v\ pos=$'1' $eRef=$'AOSQ' $val=$'2'$>$ because the node is at position 1 in the tree, the $ArrayOfStockQuote$ data type is indexed as 'AOSQ' in the WSDL document, and there are two elements of $StockQuote$ in its array. The first $<StockQuote>$ node instance in $Soap_1$ is encoded as $<v\ pos=$'2.1' $eRef=$'SQ' $val=$''$>$ (node $<StockQuote>$ is at position 2.1, its data type reference in the WSDL is 'SQ', and its value is empty because it is a complex node.) By using this tree encoding technique, the size of a SOAP message can be significantly reduced and so is the overall network traffic.

---

[1] BFS is a graph search algorithm that begins at the root node and traverses all the nearest nodes. Then for each of these neighbouring nodes, it explores their neighbouring nodes that have not been visited, and so on until the goal is found.

[2] For brevity, examples of SOAP messages described in this chapter display only the body contents of the messages, the headers are omitted.

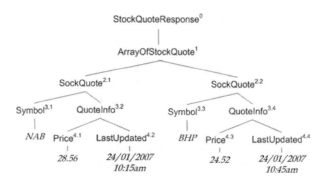

Fig. 4.5 Soap₁ XML tree, a response to getStockQuote("NAB, BHP") request, with node labels.

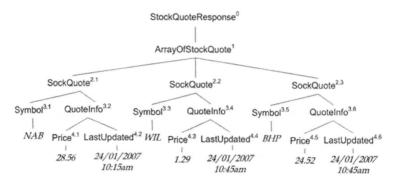

Fig. 4.6 Soap₃ XML tree, a response to getStockQuote("NAB, WIL, BHP") request, with node labels.

```
<v pos='0' eRef='SQR'>
<v pos='1' eRef='AOSQ' val='2'>
<!--First StockQuote instance -->
<v pos='2.1' eRef='SQ' val=''>
<v pos='3.1' eRef='Sbl' val='NAB'>
<v pos='3.2' eRef='QI'>
<v pos='4.1' eRef='P' val='28.56'>
<v pos='4.2' eRef='LU' val='24/01/2007 10:15am'>
<!--Second StockQuote instance -->
<v pos='2.2' eRef='SQ'>
<v pos='3.3' eRef='Sbl' val='BHP'>
<v pos='3.4' eRef='QI'>
<v pos='4.3' eRef='P' val='24.52'>
<v pos='4.4' eRef='LU' val='24/01/2007 10:45am'>
```

Fig. 4.7 Indexed version of the Soap₁ message

4.6 The Similarity-based SOAP Multicast Protocol (SMP)

The concepts and operations of SMP are explained in detail in this section. This similarity-based SOAP multicast protocol is designed to deal with SOAP performance issues by exploiting the similar structure of SOAP messages. The goal is to reduce the total traffic generated over a network when sending SOAP responses from servers to clients. SMP allows similar SOAP messages that share some parts of the SOAP template to be sent in one customised SMP message instead of being sent as multiple copies.

The objective when designing the SMP protocol is to base it on existing SOAP protocol standards so that it can integrate seamlessly with the current Web services framework. SMP should require minimal administration efforts at intermediary routers in order to enable fast deployment and easy maintenance. It is important that SMP scales well with a large number of clients. The SMP approach is to send the common message structure and data values of multiple messages and their distinctive parts in a single message instead of sending multiple messages containing duplicated copies of common parts. An important goal is to have SMP support the aggregation of multiple messages for a large number of clients.

4.6.1 SMP Message Structure and Generation

This section explains the structure of an SMP message and how it is generated.

SMP Message Structure

Clients' addresses are represented as strings and stored in the SMP header, which is encapsulated inside the SOAP message body, as shown in Figure 4.8. The SMP body is also embedded inside the SOAP message body. There are two sections in the SMP body: (1) the <Common> section containing common values and structures of all messages addressed to clients encoded in the SMP header; (2) the <Distinctive> section containing individual different parts for each response message. The outermost envelope is referred to as an SMP message. The destination of an SMP message, which is specified in the SOAP header, is the next router in a network when the message is forwarded to all clients given in its SMP header.

SOAP message Aggregation

Here we show how two SOAP messages could be merged to become an SMP message. The generation of an SMP message is explained through an example based on the network configuration shown in Figure 4.11. In this example, clients C_1 and C_5 make getStockQuote(''NAB, BHP") request to the server to retrieve the quotes for NAB and BHP stocks. Clients C_2 and C_4 request the quotes for three

SOAP Envelope

> **SOAP Header**

> SOAP Body

>> **SMP Header**

>> **SMP Body**

>>> Common Section

>>> Distinctive Section

Fig. 4.8 SMP Envelope embedded inside a SOAP envelope

stocks: NAB, WIL and BHP via the `getStockQuote(''NAB,WIL,BHP")` request. Client C_3 calls for `getStockQuote(''NAB")` request.

Figures 4.5, 4.6 and 4.9 illustrate the hierarchical SOAP trees for messages responding to the `getStockQuote(''NAB,BHP")` and `getStockQuote` `(''NAB,WIL,BHP")` and `getStockQuote(''NAB")` requests respectively. It is assumed here that the request messages arrive at the server in the order of requests from clients C_1, C_2, C_3, C_4, and C_5. Upon receiving similar requests from clients C_1 and C_2, and determining that the similarity of the two response messages $Soap_1$ and $Soap_3$ meets the *similarity threshold*, the server generates an SMP message aggregating the contents from $Soap_1$ and $Soap_3$. Figure 4.10 illustrates an SMP message, SMP_1, containing the aggregation of $Soap_1$ and $Soap_3$ messages.

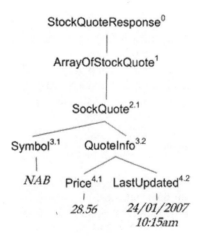

StockQuoteResponse[0]

ArrayOfStockQuote[1]

SockQuote[2.1]

Symbol[3.1]   QuoteInfo[3.2]

NAB   Price[4.1]   LastUpdated[4.2]

28.56   24/01/2007
10:15am

Fig. 4.9 $Soap_4$ XML tree, a response to the getStockQuote("NAB") request, with node labels.

```
<soap:Envelope><soap:Header>          <DPart>
  Next-hop router's address             <cPos cIds ='2' pos='2.2'>
</soap:Header>                            <part id='p4'>
<soap:Body>                                 <v eRef='SQ' val='' />
 <SMP:Header>                               <v eRef='Sbl' val='WIL' />
  <c id='1', uri='URI1' />                  <v eRef='QI' val='' />
  <c id='2', uri='URI2' />                  <v eRef='P' val='1.29' />
 </SMP:Header><SMP:Body>                    <v eRef='LU' val='24/01/2007' />
  <Distinctive>                           </part>
   <DPart>                              </DPart>
     <cPos cIds ='1,2' pos='0' />     </Distinctive>
     <part refer='p1' />               <Common>
   </DPart>                              <part id='p1'>
   <DPart>                                 <v  eRef= 'SQR' val='' />
     <cPos cIds ='1' pos='1' />          </part>
     <part>                              <part id='p2'>
      <v eRef= 'AOSQ' val='2' />           <v  eRef= 'SQ' val='' />
     <part/>                               <v  eRef= 'Sbl'  val='NAB' />
   </DPart>                                <v eRef='QI' val='' />
   <DPart>                                 <v eRef='P' val='28.56' />
     <cPos cIds ='2' pos='1' />            <v eRef='LU' val='24/01/2007' />
     <part>                              </part>
      <v eRef= 'AOSQ' val='3' />         <part id='p3'>
     <part/>                               <v eRef='SQ' val='' />
   </DPart>                                <v eRef='Sbl' val='BHP' />
   <DPart>                                 <v eRef='QI' val='' />
     <cPos cIds ='1,2' pos='2.1' />        <v eRef='P' val='24.52' />
     <part refer='p2' />                   <v eRef='LU' val='24/01/2007' />
   </DPart>                              </part>
   <DPart>                             </Common>
     <cPos cIds ='1' pos='2.2'>      </SMP:Body>
     <cPos cIds ='2' pos='2.3'>    </soap:Body>
     <part refer='p3'>               </soap:Envelope>
   </DPart>
```

Fig. 4.10 SMP$_1$: An SMP message aggregating Soap$_1$ (Figure 4.2) and Soap$_3$ (Figure 4.4) messages

The SMP protocol compares outgoing SOAP response messages in a pair-wise manner. SMP also has a user-configured time frame, denoted by t_{wait}. During this time frame, outgoing SOAP response messages are merged into an aggregated SMP message if their similarity level falls within a threshold limit. When a new request message arrives at the server, the server generates its corresponding SOAP response message and computes the new response's similarity against with the <Common> section of the existing merged SMP message. If the computed similarity satisfies the threshold then the new message is merged into the SMP message. If not, the existing merged SMP message is sent out and the last received response message is kept at the server for another t_{wait} period, waiting for new requests. The above aggregation steps can be repeatedly carried out. The SMP message will be also dispatched automatically after the defined period.

Back to the example, the response message $\texttt{Soap}_4$ for the $\texttt{getStockQuote}$ ($\texttt{``NAB"}$) request from client C_3 is highly similar to the common section of SMP_1 message. Thus, $\texttt{Soap}_4$ is merged into SMP_1 to become SMP_2 message, which is given in Appendix C. Similarly, the responses for requests from C_4 and C_5 are also merged into the SMP_2 message. The final SMP message aggregating contents of the responses to all clients is sent out from the server S to the next-hop router R_1.

4.6.2 The SMP Routing Model

The routing operation of SMP is explained in detail in this section. A network of SMP-enabled routers need to be present between the server and the client to enable the deployment of SMP. Each router along a multicast tree parses the SMP message header, partitions the client addresses into groups based on each client's next hop, replicates SMP messages if necessary, and forwards appropriate SMP messages on the next hop.

The SMP routing mechanism is described in Algorithm 1. When a router receives an SMP message, it looks in its routing table to determine the next hop for each client destination listed in the SMP header (Line 7). It then partitions the set of destinations based on the next hops (Line 9). The input SMP message that the router received is subsequently split into multiple copies depending on the number of downstream links that the router connects to (see Algorithm 2). The client list in each newly generated message header is also modified to include only those clients that will be routed through the appropriate hop. Distinctive items are also removed from the replicated messages if these items are not intended for the clients beyond the next hop. Finally, the router sends out the modified copies of the SMP messages (Line 15).

In this way, SMP eases the network's multicast states by processing each data message on the fly along the forwarding path. If the next hop is connected to a client directly, a standard indexed SOAP unicast message is sent instead of an SMP message. On the client side, the indexed SOAP message is patched with the WSDL schema to regenerate the original SOAP message. A standard SOAP message is finally passed to the client's Application layer.

Figure 4.11 illustrates the use of SMP routing algorithm. The five clients (i.e. C_1--C_5) requests for three SOAP messages (i.e. $\texttt{Soap}_1$, $\texttt{Soap}_3$ and $\texttt{Soap}_4$). The SMP message sent out by the server S has the common part for all three messages and the distinctive part for each of them. At R_1, after parsing the header of the SMP message, the router splits the SMP message into two messages targeting two separate client groups: C_1 and C_2 via R_2, and C_3, C_4 and C_5 via R_3. Once the SMP $\texttt{Message\_Splitting}$ procedure (Algorithm 2) is applied, two SMP messages are created from the original SMP message sent by the server S. The SMP message sent to R_2 contains the union of $\texttt{Soap}_1$ and $\texttt{Soap}_3$ messages only while the SMP message sent to R_3 contains the union of $\texttt{Soap}_1$, $\texttt{Soap}_3$ and $\texttt{Soap}_4$ messages. At R_3, a unicast indexed SOAP message needs to be created from the incoming SMP message to R_3 to send the content of $\texttt{Soap}_4$ to C_3 because C_3 does not share paths

---

Algorithm 1: SMP Routing Algorithm

---

begin

    $\{R$ is the set of next hop routers for the current SMP message m $\}$;

    $\{C(m)$ is the set of clients encoded in message m $\}$;

    $R \leftarrow \emptyset$;

    foreach $C \in C(m)$ **do**

        $\{r$ is the next hop router for client C $\}$;

        $r \leftarrow next\_hop(C)$;

        $\{C_r$ is the set of clients that have the next hop router as r$\}$;

        $C_r \leftarrow C_r \cup C$;

        if $r \notin R$ **then** $R \leftarrow R \cup r$;

    end

    foreach $r \in R$ **do**

        $\{m_r$ is the message to be forwarded to $r\}$;

        $\{$Call the *Message_Splitting* procedure$\}$;

        $m_r \leftarrow$ Message_Splitting(m,r,C_r) ;

        Send out m_r **to its next hop router** ;

    end

end

Algorithm 2: : SMP **Message_Splitting** Procedure

Input: m: An SMP message ;
r: An intermediary router ;
C_r: The list of clients that have r as next hop router
Output: m_r: An SMP message to forward to router r

procedure *Message_Splitting* **do**

    foreach $C \in C(m)$ **do**

        if $C \in C_r$ **then**

            $\{Dist(m_r)$ is the distinctive section in message $m_r\}$

            $\{dist(C)$ is the distinctive part of client C in $m\}$

            $Dist(m_r) \leftarrow Dist(m_r) \cup dist(C)$

        end

    end

    $\{Common(m)$ is the common section of message $m\}$

    $m_r \leftarrow Common(m) + Dist(m_r)$

    $\{$Assign r be the next hop router for message $m_r\}$

    $next\_hop(m_r) \leftarrow r$

endw

---

with any other clients any more. Similarly, at the final routers (i.e. R_4, R_5 and R_6), unicast indexed SOAP messages are sent to each client individually.

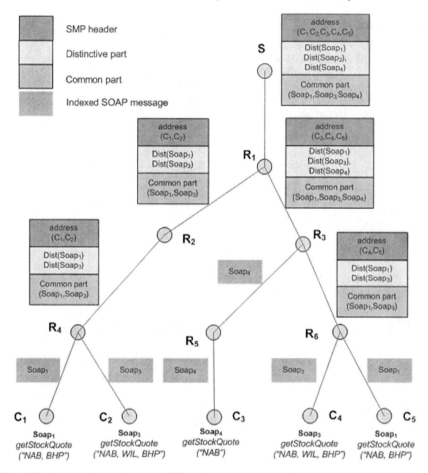

Fig. 4.11 An example showing how SMP routing mechanism works

Complexity Analysis

The complexity of SMP comes from the aggregation and splitting operations at SMP compatible servers and routers. Complexity directly affects SMP's performance in terms of processing time and required memory.

There are two steps in the aggregation process: XML template aggregation and XML data aggregation. Template aggregation (Definition 4.11) between two SOAP documents $Soap_1$ and $Soap_2$ is computed from the union and intersection of two sets of XML nodes. By simply matching between the elements of $N(Soap_1)$ and $N(Soap_2)$, the number of operations to find the union and intersection in the worst case for un-ordered sets is $|N(Soap1)| \times |N(Soap2)| = O(n^2)$, where n is the number of distinctive XML nodes in a document tree.

Data aggregation between $\texttt{Soap}_1$ and $\texttt{Soap}_2$ is a major contributor to the over-all complexity. Only the general case of string is considered here as other types of data can be represented as a string (e.g. binary data can be encoded in base64 as text). The primitive operations INSERT, DELETE, and SUBSTITUTE in tree edit distance (79) are used as the unit of complexity. The most successful tree edit distance algorithm until now, which was proposed by (101), has a complexity of $O(d^2 \times log(d))$, where d is the length of the input string.

From the above, the complexity for aggregating both the templates and data values of $\texttt{Soap}_1$ and $\texttt{Soap}_2$ is $O(n^2)+O(nd^2log(d))$, where n is the number of XML nodes in each SOAP document and d is the data size of each XML node. The number of distinctive XML nodes in a SOAP message often has an upper bound limit as the number of data types defined in the WSDL description of a service, thus n can be considered as a constant and ignored in the complexity analysis. The complexity of the SMP aggregation operation is simplified as $O(d^2log(d))$.

The SMP splitting operation is much less complex. The first step in this process is to find R the set of next hop routers for all clients encoded in the incoming SMP message m. It is assumed that the routing table is an ordered set and the time it takes to complete a search for a destination is $log_2(k)$ using a binary search, where k is the number of elements in the set. For N clients , splitting will require $Nlog_2(k)$ operations. Assuming that there is an upper bound on k, the time complexity for defining the set of next hop routers is $O(N)$. The second step in SMP splitting is to form new SMP messages where the complexity in the worst case (in which there are no common parts) is also $O(N)$. The SMP splitting operation therefore has a complexity of $O(N)$.

Combining the complexities of the SMP aggregation and splitting processes, it can be concluded that the proposed SMP routing algorithm has a complexity of $O(d^2log(d)+N)$, where d is the length of a data value in a SOAP message and N is the number of clients.

4.6.3 SMP's High Level Design

Figure 4.12 summarises the main components of SMP in a high level design. SMP lies between the SOAP engine and the Application layer. There are three main components: i) the SMP Compliant Detector; ii) the Message Handler; and iii) the Routing Adaptor. Their relationship and functionalities are explained below.

- **SMP Compliant Detector**: When a SOAP message arrives at the SOAP engine level, it will be pushed up to the SMP Compliant Detector to decide if it is a conventional SOAP message or an SMP compliant message. If it is an SMP message, this will be passed to the Message Handler; otherwise it will be passed straight to the Application layer for normal processing, thereby skipping the SMP layer.
- **Message Handler**: In case a message is received by the Message Handler, it will be analysed by the SMP algorithm as explained in Section 4.6.2 to determine if the message needs to be split before being forwarded to the next hop routers. The message handler performs this with a help from the Routing Adaptor component.

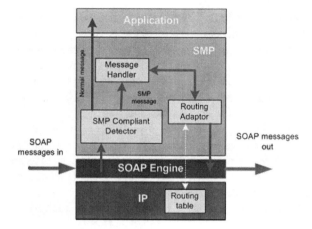

Fig. 4.12 SMP's high level design

- **Routing Adaptor**: This component is responsible for looking up the IP routing table to determine the set of next-hop routers for each client embedded in the SMP message. Additionally, the routing adaptor is in charge of routing all the outgoing SMP messages.

It is important to note that to deploy SMP in a real network, all routers in the network need to be SMP compatible. This can be done by installing an SMP software on each router to enable it to interpret SMP messages. As explained in Section 4.6.1, the SOAP header in an SMP message specifies the next hop router for the message as the message's destination. Therefore, when an intermediary router receives an SMP message, it processes the message as if it is the final destination of the message. Since an SMP-compatible router operates on the application layer, it has full access to the message's envelope and parses the SOAP body to get the list of clients encoded in the SMP header and the actual payload in the SMP body.

4.7 An Analytical Analysis

The major existing SOAP performance enhancement techniques have been reviewed in Section 4.2. To date, an evaluation of these approaches is based purely on experimental results. In contrast, this section defines and thoroughly analysed formal models of different SOAP communication schemes including unicast, multicast and the proposed SMP. Such models enable simulation results to be verified in a consistent manner and also provide a basis for comparing the different solutions in terms of average response time and total network traffic.

4.7.1 The System Model

Prior to presenting the analytical models of various SOAP communication schemes, the basic system model and assumptions made in the analysis are outlined here. Table 4.1 describes the symbols and abbreviations used in this section.

Symbol	Description
N	Number of clients.
K	Number of Web service operations.
opt_i	One in K operation responses offered by a Web service provider.
$optSize_{min}$	The minimum size of an operation response.
$optSize_{max}$	The maximum size of an operation response.
$size(opt_i)$	The size of an operation response opt_i, $optSize_{min} \leq size(opt_i) \leq optSize_{max}$.
N_i	Number of clients accessing opt_i.
s	The source node.
C	The set of clients.
φ_{query}	The mean rate of clients requests per time unit.
α	The skewness parameter of the Zipf distribution.
H	A network tree rooted at the source node s.
V	The set of nodes in the network tree H.
E	The set of links connecting any 2 adjacent nodes in H.
t_{trans}	Transmission time to transmit a message from one node to another. It is calculated as the message size divided by the bandwidth.
t_{prop}	Propagation time on each link. It is assumed to be the same for all links.
t_{link}	Total time including transmission and propagation delay for a message to pass through a link.
t_{proc}	Processing time at a node.
$p_{s.c_n}$	A path containing routers connecting the server to client c_n.
$|p_{s.c_n}|$	The number of hops between the server and client c_n.
L	A constant number representing the number of hops between the source to any client.
$n(d)$	Number of nodes at layer d in H.
$n_i(d)$	Number of nodes at layer d in multicast group tree G_i.
S_{min}	The minimum similarity between a number of SOAP messages.
S_{max}	The maximum similarity between a number of SOAP messages.
S_k	The similarity between k SOAP messages.
$aggregate\_size\{k\}$	The size of an SMP aggregated message of k SOAP original messages.
$average\_size$	The average size of a SOAP message. It is equal to $\frac{(optSize_{min}+optSize_{max})}{2}$.

Table 4.1 Legend of symbols used in theoretical models

Modelling Web Service Operations

A network of N clients that are connected to a service provider is examined in this theoretical analysis. The server (service provider) provides only one service which has K operations. Each service operation is labeled with a unique identifier, starting from opt_1 to opt_K. Operations are labeled based on their access probabilities, such that opt_1 is the most frequently accessed operation on the server, while opt_K is the least frequently accessed. N_1, N_2,..., to N_K, where $N_1 + N_2 + ... + N_K = N$, are the numbers of clients accessing operations opt_1, opt_2, ..., and opt_K respectively.

To simplify the theoretical model, it is assumed that the size of a SOAP response message, denoted as $\text{size(opt}_i)$, for one invocation of operation opt_i is uniformly distributed between optSize_{min} and optSize_{max}. Clients generate requests to access Web service operations at a mean rate of φ_{query} queries per time unit following a Poisson distribution. To model access locality, client queries are distributed among the defined Web service operations following a Zipf-like distribution (159) with a skewness parameter α. A number of studies (16, 24) report that Web requests follow a Zipf-like distribution where the number of requests to the ith most popular document is proportional to $\frac{1}{i^\alpha}$, where α is a small constant skewness factor. Recent study by (112) found the same also applies to Web services' access probability. The probability of an operation opt_i being requested by query Q_l can be calculated by substituting the number of operations, say K, and the operation ID i, into the Zipf distribution (159).

$$Pr(opt_i \in Q_l) = \frac{1}{i^\alpha} \times \frac{1}{\sum\limits_{x=1}^{K} \frac{1}{x^\alpha}} \qquad (4.8)$$

$$(4.9)$$

where $i \in 1..K$ and α is the skewness factor.

Finally, since the clients make requests to the service operations at a rate of φ_{query} requests per time unit, the rate at which a client requests an operation opt_i is equal to:

$$\varphi_i = Pr(opt_i \in Q_l) \times \varphi_{query} \qquad (4.10)$$

Based on Equations 4.8 and 4.10, and assuming that there are N clients in total, the number of clients, N_i, making requests for operation opt_i per time unit can be derived as follows:

$$N_i = N \times \varphi_i = N \times Pr(opt_i \in Q_l) \times \varphi_{query} = N \times \frac{1}{i^\alpha} \times \frac{1}{\sum\limits_{x=1}^{K} \frac{1}{x^\alpha}} \times \varphi_{query} \quad (4.11)$$

Modeling the Network

Let H denote a spanning tree representing the paths from the source s to all clients C. H can be represented as follows:

$$H = \{V, E\} \tag{4.12}$$

where V is the set of nodes including the source s and the receiver set C and E is the set of links.

Except for the source and the clients, each node in the tree corresponds to a router, which is denoted r_j, where $r_j \in V$. The spanning tree H is obtained using the Open Shortest Path First (OSPF) routing algorithm (123). A link is an ordered pair $(r_j, r_k) \in V \times V$ denoting a network link connecting the two routers r_j and r_k.

The transmission delay at any link is calculated by the size of the message passing through, divided by the bandwidth of the link, denoted by b_{link}. The transmission delay associated with a link r_j, r_k is denoted by $t_{trans}(r_j, r_k)$. A processing delay $t_{proc}(r_j)$ is also imposed on traffic passing through node router r_j using SMP or traditional multicast. It is assumed that from any node $r_j \in V$, there is at least one path p_{r_j, c_n} to client c_n. Client nodes $\forall c_n \in C$ are also nodes in the V set, but they are always end nodes. The total transmission cost along the path from node r_j to client c_n, $t_{trans}(r_j, c_n)$, is expressed as:

$$t_{trans}(r_j, c_n) = \sum_{(r_j, r_k) \in p_{r_j, c_n}} t_{trans}(r_j, r_k)$$

There are $|p_{s,c_n}|$ hops from the source s to a client c_n. For simplicity, these theoretical models assume that $|p_{s,c_n}|$ is constant at L for all clients, and expressed in Equation 4.13. If the numbers of hops from the source to each client are all different, it would be very complex to model the total network traffic of SMP mathematically due to not knowing where an SMP message will be split. Thus the size of an SMP message sent over a network link cannot be approximated correctly.

$$\forall c_n \in C, |p_{s,c_n}| = L \tag{4.13}$$

An example of H is depicted in Figure 4.13, where d indicates a node's layer, which is essentially the number of hops from that node to the clients.

4.7.2 Total Network Traffic

The total network traffic generated by the delivery of responses to all clients is the sum of traffic conveyed on each link along the paths from the source s to the respective client. A formula for the total traffic is developed here for each communication scheme.

(a) Unicast Scheme. In the unicast communication scheme, where there is no mechanism to reduce the traffic sent in the network, full SOAP response messages are sent

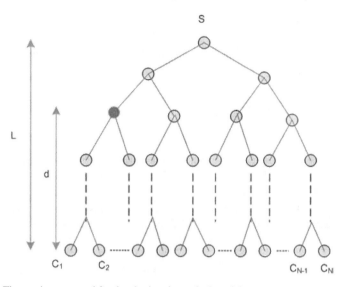

Fig. 4.13 The routing tree used for developing theoretical models

to each client as per request regardless of repetitive requests. As the result, the traffic being sent across the network for the unicast scheme is the sum of traffic generated by sending each type of operation to the clients. Therefore, we have:

$$Total\_Traffic\{Unicast\} = \sum_{i=1}^{K} Traffic\{opt_i\} \qquad (4.14)$$

As defined previously, there are L hops between the server, and each client and there are N_i clients requesting operation opt_i. Therefore, the total traffic created by sending repetitive copies of SOAP responses for opt_i to N_i clients is given by the following equation:

$$Traffic\{opt_i\} = N_i \times L \times size(opt_i) \qquad (4.15)$$

Substituting Equation 4.15 into Equation 4.14, the following function is obtained.

$$Total\_Traffic\{Unicast\} = \sum_{i=1}^{K} (N_i \times L \times size(opt_i)) \qquad (4.16)$$

(b) Multicast Scheme. Under the multicast communication scheme, the total network traffic is significantly reduced. This is because the server sends out only one copy of a response message to multiple clients that request the same operation. The theoretical model to compute the total network traffic for multicast scheme is given in this section. Note that it is not important which specific multicast protocol is used because the main objective is to derive the total traffic and average response time only.

In the theoretical models, there are K operations defined in a service offered by the server, so there are potentially K multicast groups set up in the network routing tree H. Each multicast group G_i corresponds to a multicast group delivering a SOAP response message to all the clients requesting the same operation. The overall network traffic generated by K multicast groups is then the aggregation of the total traffic created by each individual multicast tree. This is expressed by the following:

$$Total\_Traffic\{Multicast\} = \sum_{i=1}^{K} Traffic(G_i) \qquad (4.17)$$

Next, a method to compute $Traffic(G_i)$ for each multicast group is defined. As explained in Section 4.7.1 "System Model", there are N_i clients in the G_i group and every client is L hops away from the server. Consequently, G_i is an L layered multicast tree rooted at the source s and spanning N_i clients. Furthermore, it is easy to see that the number of nodes at the top layer is one (the server), the number of nodes at the bottom layer is N_i (the clients in the group), and the number of nodes at the lower layer is always greater than or equal to that at the layer above it. These observations are expressed in the following equations:

$$n_i(0) = 1 \qquad (4.18a)$$
$$n_i(L) = N_i \qquad (4.18b)$$
$$n_i(d+1) >= n_i(d) \qquad (4.18c)$$

where $n_i(d)$ is the number of nodes in the tree G_i at layer d and $0 \leq d < L$.

For a small multicast group in which the number of clients is smaller than the maximum layer in the multicast tree (i.e. $N_i < L$), we can assume that there are only N_i nodes at each layer and there is no common path among any clients. In such cases, a server needs to send unicast messages to all clients. For a larger multicast group (i.e $N_i \geq L$), since there are N_i leaf nodes in the L-layered tree, it can be assumed that there are in average $\lfloor \frac{N_i}{L} \rfloor^3$ number of nodes at each layer. These assumptions are given below:

$$n_i(d+1) = \begin{cases} N_i, & If \quad N_i < L \\ n_i(d) + \lfloor \frac{N_i}{L} \rfloor, & If \quad N_i \geq L \end{cases} where \quad 0 \leq d < L \qquad (4.19)$$

In the traditional multicast case (113, 154), the size of the message passing through the edges of a multicast group tree remains the same throughout the sub-tree, which equals to $size(opt_i)$ for the G_i sub-tree. Traffic in a multicast tree can be calculated as the sum of traffic on each layer. The traffic incurred on each layer is then equal to the message size multiplied by the number of nodes at that layer. The total traffic in

---

[3] $\lfloor x \rfloor$ is the floor function of a real number x that returns the largest integer less than or equal to x.

G_i is described by the following equation.

$$Traffic(G_i) = \sum_{d=1}^{L} traffic(d_{G_i}) = \sum_{d=1}^{L} n_i(d) \times size(opt_i) \qquad (4.20)$$

Finally, an expression for *Total_Traffic{Multicast}* that is the total traffic generated in the network by using the multicast scheme, is derived by combining Equations 4.20 and 4.17.

$$Total\_Traffic\{Multicast\} = \sum_{i=1}^{K} \sum_{d=1}^{L} n_i(d) \times size(opt_i) \qquad (4.21)$$

(c) SMP Scheme. A model for formalising the total network traffic in the SMP communication scheme is presented here. For simplicity, it is assumed that the similarity threshold is met by all N clients, meaning that all the responses to N clients can be aggregated and sent together in one SMP message.

An SMP routing tree is also assumed to be an L-layered spanning (H) tree. H is rooted at s and spans N clients. Similar to a multicast sub-tree G_i discussed above, the H tree possesses the following characteristics.

$$n(0) = 1 \qquad (4.22a)$$
$$n(L) = N \qquad (4.22b)$$
$$n(d+1) = \begin{cases} N, & \text{If } N < L \\ n(d) + \lfloor \frac{N}{L} \rfloor, & \text{If } N \geq L \end{cases} \qquad (4.22c)$$

where $n(d)$ is the number of nodes in H at layer d and $0 \leq d < L$.

A formula approximating the size of an aggregated SMP message from k original SOAP response messages is proposed here. For simplicity, the similarity between k messages is assumed to be uniformly distributed between S_k^{min} and S_k^{max}. A different distribution of message similarity can also be used , however it requires higher complexity to model. An SMP message is composed of a common section of k ordinary messages and a distinctive section that contains unique parts of each message. As portrayed in Figure 4.14, the darker color section in the diagram represents the common section (in the middle).

Assuming that all k messages have the same size, the size of the common section is then proportional to the similarity of the messages, denoted by S_k. The different part (in lighter colour) of a message is therefore proportional to $(1 - S_k)$. As a result, the total size of the aggregated message can be computed approximately as below.

$$aggregate\_size\{k\} = (S_k + k(1 - S_k)) \times msg\_size = (k - (k-1)S_k) \times msg\_size \qquad (4.23)$$

Assuming that there is a uniform distribution of message size between $optSize_{min}$ and $optSize_{max}$, the average size of a SOAP response message, msg_size, is given by the following equation.

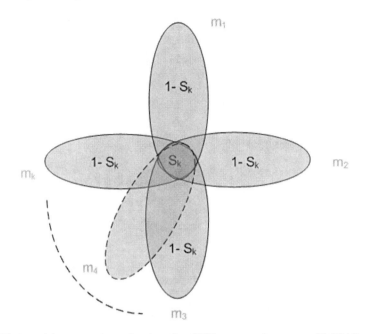

Fig. 4.14 A model to approximate the size of an SMP aggregated message of k SOAP response messages

$$msg\_size = \frac{optSize_{min} + optSize_{max}}{2}$$

With the assumptions on the tree's structure given in Equations 4.22a, 4.22b and 4.22c, the average number of clients included in an SMP message passing through each node at layer d can be given as $\lfloor \frac{N}{n(d)} \rfloor$. After substituting k with $\lfloor \frac{N}{n(d)} \rfloor$ in Equation 4.23, the total traffic sent across a link at layer d in the SMP tree becomes:

$$aggregate\_size\{\frac{N}{n(d)}\} = (\lfloor \frac{N}{n(d)} \rfloor - (\lfloor \frac{N}{n(d)} \rfloor - 1)S_{\frac{N}{n(d)}}) \times msg\_size \qquad (4.24)$$

Generalising Equation 4.24 for all incoming links from the source s to all nodes that are d hops away from s, allows us to obtain the following formula:

$$Traffic(d_{SMP}) = \begin{cases} n(d) \times (\lfloor \frac{N}{n(d)} \rfloor - (\lfloor \frac{N}{n(d)} \rfloor - 1) \times S_{\frac{N}{n(d)}}) \times msg\_size, & if \quad n(d) < N \\ \sum\limits_{i=1}^{K} N_i \times size(opt_i), & if \quad n(d) = N \end{cases} \qquad (4.25)$$

A separate formula for the cases when $n(d) = N$ is needed because a total of N unicast messages of different sizes will be sent.

The total traffic generated in the SMP tree is the sum of all traffic created at each layer. Based on Equation 4.25, an expression to compute the overall network traffic in an SMP routing tree can be obtained as follows:

$$
Traffic\{SMP\} = \sum_{d=1}^{L} \begin{cases} n(d) \times (\lfloor \frac{N}{n(d)} \rfloor - (\lfloor \frac{N}{n(d)} \rfloor - 1) \times S_{\frac{N}{n(d)}}) \times msg\_size, & if \; n(d) < N \\ \sum_{i=1}^{K} N_i \times size(opt_i), & if \; n(d) = N \end{cases}
$$

(4.26)

By not listing out the formula for $aggregate\_size\{\frac{N}{n(d)}\}$, a more compact version of the above equation is shown below:

$$
Traffic\{SMP\} = \sum_{d=1}^{L} \begin{cases} n(d) \times aggregate\_size\{\frac{N}{n(d)}\}, & if \; n(d) < N \\ \sum_{i=1}^{K} N_i \times size(opt_i), & if \; n(d) = N \end{cases}
$$

(4.27)

4.7.3 Average Response Time

Apart from ensuring that the network traffic is reduced, the response time experienced by the clients is also an important performance criterion. The response time is the time from when the server receives a request from a client to the time the client receives the response message. The lower an average response time is, the more responsive the system is to client requests. SMP is well suited to applications where there are many similar simultaneous requests to the server. In this model, it is assumed that all N clients make queries to the server at the same time. The average response time for any communication scheme is given by the following equation:

$$
Average\_Response\_Time = \frac{\sum_{n=1}^{N} response(c_n)}{N}
$$

(4.28)

The response time experienced by an individual client is composed of the delay to convey the response message in the network plus any overhead at the server and at intermediate routers if they exist. The total delay then comprises of the sum of transmission delay and propagation delay across the path from the source to the client. The transmission time, denoted by t_{trans}, of a message passing through a link is computed by dividing the size of the message, $size(opt_i)$, by the link bandwidth. It is assumed that the bandwidth on each link in the network is the same and is equal to b_{link}. The propagation delay, denoted by t_{prop}, is the time required for a message to travel from one point to another, and is assumed to be constant across all links. The time it takes to convert an indexed SOAP message to a standard SOAP message on the client side is not included in the average response time model because this time is considered considerably smaller than propagation or transmission delay. The response time experienced by each client is given by the following formula:

$$response(c_n) = t_{overhead}(c_n) + delay(c_n) = t_{overhead}(c_n) + \sum_{e \in p_{s,c_n}} (t_{prop} + t_{trans}(e))$$

$$= t_{overhead}(c_n) + \sum_{e \in p_{s,c_n}} (t_{prop} + \frac{size(opt_i)}{b_{link}}) \qquad (4.29)$$

(a) Unicast Scheme. With the unicast scheme, the processing overheads at the server and the routers are negligible and therefore ignored in our model (i.e. $t_{overhead}(c_n)\{unicast\} = 0$). N clients can be split into K groups of clients. Each group has $N_1, N_2, ...,$ and N_K clients. All clients in one group receive the same service operation response (i.e. a group with N_i clients receives a response for opt_i). Also because of the assumption that there are L hops between the source and any client, the number of links from the source s to a client c_n equals to L. Applying these to Equations 4.28 and 4.29, the average response time for the unicast scheme is computed as follows:

$$Average\_Response\{unicast\} = \frac{\sum_{i=1}^{K}(N_iL(t_{prop} + \frac{size(opt_i)}{b_{link}})}{N} \qquad (4.30)$$

(b) Multicast scheme. In the traditional multicast scenario, when a client sends a request to the server, the server will not respond to it promptly but rather it will wait for a number of other requests from other clients who are requesting the same service operation. This is because the server needs to get a reasonable number of the same requests from the clients before sending a multicast message out. This waiting period, denoted by $t_{procServer}(multicast)$, is significant and does not exist in the unicast scheme, but is included in the average response time for the multicast scheme.

Under the multicast scheme, when a message arrives at an intermediary router the router needs to process the multicast address and determines if extra copies of the message have to be created to send to branching routers. Therefore, there may be a small processing delay incurred. The average processing time at an intermediate router for multicast is denoted by $t_{procRouter}(multicast)$. The total overhead time for sending a message to a client, denoted as $t_{overhead}(c_n)$, is then the sum of the server processing time and the total router overhead over the path reaching the client, which is expressed below:

$$t_{overhead}(c_n)\{multicast\} = t_{procServer}(multicast) + L \times t_{procRouter}(multicast) \qquad (4.31)$$

In addition, the transmission delay to deliver a multicast message to a client is the same as to deliver a unicast message because the number of hops from the source to any client is assumed to be the same and the size of the message is the same in either unicast or multicast scenario. By substituting Equation 4.31 into Equations

4.28 and 4.29, the average delay experienced by each client for the multicast case can be expressed as:

$$Average\_Response\{multicast\} = \frac{1}{N} \sum_{i=1}^{K} \sum_{n=1}^{N_i} (t_{procServer}(multicast)$$
$$+ L(t_{procRouter}(multicast)$$
$$+ t_{prop} + \frac{size(opt_i)}{b_{link}}))$$
(4.32)

(c) SMP scheme. In SMP, there is an extra overhead to measure the similarity between SOAP messages when clustering the messages into groups and to generate SMP messages based on the common and different parts of the messages. This overhead at the server is denoted by $t_{procServer}(SMP)$. The value of this variable depends on the number of outgoing response messages and work required to measure message similarities.

The overhead at intermediary routers in the SMP case is also similar to that in the traditional multicast case. However, $t_{procRouter}(SMP)$ may be greater than $t_{procRouter}(multicast)$ because more time is required to split SMP messages to branching routers. Similar to multicast, the total overhead time, $t_{overhead}(c_n)$, for sending a message to a destination in the SMP case is expressed as follows.

$$t_{overhead}(c_n)\{SMP\} = t_{procServer}(SMP) + L \times t_{procRouter}(SMP)$$
(4.33)

The total transmission time of all messages in the SMP case is computed by dividing the total transmitted traffic by the network bandwidth. The total transmitted traffic here is the sum of traffic sent to all clients. In a case of aggregated messages passing through a layer (i.e. $n(d) < N$), the total transmitted traffic is computed by multiplying the traffic generated on that layer, as given in Equation 4.27, by the average number of clients, denoted as $\lfloor \frac{N}{n(d)} \rfloor$, encoded in each message. In a case when unicast messages are sent at a layer, the total transmitted traffic on that layer is the same as the one given in Equation 4.27 (in $n(d) = N$ case). Therefore, the total transmission time experienced by all clients is given by the following formula:

$$t_{trans}\{SMP\} = \frac{1}{N \times b_{link}} \sum_{d=1}^{L} \begin{cases} \lfloor \frac{N}{n(d)} \rfloor \times n(d) \times aggregate\_size\{\frac{N}{n(d)}\}, & if \ n(d) < N \\ \sum_{i=1}^{K} N_i size(opt_i), & if \ n(d) = N \end{cases}$$
(4.34)

Combining Equations 4.28, 4.29, 4.33 and 4.34, the formula for computing SMP's average response time is given by the following:

$$Average\_Response\{SMP\} = t_{procServer}(SMP) + L(\,t_{procRouter}(SMP) + t_{prop}\,) \tag{4.35}$$

$$+ \frac{1}{N \times b_{link}} \sum_{d=1}^{L} \begin{cases} \lfloor \frac{N}{n(d)} \rfloor \times n(d) \times aggregate\_size\{\frac{N}{n(d)}\}, & if \quad n(d) < N \\ \sum_{i=1}^{K} N_i size(opt_i), & if \quad n(d) = N \end{cases} \tag{4.36}$$

4.8 Simulation and Results

To evaluate the performance of the proposed method, extensive experimentation has been performed. This section describes the simulation model and summarizes the results obtained from simulation of SMP, traditional multicast, and unicast. The simulation was implemented using the OMNet++ discrete event simulator.

This section provides an experimental evaluation of the SMP protocol. This obviously a good complement of the analytical evaluation provided in the previous section. To model access locality, client queries are distributed among data objects following a zipf-like distribution with skewness parameter α. Existing research found this distribution to be a good representation of access pattern of Web users.

4.8.1 Experimental Setup

It is important to choose a valid test data domain because it needs to be suitable for the use of SMP. SMP is best suited in high-transaction services where the server needs to send many syntactically similar response messages to a large number of clients in a short period of time. Hence, data obtained from the Australian Stock Exchange has been chosen for testing the `StockQuote` application to evaluate the performance of SMP.

The OMNeT++ (8) simulation program was used to randomly generate different hierarchical network topologies with different numbers of network layers to carry out the experiments. Figure 4.15 illustrates a simple network of 20 clients used for testing. For each network topology setup, tests of SMP, traditional multicast (which uses IP multicast), and unicast communication schemes were performed. The simulation model consisted of N clients making queries to K operations. Queries were made, based on a Zipf distribution (159), among all operations offered by the Web service server. The message size and the number of clients were varied in different tests. For each test, 20 experimental runs were performed and the result presented is the average of these runs. The simulation parameters and their values are listed in Table 4.2.

4.8.2 Experimental Results

This section examines the performance of SMP by measuring the total network traffic and the average response time of each communication scheme. The total network traffic is the sum of all the sizes of messages sent to clients. The average response

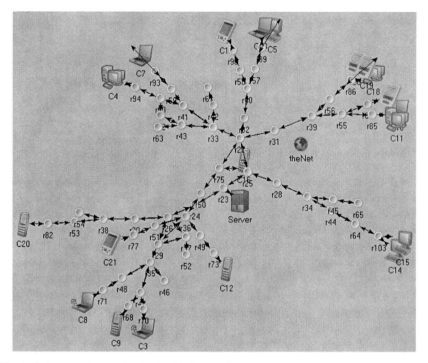

Fig. 4.15 An example of a simple simulated network

Parameter	Default	Range
Number of simulation runs per data point	20	
Number of queries in a simulation period	300	20–500
Number of clients (N)	50	10–200
Number of service operations (K)	10	5–50
Size of a SOAP response message (K)	30Kb	20–50Kb
Number of routers between the source and a client (tree depth)	10	5–15
Bandwidth of a link (b_{link})	1.5Mbps	
Propagation time through a link (t_{prop})	1 ms	
Processing time at routers in multicast scheme ($t_{proc}multicast$)	0.1 ms	
Processing time at routers in SMP scheme ($t_{proc}SMP$)	0.2 ms	
Similarity threshold	0.7	0.3–1
Zipf parameter (α)	1	0.4–1.8

Table 4.2 Simulation Parameters

time is the time from when the server sends a response message until the message reaches its targeted client. It is computed by dividing the total delay experienced by the number of clients. Response time includes propagation and transmission delays on each link and processing delays at the server and intermediary nodes.

(a) **Total Network Traffic.** Figure 4.16 shows the simulation results giving the total network traffic for the three communication schemes. The unicast scheme produces the greatest volume of traffic, which is proportional to the number of receivers. The traditional multicast protocol represents an improvement of around 30% over unicast. SMP reduces traffic by up to 50% over unicast. With a small network (10 to 50 clients), the reduction in traffic of SMP over unicast or multicast is already noticeable, up to 35%. With larger networks (100 to 200 clients) SMP's performance gain over unicast in traffic becomes even more significant, between 45–50%. Comparing SMP to multicast, the difference in traffic generated is not noticeable with small networks of 10 or 20 clients. When the client numbers increase to over 100 clients, SMP outperforms traditional multicast by around 25%. In general, the larger the network is, the higher performance SMP offers in terms of the reduction of network traffic.

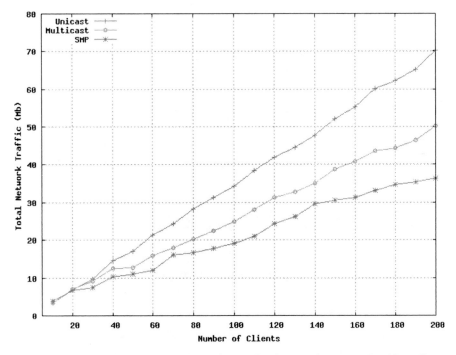

Fig. 4.16 Total network traffic for SMP, multicast and unicast routing protocols with medium messages of 20–50Kb.

(b) Average Response Time. The graph in Figures 5.8 displays the simulation results for the average response time when different SOAP communication schemes are used. The unicast method has the lowest average response time at approximately 86ms for networks with 100 clients and 116ms for networks with 200 clients. Corresponding results for multicast and SMP are 103ms (100 clients), 153ms (200 clients) and 114ms (100 clients), 175ms (200 clients) respectively. That is, the traditional multicast protocol is about 1.3 times slower than unicast.

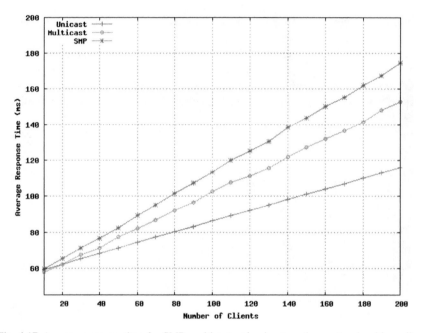

Fig. 4.17 Average response time for SMP, multicast and unicast routing protocols with medium messages of 20–50Kb.

SMP's weakness of having higher processing overhead at the server and intermediate nodes causes the average response time of SMP to be slightly higher than that of the multicast and unicast method. However, the delay penalty is negligible when the number of clients is small (under 40 clients). When the network size increases to 100 clients, SMP experiences 1.5 times higher response time than unicast and 1.15 times higher than multicast.

(c) Payload Size Factor. The performance of SMP is analyzed here in two scenarios: small messages (0.6–1Kb) and large messages (100–300Kb). In the small message scenario, the message schema and other parameters are unchanged. Only the message payload is changed, with size ranging from 0.6 to 1Kb. Figures 4.18(a) and 4.18(b) show the results for total network traffic and average response time for different routing protocols in this scenario. As shown by the graph, the performance gain of SMP over multicast is marginal, under 10% improvement for networks of under 80 clients. Compared to unicast, SMP can reduce total traffic by only 40% in the small message scenario, compared to 50% in the normal scenario presented above. Since SMP messages include extra XML encoding for grouping common and distinctive sections, an SMP message aggregating SOAP messages with small payload does not result in a significant size reduction compared to the combined size of all individual messages. The average response time of SMP in the small message case is slightly smaller than that in the medium message case because of less work involved in the measurement of similarity between payload data.

Figure 4.19(a) displays the total network traffic of SMP against multicast and unicast in the large message scenario. In this scenario, large payload data was simulated for the same service schema. Message sizes ranged from 100 to 300Kb. SMP shows better performance with large payload size compared to other scenarios. As shown in Figure 4.19(a), even with small networks (under 50 clients) SMP outperforms unicast by 60%. Furthermore, a close to 70% reduction in network traffic can be achieved for large networks (more than 150 clients). In the large message scenario, SMP performs slower than in other scenarios by around ten milliseconds — 1.6 times higher in response time, which is not significant in many applications.

4.8.3 Results Validation

The experimental results are compared to the analytical results presented in Section 4.7. Figures 4.20 and 4.21 show both the analytical and experimental results in total network traffic and average response time for all three communication schemes. Table 4.3 outlines the values of the key parameters used when obtaining the graphs.

Parameter	Value
$size_{msg}$	35Kb
b_{link}	1.5Mbps
t_{prop}	5ms
$size(opt_i)$	35Kb
$t_{procServer}(multicast)$	0.5ms
$t_{procRouter}(multicast)$	0.1ms
$t_{procServer}(SMP)$	0.6ms
$t_{procRouter}(SMP)$	0.2ms

Table 4.3 Assumptions of parameters used to obtain the theoretical results

As seen from Figure 4.20, the simulation results generally follow the patterns predicted by the analytical results. However, there is a large difference between the experimental and analytical results of multicast for networks over 100 clients. This is due to assumptions made (for simplicity) about the fixed network topology in the theoretical analysis (see Section 4.7.2). In the simulations, generated network topologies did not strictly follow the assumption on the number of nodes in each layer because in the experiments, the network topologies were randomly created.

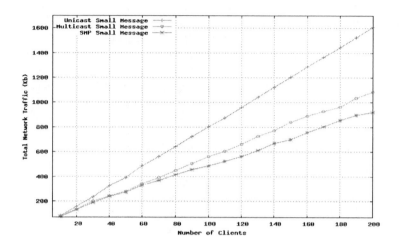

(a) Total network traffic

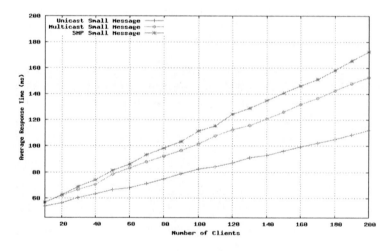

(b) Average response time

Fig. 4.18 Total network traffic and average response time for SMP, multicast and unicast routing protocols with small messages of 0.6–1Kb.

Therefore, some discrepancies between the analytical and simulated results are expected.

Similarly, the average response times in simulations closely follow the expected trends in the analytical results as shown in Figure 4.21. These results prove that SMP outperforms both unicast and traditional multicast methods in terms of total network traffic in both experimental and theoretical analysis.

4.9 Discussion

SMP is a SOAP multicast protocol that makes use of the similarity of SOAP messages to reduce network traffic significantly and to increase overall SOAP performance. In addition, SMP uses a combination of both multicast and unicast concepts to actually 'multicast' messages without using multicast addresses. As discussed in the experimental results section, SMP reduces the consumption of network bandwidth by i) around 20% for small networks with small data payload (0.6–1Kb); ii) by over 40% for networks with medium-size messages (20–50Kb); and iii) by 50–70% for large networks with large-size messages (100–300Kb). SMP's performance gain in network traffic improvement is proportional to the number of clients in the multicast group.

The improvement in total network traffic of SMP over unicast is obvious because under SMP, messages of similar content are grouped and sent together. Therefore, duplicate messages are avoided and more bandwidth can be saved. SMP can reduce further traffic than conventional IP multicast because SMP can 'multicast' SOAP messages of slightly different contents as well as identical messages while IP multicast can send only same messages. Common parts (templates or data values) in different outgoing SOAP messages are efficiently reused and only one copy of the common parts is sent out. In addition, SMP employs an indexing technique that only compact representations of SOAP documents are sent, therefore the total size of messages can be reduced further.

SMP can support a very large number of receivers because there is no limit on the number of addresses that could be embedded in a SOAP message (SMP header), while the size of Xcast (a small group multicast protocol, see Section 4.3.1) packet headers is limited to the size of an IP header, so the number of receivers that can be stored inside an Xcast header is limited. SMP addresses the scalability problem of Xcast. Placing client addresses inside SOAP messages is also beneficial for reliability since the senders always have the addresses of the receivers for retransmission purposes. It is important to note that no state maintenance is required at forwarding routers under SMP. In contrast, under IP multicast each router on multicast trees needs to maintain a list of clients that belong to the multicast group.

A drawback of SMP is that it requires additional processing time at each router, to perform unicast table lookups, to parse the SMP header, and to split SMP messages into multiple copies. Thus, SMP produces higher average response time than unicast. SMP provides a multicast solution with minimal usage of network bandwidth and a low delay trade-off. It is especially suitable for applications that do not have strong constraints in delay, as well as for wireless environments (ad-hoc networks, wireless LANs and wide-area cellular networks) which are scarce in bandwidth.

4.10 Summary

This chapter of this book provided details of the SMP model, which is a new multicast protocol for Web services to efficiently send similar SOAP messages to a large number of clients. The contribution of this chapter is three-fold. Firstly, a novel algorithm for measuring the similarity of SOAP messages was presented. Using this similarity measurement between outgoing SOAP messages, servers can determine if these messages have the XML structure or payload values in common. Secondly, a new similarity-based multicast routing protocol (SMP) for SOAP is proposed to take advantage of common message structures and values among response messages. SMP sends the contents of multiple similar responses in one aggregated message, called an SMP message, instead of sending each of them individually, thus significantly reducing network traffic.

The SOAP indexing technique enables fast merging and splitting of SMP messages. Each data type definition in a WSDL service description is indexed with a unique identifier. Each XML node in a SOAP message is also labeled with a position, and is presented in a compact form that includes: (1) the node data type ID referenced back to the WSDL document, (2) the position of the node in the SOAP message and (3) the node value. The indexed representation of a SOAP message not only reduces message size due to the omission of full XML tag names, but also leverages the organization of common and distinctive data in SMP messages. To the best of our knowledge, SMP is the first similarity-based SOAP multicast protocol that has been proposed in the Web services.

SMP's main advantage is that it reduces the traffic generated over a network by 50–70% compared to unicast in large networks (over 100 clients) with large payload (over 100Kb). The performance trade-off of SMP is its higher response time. However SMP's performance penalty in response time is relatively small (1.5 times slower) compared to its performance gain in network traffic (3 times less traffic), when being compared with unicast. The use of SMP is justifiable for Web service applications that are not time critical, are constrained in bandwidth and deal with large amount of data.

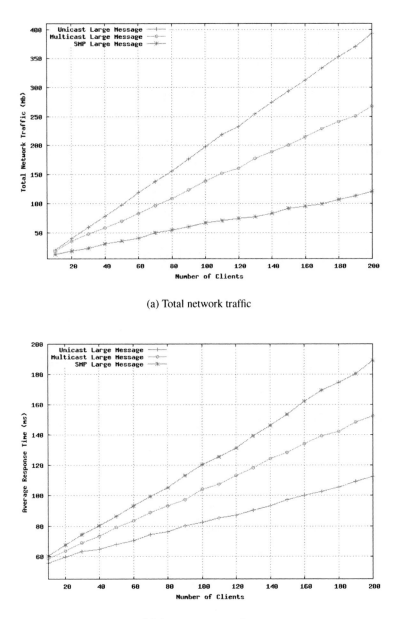

(a) Total network traffic

(b) Average response time

Fig. 4.19 Total network traffic and average response time for SMP, multicast and unicast routing protocols with large messages of 100–300Kb.

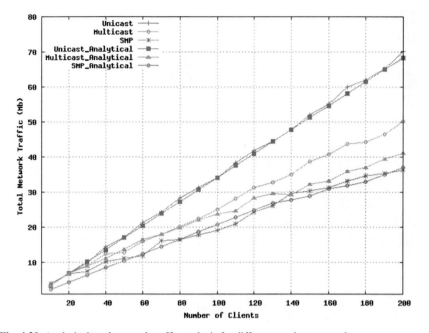

Fig. 4.20 Analytical total network traffic analysis for different routing protocols.

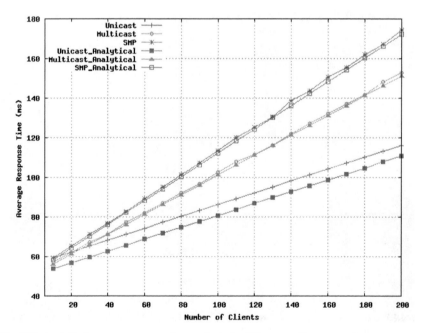

Fig. 4.21 Analytical average response time analysis for different routing protocols.

Chapter 5
Network Traffic Optimisation

*There are two ways to live: you can live as if nothing is a
miracle; you can live as if everything is a miracle.*

Albert Einstein

This chapter discusses in details a traffic-constrained SOAP multicast routing protocol, called tc-SMP[1], which is an extension of the similarity-based SOAP multicast
protocol (SMP) proposed in the previous chapter. Tc-SMP offers improvements over
SMP in terms of network traffic size by using its own routing protocol instead of the
shortest path algorithm that conventionally sends messages between nodes along
shortest paths first. Tc-SMP looks at the network optimisation aspect of the SMP
protocol and proposes alternative message delivery paths that minimise the number
of bytes transmitted over the network. Two tc-SMP algorithms, *greedy* and *incremental* approaches, are proposed and compared for their efficiency and performance
advantages over SMP. Simple heuristic methods are also proposed for incorporat-
ing with the two tc-SMP algorithms to improve results. Theoretical analysis is also
presented to show the differences in total traffic and average response time between
tc-SMP and SMP. From extensive experiments, it is shown that tc-SMP achieves a
25% reduction in total network traffic compared to SMP, with a trade-off of 10%
increase in average response time. Compared to conventional unicast, bandwidth
consumption can be reduced by up to 70% using tc-SMP and 50% using SMP.

5.1 Motivation

The SMP protocol described in Chapter 4 uses the Open Shortest Path First (OSPF)
protocol to route messages. This protocol is based on Dijkstra's algorithm (37), and
it routes a message using the shortest path from a source to a destination. Therefore,
the routing path selected by such an algorithm may not be the best in terms of traffic
optimisation. It is important to note that two nodes of a network are connected with
multiple paths in most cases.

The routing protocol plays a critical role in SMP. In particular, the more similar
SOAP messages can be combined over specific links the more network bandwidth
can be saved. However when OSPF is used, some SOAP messages that are very
similar in content and follow the shortest paths, there may not be many common

---

[1] In earlier publication of this work, tc-SMP was called eSMP (117).

links shared by these messages. By restricting ourselves to the OSPF routing paths, we may miss other feasible paths that may result in further reduction in the total traffic. Using other paths may permit the aggregation of SOAP messages with a higher level of similarity and their transmission along more common links.

This chapter describes an extension of SMP, called tc-SMP, which includes an efficient routing algorithm for delivering SMP messages. Simulations have shown that tc-SMP can reduce network traffic, when compared to SMP, by more than 25% with a small increase in response time (namely 10%). In addition, tc-SMP can reduce the traffic by up to 70% compared to unicast, and 40% compared to traditional multicast, the corresponding results for SMP are 60% and 30% respectively.

The rest of this chapter is organised as follows. The next section discusses related work on QoS-based routing. The tc-SMP routing algorithm is then presented in Section 5.4. Analytical comparisons between the tc-SMP algorithms and the SMP algorithm are presented in Section 5.5. Performance experiments and results are detailed in Section 5.7. Afterwards, the experimental results are analysed in the Discussion section to highlight the strengths and weaknesses of tc-SMP. The chapter concludes with a summary that remarks on tc-SMP and its benefits.

5.2 Related Work

This section gives an overview description of QoS-based routing and discusses existing popular QoS-based routing solutions in multicast. In recent years, there has been a rapid growth in multimedia and real-time applications such as video teleconferencing, real-time remote control systems, and interactive distributed games. This evolution of digital technologies has arisen a need to satisfy certain quality-of-service (QoS) requirements for individual customers who are willing to pay more for better services such as faster response time or higher bandwidth. Service providers may have other QoS requirements that relate to the whole session, such as minimal transmission cost. By adding such constraints to the original problem of routing, the problem is re-formulated as a QoS-constrained routing problem.

QoS-based Routing

The main objective of QoS routing is to find the selection of paths that satisfy multiple QoS requirements in a network, while contributing to improved network resource utilisation. QoS requirements are given as a set of constraints which can be link constraints, path constraints or tree constraints. (31) define a *link constraint* as a restriction on link usage such as link bandwidth, while a *path constraint* is an end-to-end requirement on a single path such as end-to-end delay bounds or delay jitter. A *tree constraint* specifies a QoS requirement for an entire multicast tree, for example total traffic over a network or loss ratio. Resource utilisation is often computed by an abstract cost metric (33). The optimisation of QoS routing is then to find the lowest-cost path among all the feasible paths.

QoS-based Multicast Routing

The basics of many commonly-used multicast routing protocols such as DVMRP (Distance-Vector Multicast Routing Protocol), MOSPF (Multicast Extension to OSPF), and PIM (Protocol Independent Multicast) have been discussed in Section 2.3 of Chapter 2, Background. This section explains in more detail, how a multicast tree which is rooted at a source and spans multiple destinations is actually built.

There are several well-known multicast routing problems. The *Steiner tree* problem (also called the *least cost* multicast routing problem) is to find the tree that spans a set of destinations with the minimum total cost over all links (70). The *constrained Steiner tree* problem (often called the *delay-constrained least-cost* routing problem) is to find the least cost tree with bounded delay.

Multicast routing algorithms can be grouped into two categories: *source routing* and *distributed routing*. Source routing is a strategy that requires each node to maintain the global state of the network topology, and link state information. Feasible paths to each destination are computed at the source node, based on the global state information. Routing decisions are then communicated to intermediate nodes via a control message. Contrasting to source routing, in distributed (or hop-by-hop) routing each node maintains state information for nearby nodes, exchanged via control messages. Each packet contains the address of its destination, and every node maintains a forwarding table that maps each destination address into transmitting-neighbour nodes. Forwarding decisions are made by each node, upon the receipt of a packet, the destination of the packet is considered. Examples of QoS source routing algorithms are presented in (34, 86, 158). Work in QoS hop-by-hop routing can be found in (76, 128). These studies are described in detail in subsequent sections.

The class of QoS multicast routing problems has been shown, in general, to have high computational complexity (NP-hard) (153). Hence these algorithms usually use heuristics to reduce the complexity of the path computation problem, at the expense of not achieving an optimal solution but just a feasible solution (116). Next, main contributions in solving constrained multicast routing problems both by source and distributed routing strategies will be discussed.

QoS-based Multicast Source Routing

In this section, some important work on source routing algorithms for multi-constrained multicasting is discussed.

(34) proposed an algorithm, called QoS-based Dynamic Multicast Routing (MQ-DMR), that builds a dynamic multicast tree which satisfies multiple QoS requirements and efficiently distributes traffic throughout the network . It operates when adding a new node to the existing multicast tree. The two objectives of MQ-DMR are to minimise the overall network traffic when connecting a new receiver, and to connect a new node to the source so that QoS constraints are satisfied. In their model, a link cost is the inverse of the available bandwidth on that link. They aim to use part of the existing multicast tree to share the same path from the source to a

newly added client, such that the additional traffic is minimised. The authors developed a model that dynamically assigns cost to a link based on the duration for which it would be in use. MQ-DMR operates in a similar way to the Bellman-Ford shortest path algorithm (19). In the first iteration, it tries to find one-hop least cost paths to all destinations. In the next iteration, it aims to find two-hops least cost paths with a tendency to select links that are already in use in the multicast tree. Subsequent iterations are similar. The maximum number of iteration steps can be determined based on the pre-defined allowable delay jitter.

In their experiments, Chakraborty et al. simulated their proposed MQ-DMR algorithm against Greedy (141) and Naive (43) multicast routing and DMG (28). DMG, which was described earlier by the same authors, is an algorithm that works similarly to MQ-DMR but is based on Dijkstra's shortest path algorithm and is not QoS-based. Greedy and Naive algorithms are dynamic multicast routing algorithms but do not take QoS requirements into account. In the Greedy algorithm, a new node joins with the shortest path to the nearest node that is in a multicast tree while in the Naive algorithm, a new node is added to a multicast tree through the shortest path from the source. Even though MQ-DMR is compared with three un-constrained algorithms, the results show that MQ-DMR performs as efficiently as the Naive, Greedy and DMG algorithms. The average tree cost results are dependent on the strictness of the QoS requirements. Regarding results, the average number of hops produced by MQ-DMR is very similar to that of the Naive algorithm.

Chakraborty et al.'s approach is quite similar to the proposed SMP, however SMP incorporates the actual size of traffic passing through a link in the cost function. SMP algorithm is based on Dijkstra's algorithm to find paths connecting a new client to an existing SMP tree through a node that is not necessarily the source.

Delay and delay variation constrained shortest path multicast routing is also a popular problem that attracts great interest from many researchers. Mokbel et al. proposed a heuristic algorithm called DVCSP that solves the problem in polynomial time and returns a near optimal tree (86). The DVCSP approach includes two main phases. First, it finds a set of potential paths that satisfy the delay constraint for all destinations. This phase is facilitated by K maximum tokens kept in each node. A token at a node is used to keep track of the cost and delay experienced so far, as well as the path it has traversed from the source to the current node. Tokens are continuously duplicated from node to node until the path reaches its destination. Next, among a set of tokens arriving at a destination, one that satisfies the delay constraint variation will be chosen as the routing path reaching to that destination. The complexity of the algorithm is $O(K^2M^2)$ if $KM^2 > N^2$ and $O(KN^2)$ if $KM^2 < N^2$, where K is an integer value ranging from 1 to N, M is the number of nodes in the multicast group and N is the number of nodes in the network. Mokbel et al. compared their algorithms with other delay constrained shortest path solutions and consider two performance factors: failure rate and average cost per path. DVCSP has an additional cost to satisfy the additional constraint of delay variation.

A bounded shortest path algorithm (BSMA) to find a Delay-Constrained Least Cost (DCLC) path is proposed by (158). Their original approach uses a loop-less k-shortest-path (KSP) algorithm (46) to list all possible shortest paths in order of increasing cost, then picks the first path that satisfies all delay requirements. The same authors proposed an alternative implementation for the BSMA heuristic bounded shortest path algorithm to reduce the time complexity of BSMA but still maintain cost performance (48). A comprehensive comparison of different heuristics and algorithms for multicasting can be found in work of (124).

QoS-based Multicast Hop-by-hop Routing

Though many proposed source routing algorithms to solve QoS-constrained multicast routing problems, provide promising results, they have a common lack of scalability. This weakness stems from the fact that frequent updates of global states need to be made at the source to cope with the dynamics of network and that means high computation overhead at the source (116). To avoid this overhead, there have been attempts to solve the QoS-constrained multicast problems in a distributed manner. Two important work in this area is presented here.

(128) presented a destination-driven multicast routing algorithm (DDMC) that optimises total tree cost. Most of the proposed heuristics that solve the minimum multicast tree problem assume the use of global cost information by the source, but DDMC uses only cost information from nearby nodes. The DDMC algorithm uses a greedy strategy based on Dijkstra's shortest path and Prim's minimal spanning tree algorithms. In DDMC, the costs at destination nodes are reset to zero to encourage the selection of paths that go through destination nodes. Their justification for this approach is that nodes reached from another destination node experience only an incremental additional cost, thus the total tree cost can be reduced. However this method may result in a tree with long paths connecting multiple destination nodes, so it may not meet the end-to-end delay constraint. Additionally, in their tree model, cost is not associated with any specific network parameter - however different cost metrics may have different meanings and implications on the overall performance of an algorithm. Shaikh and Shin did not provide results about the algorithm's performance on different cost metrics such as link capacity, hop distance, inverse of link bandwidth, or congestion rate; which would be beneficial to other researchers.

A distributed heuristic algorithm for solving the delay-constrained Steiner tree problem was proposed in a study by (76). In their algorithm, every node maintains a distance vector giving the minimum delay to other nodes. The algorithm begins with only the source node in the tree and iteratively adds new links to the tree through three phases. First, the source sends a "Find message" to all nodes in the network. Upon the receipt of the "Find message", each intermediary node finds the adjacent link that can connect to a new destination (not yet included in the tree), which meets the delay constraint and minimises a selection function. Next, the links found by all nodes are submitted to the source where the best link, the one that minimises the selection function, is chosen. Last, an "ADD message" is sent to add the best link to the tree. The algorithm takes $O(n^3)$ time to build a tree to all destinations, where n is the number of vertices in a network.

The problem addressed in this chapter, that is *finding a minimum traffic cost multicast tree for sending similar SOAP messages*, can be categorised as a QoS-based routing problem. The solutions for this problem presented here are not dynamic because in every multicast session, the number of receivers are known and fixed in advance by the message aggregation process. Once the similarity of N outgoing SOAP messages is determined to be over a threshold level, a multicast tree for the client destinations of these N messages will be formed. In addition, the proposed algorithms use the source routing strategy and assume that the source has the global state information provided by a link-state routing protocol.

5.3 Notations and Problem Definition

Here a formalisation of the underlying tc-SMP model is given. The most difficult problem in tc-SMP is to find routing paths linking a source to a set of clients while simultaneously minimising a total traffic cost function. To achieve this objective, a tree connecting the source and client nodes needs to be computed. A mathematical formulation of the *traffic-constrained similarity-based SOAP multicast* routing tree problem based on graphs can be given as follows.

Let $G(V,E)$ be a network graph, where V is the set of nodes and E is the set of edges, s is the source node, $C = \{c_1, c_2, c_3, ... c_N\}$ is the set of clients (or destinations) in the network, so $s \cup C \subseteq V$. A tree $T(s,C) \subseteq G$ originates at s and spans all members of C. Let $P_T(c_i) \subseteq T$ be the set of links in T that constitutes the path from s to client $c_i \in C$. The $tr(e)$, where $e \in E$, is a function that gives the number of bytes transmitted through link e. The total traffic generated in the tree T, denoted by $Traffic(T)$, is defined as the sum of the traffic transmitted on all links in the tree, given by the expression $Traffic(T) = \sum_{e \in T} tr(e)$. The objective of the tc-SMP problem is to construct a tc-SMP tree $T(s,C)$ such that the tree's network traffic, $Traffic(T)$, is minimised.

The traditional multicast routing tree problem (which sends *identical* messages to multiple receivers from a source while simultaneously minimising some cost function) is an NP-hard problem (113). The following lemma proves that tc-SMP is also NP-hard.

Lemma 1 *The minimum traffic-constrained similarity-based SOAP multicast routing problem (tc-SMP) is NP-complete.*

Proof. This lemma is proved by method of reduction from the Steiner problem which is NP-hard (70). The Steiner tree problem deals with a weighted graph $G(V,E,w)$, where w is a weight function: $E \rightarrow R_+$ and a subset of vertices $D \subseteq V$. The objective of the Steiner problem is to find a minimal weight tree that includes all vertices in D (70).

Using reduction method, one of the nodes $s \in D$ is chosen to be the source, and the rest of the nodes in D are assigned to be clients: $C = D \setminus s$. The $tr(e), e \in E$, function in the traffic-constrained SMP (tc-SMP) problem corresponds to the weight function in the Steiner problem. Therefore, the tc-SMP problem can be mapped into the Steiner problem. In addition, the weight function in the Steiner problem is static while the $tr(e)$ function in the tc-SMP problem is dynamic, depending on which message is sent across link e. Hence, the tc-SMP problem is even more complex than the Steiner problem. Thus, it can be concluded that the traffic-constrained SMP problem is NP-complete.

To cope with the NP-completeness of the problem, heuristic algorithms are developed to solve the problem in polynomial time. They are described in Section 5.4. A tc-SMP routing tree and a branching node, used in the tc-SMP algorithms, are defined as the following:

Definition 5.1. [*tc-SMP Tree*]: A tc-SMP tree is a tree of tc-SMP nodes. A tc-SMP r_j node is a data structure $[r_j.router, r_j.clients, r_j.cost]$ where:

- $r_j.router$: corresponds to a physical router in the network topology,
- $r_j.clients$: is a set of clients that r_j forwards SMP messages to, and
- $r_j.cost$: is the total traffic already generated in a network when an SMP message arrives at r_j.

Definition 5.2. [*Branching Node*]: A node B is a branching node of a client C with respect to a tc-SMP tree T if the following conditions are met:

- $B \in T$.
- C is connected to the tree T through B and this connection introduces minimum additional traffic to the total tree traffic cost compared to other link connections.

5.4 Tc-SMP Routing Algorithms

Here two algorithms, *greedy* and *incremental* tc-SMP algorithms, are described to build a minimum traffic tc-SMP routing tree. The *greedy* algorithm is a simple approach where clients are added to a tc-SMP tree, one after another, taking the shortest path to a branching node in the tree. The *incremental* approach is however more complex, because it builds the shortest path SMP tree using the OSPF protocol first. The incremental algorithm then builds a tc-SMP tree gradually from branches of the SMP tree to ensure that the final tc-SMP tree always has less total traffic than or at least equal to that of the SMP tree. First, the two tc-SMP algorithms without using heuristics will be explained. Next, two simple heuristic methods will be proposed for use in conjunction with the tc-SMP algorithms, to improve performance.

5.4.1 The Greedy tc-SMP Algorithm

The algorithm presented in this section takes a simple approach in solving the minimal traffic-constrained SMP problem. Its objective is to add a new client to the tree along a path that introduces the least additional traffic.

The multicast session begins with only the source node whose cost is initially set to zero. The greedy tc-SMP algorithm goes through multiple iterations to add paths with minimal traffic connecting each client to the tree one by one. A client may join a tc-SMP tree via a branching node (see Definition 5.2) where the additional traffic introduced by adding the new client is smaller than the traffic created by adding the client via other existing nodes in the tree. In order to compute the additional traffic each time a client is added, each tc-SMP node maintains two parameters (see Definition 5.1): (1) the list of clients that the node conveys messages to and (2) the accumulated traffic cost generated along the path from the source to the current node. In this way, the added traffic generated by a new client can be computed as the difference between the new cost and the old cost at the branching node plus the traffic generated along the shortest path from the branching node to the new client. The algorithm finishes when all clients have been successfully added to the tree.

The pseudocode of the *greedy* tc-SMP is described in Algorithm 3 that calls another main procedure, namely `UpdateTreeNodeCosts` which is defined in Algorithm 4. There are three main phases in each iteration adding a new client to an existing tc-SMP tree.

- **Phase 1**: Finding the branching node (Lines 2 to 17 of Algorithm 3).
- **Phase 2**: Updating tree nodes' costs (Line 19 of Algorithm 3, or full Algorithm 4).
- **Phase 3**: Adding routers along the shortest path to the tree (Lines 20 to 24 of Algorithm 3).

Other functions called by the tc-SMP algorithm and the `UpdateTreeNodeCosts` procedure are defined below.

- `ComputeCost (r, C)` is a function that computes the accumulated cost in traffic from the source to a node r to deliver messages to a set of clients C.
- `FindSP (r, c)` is a function to find the set of router nodes along Dijkstra's shortest path from a branching node r to a new client c.
- `SPCost (r, c)` is a procedure that computes the amount of traffic created by sending a unicast SOAP message from a branching node r to a new client c following the shortest path.
- `Descendants(r)` function returns a list of child nodes of an input node r in a tree.
- `SubTree(r)` gives all the nodes in the sub-tree rooted at an input node r.
- `size(m_i)` represents the original size of a SOAP response message m_i.
- `hops(r, r_k)` returns the hop count between two input nodes.
- `parent(r)` returns the lowest ancestor node of the input node r.

In addition, the following notations and assumptions are made for the proposed *greedy* tc-SMP routing algorithm:

- Let T be the set of nodes in a tc-SMP spanning tree.
- Let $M_K = \{m_1, m_2, m_3, ..., m_K\}$ be a set of SOAP response messages to be sent to all clients, and m_i be the response message for client c_i.
- Let $C_K = \{c_1, c_2, c_3, ..., c_K\}$ be a group of clients to which the SOAP messages in the M_K set are sent.
- Let added_*cost* be the additional traffic generated in the network as the result of adding client c_i into T.

- Let $\texttt{min\_cost}$ be the minimum additional network traffic as a result of adding c_i into T (the minimum of all possible *added_cost* values).

The objective of the greedy tc-SMP algorithm is to find $T = \{s, c_1, c_2, ..., c_K, r'_j, .., r'_h\}$, where r'_j is a tc-SMP node, so that $\texttt{Traffic}(T)$ is minimized. Now, the steps involved in each phase are described in detail.

Algorithm 3: tc-SMP: Minimum-traffic tc-SMP routing tree algorithm

---

$T \leftarrow \{s\}$;

foreach $c_i \in C_K$ **do**
    min_cost $\leftarrow \infty$;
    branch_node $\leftarrow NULL$;

    foreach $r'_j \in T$ **do**
        if $|T| = 1$ **then**
            branch_node $\leftarrow s$;
            break;
        else
            old_cost $\leftarrow r'_j.cost$;
            new_cost $\leftarrow \texttt{ComputeCost}(r'_j, r'_j.clients \cup c_i)$;
            diff_cost $\leftarrow$ (new_cost $-$ old_cost) ;
            sp_cost $\leftarrow \texttt{SPCost}(r'_j, c_i)$;
            added_cost $\leftarrow$ diff_cost $+$ sp_cost ;

            if added_cost $<$ min_cost **then**
                min_cost $\leftarrow$ added_cost ;
                branch_node $\leftarrow r'_j$;
            end
        end
    end
    $T \leftarrow T \cup c_i$;
    $\texttt{UpdateTreeNodeCosts}(\text{branch\_node}, c_i, s)$;
    $R = \texttt{FindSP}(\text{branch\_node}, c_i)$;
    foreach $r_k \in R$ **do**
        $r'_k.clients \leftarrow c_i$;
        $r'_k.cost \leftarrow \texttt{size}(m_i) \times \texttt{hops}(\text{branch\_node}, r_k) + \text{branch\_node}.cost$;
        $T \leftarrow T \cup r'_k$;
    end
end

The first phase (Lines 2-17 of Algorithm 3) is to find the branching node through which a new client can connect to a tree such that this connection introduces the smallest additional traffic to the network compared to connections via other nodes in the tree. A random client, say c_1, is the first joining the source node. A heuristic method, which will be discussed later, can be applied to assist in choosing the first client. But, here it is assumed that there is no heuristic method applied to the greedy tc-SMP routing algorithm. The branching node for the first client is the source.

Algorithm 4: *UpdateTreeNodeCosts* Procedure: Update the costs of all nodes in a tree

---

Input: s: The source ;
branch_node: Branching node ;
c: The newly added client ;

procedure *UpdateTreeNodeCosts* **do**
    previous_root ← *NULL*;
    r ← branch_node ;
    while $r = s$ ‖ parent(r) ∈ T **do**
        old_cost ← *r.cost*;
        r.clients ← *r.clients* ∪ c;
        r.cost ← ComputeCost(r, *r.clients*) ;
        diff_cost ← (*r.cost* − old_cost);
        foreach u ∈ Descendants(r) **do**
            if u ≠ previous_root **then**
                foreach v ∈ SubTree(u) **do**
                    v.cost ← *v.cost* + diff_cost ;
                end
            end
        end
        if r ≠ s **then**
            previous_root ← r ;
            r ← parent(r) ;
        end
        else quit
    end
endw

The first client is always added to the tree via the shortest path based on Dijkstra's algorithm.

For subsequent clients, a branching node for a client is determined by examining through all existing tc-SMP tree nodes, (excluding leaf nodes which are clients), from top to bottom searching for potential branching nodes. A node among these potential branching nodes is then chosen to be the branching node from which the new client connects to the tree. A node is considered a potential branching node if there exists an off-tree path (none of the link resides in the tree yet) from it to the new client.

At each potential branching node, the additional traffic (`added cost`) introduced to the network as a result of adding the new client to the tree is computed. `Added cost` is calculated as the sum of the difference of the new and old costs at the branching node and the total shortest path cost from the branching node to the client. This is shown in Line 14 of Algorithm 3. Our strategy to ensure the total traffic size is as small as possible is to minimize the number of bytes sent every time a new client is added to the tree. Therefore, among all potential branching nodes, the node that has the smallest `added cost` is selected.

The second phase (Line 19 of Algorithm 3 and Algorithm 4) is to update the costs of all existing nodes in the tree to reflect the addition of the new client. This pseudocode for this phase is given in Algorithm 4 (UpdateTreeNodeCosts). It updates the clients lists, denoted as r.clients, and calculates the accumulated costs, r.cost, of a branching node and its ancestors (Lines 6-7 in Algorithm 4). A clients list is a list of clients that a node forwards SMP messages to and the accumulated cost of a node is the total traffic generated over the network when an SMP message arrives at the node as defined in Definition 5.1. The costs of nodes that are in the sub-trees of the ancestor nodes of the branching node are also incremented by a diff_cost amount (Lines 9-12). Diff_cost is computed as the difference between the cost of the ancestor node before the update and the new updated cost.

The third phase (Lines 20-24 of Algorithm 3) is to add the nodes, that are along the shortest path from the branching node to the new client, to the tree. The clients list, r'_k.clients, of a node r'_k among these newly added routers will include only the new client. The accumulated cost of r'_k, r'_k.cost, is the sum of the branching node's accumulated cost and the multiplication of h and the size of a unicast SOAP message, where h is the number of hops from r'_k to the branching node.

Example Illustration

The diagram in Figure 5.1 is an example to illustrate the greedy algorithm. If a router r_i from the topology is included in the spanning tree T, it corresponds to a node r'_j in the tree T where $r'_j.router = r_i$. At the beginning, the tree includes only the source node: $T = \{r'_0\}$, and c_1 is the first client to be added to T. The shortest path from the source s to the client c_1 (highlighted in the bold line) is then added to the tree. The spanning tree T is then updated to include $\{r'_0, r'_1, r'_2, r'_3, r'_4\}$. The cost at node r'_1 is the amount of traffic created by sending a message addressed to c_1 over link l_{s-r_1}. The cost at node r'_2 is the total size of traffic generated by sending a message to c_1 over links l_{s-r_1} and $l_{r_1-r_4}$.

The next client to be added to the tree is c_2. The routing path for c_2 will be chosen in consideration of the path already determined for c_1, so that the total traffic volume created as the result of sending messages to these two clients is minimal. From the network topology in Figure 5.1, there are two feasible paths to client c_2 from the source s via different forwarding routers r_1 and r_2. The source node must decide on path that will create the smallest amount of traffic together with the message for client c_1.

The dotted lines represent paths from two potential branching nodes, s and r_5 in the network topology, for connecting client c_2 to the existing tc-SMP tree T. Assuming that messages to c_1 and c_2 are exactly the same, r_5 [r'_3] will be chosen as the branching node because it has the smallest additional traffic cost when including c_2 in the client list. Node c_2 [r'_5] will be added as a new node in T as well.

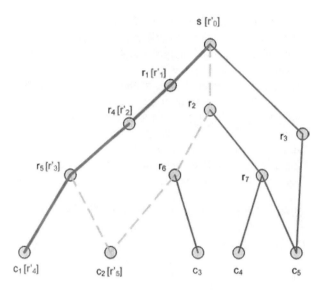

Fig. 5.1 A sample network used to illustrate tc-SMP routing

Finally, all routers that are on the newly found optimal path from the branching node to the new client will also be added to the spanning tree. The costs of all nodes in T will be updated to reflect the new status of the tree in terms of traffic (with the inclusion of the new client). Repeating this process for the rest of the clients. Adding clients one by one to the spanning tree will result in a full spanning tree to all destinations in the group. The complexity of the *greedy* algorithm is analysed in later sections.

5.4.2 The Incremental tc-SMP Algorithm

The second approach to solve the tc-SMP problem is called `incremental` tc-SMP. While the greedy algorithm builds a tc-SMP tree from scratch, the incremental algorithm builds a tc-SMP tree based on a shortest path SMP tree. The incremental tc-SMP algorithm iteratively examines each branch in the SMP tree connecting to a client and determines if the branch can be replaced by an alternative path in the network to reduce the traffic created when transmitting an SMP message to that client. If there is no such a substitute branch, the shortest path to the client from the SMP tree will be added to the tc-SMP tree. Therefore, in the worst scenario, incremental tc-SMP produces the same results as SMP.

Algorithm 5 formally shows the steps involved in this algorithm. The steps are grouped into three main phases as presented in the following list. The details of each phase are elaborated in the subsequent paragraphs.

- **Phase 1**: Setting up an SMP tree based on shortest paths (Line 1 of Algorithm 5).

- **Phase 2**: Finding alternative paths connecting to each client (Lines 15-16 of Algorithm 5).
- **Phase 3**: Building a temporary tree, T_{temp}, which includes the newly found alternative path to the client (Lines 18-19 of Algorithm 5 and Algorithm 6).
- **Phase 4**: Selecting the branch that connects to the client with the least traffic to add to the tc-SMP tree (Lines 20-23 of Algorithm 5).

Algorithm 5: Incremental tc-SMP algorithm

$T_{SMP} = \{r_k, r_{k+1}, ..\}$: an SMP tree ;
$T_{temp} \leftarrow T_{SMP}; T_{tc-SMP} \leftarrow \emptyset$;
foreach $c_i \in C_K$ **do**
$\quad$ **if** $T_{tc-SMP} = \emptyset$ **then**
$\quad\quad$ **foreach** $r_j \in p_{s,c_i}$ **do**
$\quad\quad\quad$ $\{p_{s,c_i}$ is the shortest path from s to $c_i \}$;
$\quad\quad\quad$ $T_{tc-SMP} \leftarrow T_{tc-SMP} \cup r_j$;
$\quad\quad$ **end**
$\quad\quad$ $T_i \leftarrow T_{SMP}$;
$\quad\quad$ **continue** ;
$\quad$ **else**
$\quad\quad$ $\{p_{s,c_i}^{min}$ is a path from s to c_i that introduces the least traffic in the tree$\}$;
$\quad\quad$ $p_{s,c_i}^{min} \leftarrow p_{s,c_i}$, where $p_{s,c_i} \in T_{i-1}$;
$\quad\quad$ $T_i \leftarrow T_{i-1}$;
$\quad\quad$ **foreach** $r_j \in T_{tc-SMP}$ **do**
$\quad\quad\quad$ **if** $r_j \neq s$ && $r_j \notin C_k$ && $r_j \notin p_{s,c_i}$ **then**
$\quad\quad\quad\quad$ $R = \text{FindSP}(r_j, c_i)$;
$\quad\quad\quad\quad$ **if** $R \neq \emptyset$ **then**
$\quad\quad\quad\quad\quad$ $T_{temp} \leftarrow \text{RemoveClientFromTree}(T_{temp}, c_i)$;
$\quad\quad\quad\quad\quad$ $T_{temp} \leftarrow T_{temp} \cup R \cup p_{s,r_j}$;
$\quad\quad\quad\quad\quad$ **if** $\text{Cost}(T_{temp}) < \text{Cost}(T_i)$ **then**
$\quad\quad\quad\quad\quad\quad$ $p_{s,c_i}^{min} \leftarrow p_{s,r_j} \cup p_{r_j,c_i}$;
$\quad\quad\quad\quad\quad\quad$ $T_i \leftarrow T_{temp}$;
$\quad\quad\quad\quad\quad$ **end**
$\quad\quad\quad\quad$ **end**
$\quad\quad\quad$ **end**
$\quad\quad$ **end**
$\quad\quad$ $T_{tc-SMP} \leftarrow T_{tc-SMP} \cup p_{s,c_i}^{min}$;
$\quad$ **end**
end

The following notations and assumptions are made for the *incremental improvement* tc-SMP routing algorithm:

- Let T_{tc-SMP} be the set of routers in the tc-SMP spanning tree.
- Let T_{temp} be a temporary tree built during the path finding process for each client.

Algorithm 6: *RemoveClientFromTree* Procedure: Remove nodes spanning a client from a tree

---

Input: T: the input tree ;
c: The client to be removed from T;
Output: T: The resulted tree after removing c;

procedure *RemoveClientFromTree* **do**
    foreach $r_i \in p_{s,c}$ **do**
        if $|r_i.clients| = 1$ **then**
            {There is only c passing through this router } ;
            $T \leftarrow T \setminus r_i$;
        end
    end
endw

- Let T_i be a tree generated after each iteration of adding a new client to the tc-SMP spanning tree.
- Let $C_K = \{c_1, c_2, c_3, ..., c_K\}$ be a group of clients that have requested for $|M_K|$ SOAP messages which have a similarity level greater than or equal to the required threshold and can be aggregated into one SMP message.
- Let $M_K = \{m_1, m_2, m_3, ..., m_K\}$ be the set of SOAP response messages to be sent to all clients; m_i is the response message for client c_i.
- Let $Cost(T)$ be a function of the total traffic cost of the whole tree T.
- Let $FindSP(r_j, c_i)$ be a function to find a list of routers connecting router r_j to client c_i along its shortest path.

In the first phase, the source establishes a routing tree, called T_{SMP}, where every path from the source to each client is based on Dijkstra's shortest path first algorithm, similar to the original SMP algorithm. This phase can be easily completed by using the OSPF routing protocol deployed in most networks. Each node r_j in the T_{SMP} tree also maintains the properties $r_j.router$, $r_j.clients$ and $r_j.cost$ as defined in Definition 5.1.

The tc-SMP tree, T_{tc-SMP}, is initially empty. Each client is added to the tc-SMP tree, one after another. In the first iteration, from K clients, a random client c_1 is chosen as the first client to be added to the T_{tc-SMP} tree. The first client is a special case where the tc-SMP path to c_1 is the same as the SMP path to c_1 (see Lines 4–7 of Algorithm 5). This is similar to the greedy approach in that the first client is always added to the tree using the shortest path first algorithm. The current total cost in terms of traffic in the tree will be calculated and denoted by $Cost(T_1)$.

In the next iteration, the algorithm attempts to finding an alternative path for another client, say c_i, as illustrated from Lines 11–23 of Algorithm 5. T_{temp} is denoted as a temporary tree which is built during the process of finding an alternative path for a client c_i. The tc-SMP algorithm examines if there exists a path from a node (excluding the source and the clients), r_j, that is already in T_{tc-SMP}, to the client c_i. Also, the algorithm ignores r_j if it resides on the original shortest path p_{s,c_i} from the previous tree.

If there is a path from r_j to c_i that meets the criteria in Line 15 of Algorithm 5, the T_{temp} is then built based on T_{i-1}, which is the resulted tree from the previous iteration, but excluding the path spanning c_i (see Line 18 of Algorithm 5 and full Algorithm 6). Subsequently, the path p_{r_j,c_i} is added to T_{temp}. The total cost of T_{temp} is then calculated as a result of this and compared to the cost of T_{i-1}. If $Cost(T_{i-1})$ is greater than $Cost(T_{temp})$, T_{temp} will be assigned to T_i. This process continues until all the clients in the list are examined for alternative paths.

Example Illustration

Figures 5.2 and 5.3 show an example of how the incremental tc-SMP algorithm operates. In this example, there are 4 clients c_1, c_2, c_3 and c_4 all requesting the same SOAP message. Let ω denote the size of each SOAP response message. To make the example easy to follow, the size of an aggregated SMP messages of any number of standard SOAP messages is still ω. First, an SMP tree, denoted by T_{SMP}, is built by using the OSPF protocol. T_{SMP} roots at the source s and spans all four clients on the shortest paths, as shown in solid lines in Figure 5.2(a). The cost in terms of the total traffic created if SMP messages are sent following the paths in T_{SMP} is then computed $(Cost(T_{SMP}) = 10\omega)$. Next, a tc-SMP tree, denoted by T_{tc-SMP}, will be built gradually by adding the clients to the tree one after another. The first client, c_1, is added to the tc-SMP tree through the shortest path, therefore, the source s, routers r_1 and r_4 and client c_1 are included in the T_{tc-SMP} tree.

To add client c_2 to T_{tc-SMP}, the algorithm examines if there exists a path from a node, that resides in T_{tc-SMP} and satisfies the criteria on Line 15 of Algorithm 5, to c_2. Routers r_1 and r_4 both have paths to c_2. Let us consider r_4 as the branching node for linking c_2 as r_4 is closer to c_2 than r_1 is. A temporary tree, denoted by T_{temp}, is built by removing the single path spanning c_2 in the T_{SMP} tree and adding the new path connecting r_4 to c_2. This T_{temp} tree is depicted in Figure 5.2(b). The cost of this temporary tree is computed and equal to 11ω which is higher than the cost of the initial T_{SMP} tree (10ω). Therefore, in this iteration the shortest path from the source to client c_2 is added to T_{tc-SMP}. If the greedy tc-SMP algorithm was used instead, r_4 would be chosen as the branching node over the source because the greedy algorithm only considers the total traffic cost for clients that it has added so far instead of the whole client set.

Client c_3 can be added to T_{tc-SMP} easily because there is only one path from the source to c_3. There are two paths spanning client c_4, and it is trivial to realise that c_4 will be added to T_{tc-SMP} via r_5. The final incremental tc-SMP tree is illustrated in Figure 5.3 along lines with arrows.

5.4.3 The Heuristics

The basic functionalities of the two tc-SMP routing algorithms without using a heuristic have been described. Here, two simple methods, which can be applied

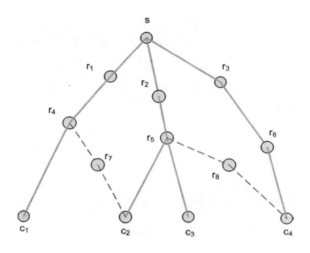

(a) Initial SMP tree (in solid lines)

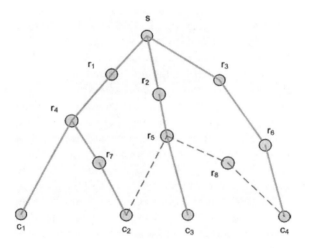

(b) A temporary tree (in solid lines)

Fig. 5.2 An SMP tree and a temporary tree built by the incremental tc-SMP algorithm in a sample network

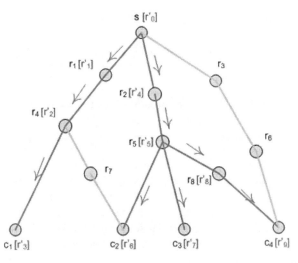

Fig. 5.3 A tc-SMP tree (lines with arrows) finally built by the incremental tc-SMP algorithm in a sample network

to both algorithms to determine the order of clients in a distribution list to be added to a tree, are proposed.

- *Message size-based Heuristic Approach.* This approach is based on the sizes of response messages. First the K SOAP response messages are sorted in a descending order according to their size. Clients are added to the tree in order by their descending message size. Using this method, large messages are sent out first along the least hop paths. Thus less additional traffic is generated later.
- *Similarity-based Heuristic Approach.* This heuristic method is based on the similarities between response messages. The first client to be added to a tree is the one that has the largest message size. Then subsequent clients are added to the tree in order by descending message similarity with existing clients' messages in the tree. With this method, messages with higher similarity tend to be sent along paths that have more common links, thus more network bandwidth can be saved.

For both algorithms, a number of tc-SMP trees may need to be built to deliver all the responses to the clients. This is because a tc-SMP multicast tree is only for a group of clients whose SOAP response messages can be combined. Information about the tree will be pigged-back on SMP messages so that intermediary routers can look up the routing information and determine next-hop routers for each client embedded in the messages.

The main difference between the *greedy* and *incremental* algorithms is that the *greedy* one builds a tc-SMP tree from scratch while the *incremental* one builds a tc-SMP tree based on an established SMP tree and adds paths that minimize the total cost of the tc-SMP tree. The *incremental* algorithm guarantees that every time a path for a client is chosen, a tc-SMP tree produces an equal to or smaller traffic volume than an SMP tree.

5.5 Complexity Analysis

The time complexity of the algorithms to build a tc-SMP routing tree is analysed here. The computation time for the algorithms is shown to be polynomial by proving the following lemmas.

Lemma 2 *The time complexity of the greedy algorithm to build a traffic-constrained SMP routing tree is $O(n(m+nlogn))$, where m is the number of edges and n is the number of nodes in a network.*

Proof. In a network graph $G = (V,E)$, where $|V| = n$ and $|E| = m$. In the worst case, all clients in the set C will be added to a tc-SMP tree. The *for-loop* from Lines 2 to 24 of Algorithm 3 is executed once for each client and hence for a total of N times. The *for-loop* of Lines 5–17 of the same algorithm, in the worst case, is performed n times if all the nodes in the set V are already included in the routing tree. In each round of this loop, an execution of finding the shortest path between the current node to a client takes place. Dijkstra's shortest path algorithm is run in $O(m+nlogn)$ time using a Fibonacci heap implementation (37). Therefore, the complexity to complete the full *for-loop* of Lines 5–17 is therefore $O(n(m+nlogn))$. The *UpdateTreeNodeCosts* procedure in the worst case needs to update all the nodes in the network, thus has a time complexity of $O(n)$. Hence, total execution time of the entire algorithm is $O(N(n(m+nlogn)+n))$, which can be simplified to $O(n(m+nlogn))$ since N can be considered as a constant as there is always a limit on the number of messages aggregated in an SMP message. In conclusion, the greedy tc-SMP algorithm runs in polynomial $O(n(m+nlogn))$ time.

Lemma 3 *The time complexity of the incremental algorithm to build a traffic-constrained SMP routing tree is $O(n(m+nlogn))$ where m is the number of edges and n is the number of nodes in a network.*

Proof. The worst case for this algorithm is when building a tc-SMP tree that spans all N clients. Considering the main for-loop, Lines 3–23 of Algorithm 5. This *for-loop* is executed once for each client and hence for a total of N times. As explained above, N is considered as a constant in this analysis as there is often an upper bound on the number of clients that can be aggregated in an outgoing SMP message from the server. Inside this loop, the algorithm runs through all the nodes that already exist in the tc-SMP tree, which in the worst case would have n nodes. Finding the shortest path from a node to a client (as presented in Line 16 of Algorithm 5) requires $O(m+nlogn)$ time using a Fibonacci heap implementation (37). Line 18 calls the *RemoveClientFromTree* procedure, described in Algorithm 6, which requires $O(L)$ time where L is the largest number of hops from the source to any client in the network. The time complexity required to measure the cost of a temporary tree, Line 20, is $O(n)$. Therefore, the *for-loop* of Lines 3–23 takes $O(n(m+nlogn)+L+n)$, simplified to $O(n(m+nlogn))$, to complete. In conclusion, execution time of the incremental tc-SMP algorithm is of the order $O(n(m+nlogn))$ time.

The proposed algorithm is more complex than the OSPF algorithm, because the OSPF problem finds the optimal path for each destination independently. In contrast, the traffic-constrained SMP problem involves path optimisations for multiple destinations the paths of which are dependent on each other and there is a common tree constraint of reducing the overall network traffic.

5.6 An Analytical Study

In this section, the analytical models of the total network traffic and the average response time for the tc-SMP routing protocol are presented and compared with the analytical models of SMP, multicast and unicast protocols, which were presented in the previous chapter. These models will enable a comparison to be made between various SOAP multicast schemes without the need for simulation. This analysis will also provide a general framework for analysing the performance of these schemes under different workloads and network sizes and will be used to verify the accuracy of simulation results.

Table 5.1 outlines the definitions of symbols and notations used in the analytical study. In addition, the network and Web service operation models are defined as per in Chapter 4.

Symbol	Description
N	Number of clients.
K	Number of operations.
opt_i	One in K operations offered by a Web service provider.
N_i	Number of clients accessing opt_i.
s	The source node.
C	The set of clients.
$Traffic\{A\}$	The total network traffic when using routing protocol A.
$Diff\_Traffic\{A,B\}$	The difference in total traffic between routing protocols A and B.
$size_{msg}$	The average size of a SOAP message.
h	Number of hops along the shortest paths from a source to all clients except c_1, $\{C \setminus c_1\}$, in the best case total traffic scenario.
$Diff\_response\{A,B\}$	The difference in average response time between A and B.
$t_{procServer}(A)$	The server processing overhead when using routing protocol A.
$t_{procSim}$	The processing overhead to measure the similarity between messages (common for both SMP and tc-SMP).
$t_{treeBuilder}$	The processing overhead to build a routing tree under tc-SMP.
t_{path}	The time it takes to find the shortest path from a router to a client and to measure the additional cost added to a tree if the client is added through that router.
n	Number of nodes in a network graph.

Table 5.1 Legend of symbols used in tc-SMP theoretical models

5.6.1 Total Network Traffic

Computing the performance metrics (traffic and response time) of tc-SMP theoretically is a complex task. To compare tc-SMP against SMP, it is necessary to model a tc-SMP routing tree based on the same network which was used to model SMP. It is relatively straightforward to model an SMP routing tree in a network where multiple paths exist from one node to another. In such a tree, the source as the root is connected to its clients through the shortest paths. The shortest paths can be easily found using Dijkstra's algorithm, as explained in Chapter 4. However, it is difficult to estimate the average response time and total bandwidth of a tc-SMP tree due to the influence of many parameters (such as the layout of the network, and the similarity level between SOAP messages).

The complexity of a network topology presents a challenge in computing the total network traffic. Assuming a fixed network topology such as a binary tree network, is a poor option because it does not provide a generalisation of the problem. In this chapter, theoretical models for tc-SMP are based on the models previously used for SMP in Chapter 4, Section 4.7. The difference in total network traffic between the tc-SMP and SMP routing schemes is then determined. Specifically, worst and best case scenarios are approximated to find the range of difference in total network traffic between the two.

A) Worst case

The worst case, analysed in this section, refers to the case where the difference in traffic, $Diff\_Traffic\{SMP, \text{tc-SMP}\} = Total\_Traffic\{SMP\} - Total\_Traffic\{\text{tc-SMP}\}$, is smallest. The worst case scenarios for both greedy and incremental algorithms are examined.

Greedy tc-SMP Algorithm: The scenario where the *greedy* tc-SMP algorithm performs worse than SMP is when the shortest-path tree built by SMP is already an optimal tree, and the tc-SMP tree built using the greedy algorithm is only a near optimal one. Since, under the greedy approach, a source does not have a full view of routing paths to all clients, when adding a new client to a tree, the greedy algorithm can only optimize the traffic for clients that already exist in the tree, not all clients. Therefore, it is not expected that traffic in the greedy tc-SMP tree is always smaller than that in the SMP tree. The worst difference in traffic for the greedy algorithm is given below:

$$Total\_Traffic\{SMP\} \leq Total\_Traffic_{worstcase}\{\text{tc-SMP}(greedy)\} \qquad (5.1)$$

The above inequality can be re-written as follows:

$$Diff\_Traffic_{worstcase}\{SMP, \text{tc-SMP}(greedy)\} \leq 0 \qquad (5.2)$$

Incremental tc-SMP Algorithm: Since the *incremental* tc-SMP algorithm builds a tc-SMP tree based on an SMP tree, in the worst case, the traffic of the tc-SMP tree is equal to that of the SMP tree. Therefore, the following inequality can be drawn for the difference in total traffic between the *incremental* tc-SMP algorithm and SMP given the same number of clients and network topology.

$$Diff\_Traffic\{SMP, tc\text{-}SMP(incremental)\} \geq 0 \qquad (5.3)$$

B) Best case
The best-case scenario here implies the case when the difference in traffic between SMP and tc-SMP, denoted as $Diff\_Traffic\{SMP, tc\text{-}SMP\}$, is largest. This scenario occurs when all messages to N clients can be sent as an aggregated message along h hops from a source to router r_h, where the SMP message is split into N individual unicast messages to all the clients. Figure 5.4 depicts this scenario, the solid lines represent the tc-SMP paths. There are $h+1$ hops from the source to any of the clients using tc-SMP routing. SMP routing paths are represented by dashed lines. The SMP

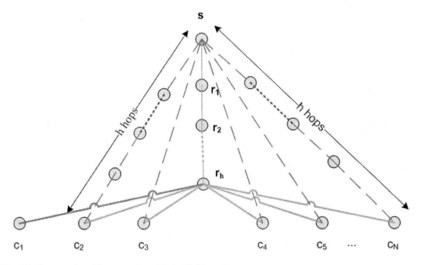

Fig. 5.4 Best total traffic scenario with tc-SMP routing

routing tree has only one common path, which is p_{s,c_1} connecting the source to the first client c_1, with the tc-SMP routing tree. Other paths in the SMP tree are h-hop shortest paths from the source to all clients in $\{C \setminus c_1\}$. For simplicity, it is assumed that the size of each original SOAP response message is all the same and is equal to $size_{msg}$. The total traffic generated by the SMP paths is given by the following equation:

$$Total\_Traffic\{SMP\} = (h+1)size_{msg} + h(N-1)size_{msg} = (1+h \times N)size_{msg} \quad (5.4)$$

The total traffic generated on the tc-SMP paths is equal to the sum of the traffic along the common path from s to r_h and the traffic at the final hops from r_h to each of the clients. Along the common path, the size of the aggregated message is assumed to be $\alpha \times size_{msg}$, where $1 \leq \alpha < N$ (the aggregated message size is always equal to or greater than the original response message size and less than the sum of all original SOAP messages). The total traffic for tc-SMP is given by the following equation:

$$Total\_Traffic\{tc\text{-}SMP\} = h \times \alpha \times size_{msg} + N \times size_{msg}$$

In the best-case scenario, the similarity among all messages is 1, so $\alpha = 1$, and the above formula becomes:

$$Total\_Traffic\{tc\text{-}SMP\} = h \times size_{msg} + N \times size_{msg} = (h+N) \times size_{msg} \qquad (5.5)$$

From Equation 5.4 and Equation 5.5 the best case traffic difference between tc-SMP (both greedy and incremental algorithms) and SMP is given by:

$$Diff\_Traffic\{SMP,tc\text{-}SMP\} \le (h \times N + 1 - h - N) \times size_{msg} \qquad (5.6)$$

In conclusion, from Equations 5.2, 5.3, and 5.6, the ranges of differences in total network traffic generated between SMP and greedy tc-SMP algorithms; and between SMP and incremental tc-SMP are shown below:

$$a \le Diff\_Traffic\{SMP, tc\text{-}SMP(greedy)\} \le (h \times N + 1 - h - N) \times size_{msg} \qquad (5.7)$$
$$where \ a \ \le 0$$
$$0 \le Diff\_Traffic\{SMP, tc\text{-}SMP(incremental)\} \le (h \times N + 1 - h - N) \times size_{msg} (5.8)$$

Expression 5.7 implies that greedy tc-SMP generally outperforms SMP by a certain amount of traffic up to $(hN + 1 - h - N)size_{msg}$ units of bytes, but in some cases, greedy tc-SMP can be outweighed by SMP. On the other hand, Expression 5.8 shows that incremental tc-SMP always produces less traffic than or equal to SMP.

5.6.2 Average Response Time

Modelling a function to accurately compute average response time is a complex task, since the result is influenced by the topology of a network. The difference in average response time between SMP[2] and tc-SMP is mainly due to the overhead at the server for building tc-SMP routing trees. For simplicity, it is assumed in this model that the total transmission delay, propagation delay and processing delay at intermediate nodes experienced by a client are the same in both tc-SMP and SMP. Therefore, the difference in average response time between SMP and tc-SMP is also the difference in the server processing overhead time between them. This is shown in the following expression:

$$Diff\_response\{SMP,tc\text{-}SMP\} = t_{procServer}(SMP) - t_{procServer}(tc\text{-}SMP) \qquad (5.9)$$

Both SMP and tc-SMP have the same overhead in measuring message similarity and in determining which messages can be aggregated. This time is denoted by

---

[2] Under SMP, messages are routed automatically using OSPF, a common routing protocol employed by most networks.

$t_{procSim}$, which is the same as $t_{procServer}(SMP)$ defined in Section 4.7.3. Therefore, the following equation is obtained:

$$t_{procSim} = t_{procServer}(SMP) \qquad (5.10)$$

Under tc-SMP, extra time overhead, denoted by $t_{treeBuilder}$, is required to build a tc-SMP routing tree. As proved previously, both greedy and incremental tc-SMP algorithms have the same time complexity. Therefore, the server processing overhead experienced by a client for both tc-SMP algorithms can be expressed as follows:

$$t_{procServer}(\text{tc-SMP}) = t_{procSim} + t_{treeBuilder} \qquad (5.11)$$

The process of finding the branching node for a new client in tc-SMP involves searching each existing node in a T_{tc-SMP} tree to find the shortest path from the node to the client, and computing the traffic cost introduced by adding this shortest path to the tree. The time it takes to do this on each router is called t_{path}. The maximum number of nodes to be processed when a client is added to the tree is n, which is the number of vertices in a network graph. Therefore, in the worst case, the processing overhead to build a tc-SMP tree for N clients can be given as:

$$t_{treeBuilder} = N \times n \times t_{path} \qquad (5.12)$$

Combining Equations 5.9, 5.10, 5.11 and 5.12, the average response time difference between SMP and tc-SMP is given as below:

$$Diff\_response\{SMP,tc\text{-}SMP\} = t_{procServer}(SMP) - t_{procSim} - N \times n \times t_{path} \quad (5.13)$$

As explained in Equation 5.10 $t_{procServer}(SMP) = t_{procSim}$, Equation 5.13 can be rewritten as:

$$Diff\_response\{SMP,tc\text{-}SMP\} = -N \times n \times t_{path} \qquad (5.14)$$

Equation 5.14 shows that tc-SMP experiences slower average response time than SMP by $N \times n \times t_{path}$ time units.

5.7 The Experimental Results

The purpose of this section is to identify the characteristics of the routing algorithm and evaluate its performance under various network conditions. To test the effectiveness of tc-SMP over SMP, its performance is evaluated and compared with SMP, traditional multicast and unicast communications.

5.7.1 Experimental Setup

The OMNeT++ (8) simulation program was used to randomly generate different hierarchical network topologies to carry out experiments. Figure 5.5 illustrates a sample network of 40 clients used for testing. In these topologies, the maximum number of hops in the shortest paths from the source to any client is 10. The propagation delay, which is the time that a network message takes to travel from one node to another is constant at $t_{prop} = 5ms$. The topologies were generated such that there were always multiple paths to convey a message from the source to most of the clients. The number of clients in the network ranged from 10 to 200. For each network topology, six tests were performed. They were greedy tc-SMP without heuristic, incremental tc-SMP without heuristic , greedy tc-SMP with the message size-based heuristic, incremental tc-SMP with the message size-based heuristic, greedy tc-SMP with the similarity-based heuristic and incremental tc-SMP with the similarity-based heuristic. The test results for SMP, traditional multicast and unicast were obtained from the experience described in the previous chapter. For each test, 20 experimental runs were performed and the result given is the average of these runs.

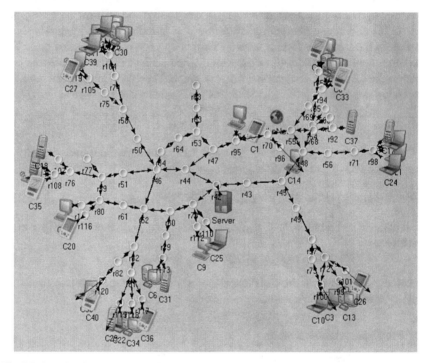

Fig. 5.5 Sample of a simulated network topology

Client requests to the Web service operations followed a Zipf distribution (159) with a skewness factor of $\alpha = 1$. There were 10 operations defined in the Web service's description document in the experiments. These operations correspond to 10 SOAP response messages denoted by $m_1, m_2, \ldots, m_{10}$ in which m_1 is the most frequently requested message and m_i is the ith frequently accessed one. The size of the messages ranged from 20Kb to 50Kb. The similarity threshold used for SMP and tc-SMP methods is 0.7. The similarity between messages depends on the requested service operation and on its input parameters. The simulated bandwidth available on each link was 1.5Mbps.

5.7.2 Experimental Results

The total network traffic and the average response time for each client are the two metrics used to examine the performance of the tc-SMP algorithm and to compare with SMP, multicast and unicast. The network load is the total size of all messages passing through all links in the routing tree when sending responses to all the clients. The average response time is the average time it takes from the server sending a response message out, until the message reaches the destined client. It is computed by dividing the sum of the delays that each client experiences by the number of clients. The response time includes propagation and transmission delays on each link and processing delays at the server and at intermediary nodes.

A) General Case
This section presents the results for experiments in the general cases as outlined in Section 5.7.1.

Total Network Traffic: Figure 5.6 shows the total network traffic for greedy and incremental tc-SMP algorithms compared to SMP, multicast and unicast schemes. As expected, unicast produces the greatest volume of traffic, that is proportional to the number of receivers. Traditional multicast protocol represents an improvement of around 30% over unicast, while SMP and tc-SMP can reduce traffic by up to 50% and 65% respectively. With a small network of under 50 clients, the reductions in traffic between tc-SMP and SMP over unicast are quite small, with little difference between them (around 15%).

With larger networks (100 to 200 clients) tc-SMP's and SMP's performance gain over unicast in traffic is more significant — over 60% for tc-SMP and over 45% for SMP. Comparing tc-SMP to SMP, the difference in bandwidth consumption is not noticeable with small networks of 10 or 20 clients. When the client numbers increase to 50, 100 and 200, tc-SMP (both greedy and incremental algorithms) outperforms SMP by around 10%, 20%, and 25% respectively. As shown from Figure 5.6, the *incremental* tc-SMP algorithm in general performs better than the *greedy* tc-SMP algorithm by 2–4% across all network sizes.

Figure 5.7 compares the total network traffic for different tc-SMP algorithms with and without heuristics. In general, there is no significant difference between the network traffic results with or without tc-SMP heuristics. A close look reveals that the similarity-based heuristic method presents an improvement of approximately 3% over its message size-based heuristic method counterpart. For example, with a network of 100 clients, the *greedy* tc-SMP with message-size based heuristic produces 14.74Mb traffic while the similarity-based heuristic for the same tc-SMP algorithm produces only 13.68Mb traffic. Similarly, with a network of 150 clients, the *incremental* tc-SMP algorithm with message-size based heuristic and similarity based heuristic generate 21.9Mb and 19.23Mb traffic respectively. It is evident that the

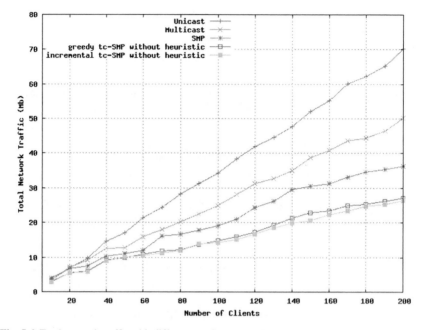

Fig. 5.6 Total network traffic with different routing protocols.

incremental tc-SMP algorithm with the similarity based heuristic method produces least traffic of the tc-SMP variations by a margin of around 5%.

Average Response Time: The average response times observed in the experiment is displayed in Figure 5.8. The unicast method has the lowest average response time at approximately 59ms for networks with 10 clients and 116ms for networks with 200 clients. The traditional multicast protocol is about 1.3 times slower than unicast. SMP performs slightly slower than multicast with about 10% higher average response time. The response times for different variations of the tc-SMP methods are fairly close, on average about 2.0 to 2.5 times higher than the unicast method. This represents an average increase of 15% in response time over multicast.

SMP and the two versions of tc-SMP have significant processing overhead at the server required to measure the similarity between messages and to aggregate the similar ones. Small additional processing time at intermediate nodes is required because midway routers need to split incoming SMP messages into multiple outgoing messages for next-hop routers. Similar overhead also occurs in traditional multicast routing but is slightly smaller at transitional routers.

The performance penalty of tc-SMP over SMP is primarily its overhead in setting up the routing tree initially at the server. However, the difference in the average delays is not significant. For tc-SMP without heuristic, the average delay a client experiences ranges from 60ms to 195ms for networks of 10 clients to 200 clients. The corresponding results for SMP are 59.5ms to 175ms. On average, using the tc-SMP algorithms raises the average response by around 10% compared to SMP.

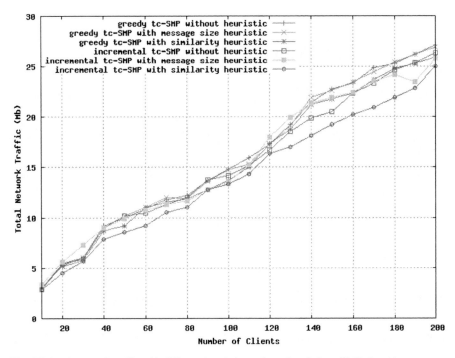

Fig. 5.7 Total network traffic with different heuristics and non-heuristic tc-SMP algorithms

Figure 5.9 shows the response times for different variations of tc-SMP algorithms with and without heuristics. As shown in the graph, the *incremental* algorithm responds more slowly than the *greedy* one. This is because the *incremental* method needs to build an SMP tree first based on Dijkstra's algorithm, before incrementally building a tc-SMP tree. In addition, between the two heuristics used for selecting the order in which clients are added to a tc-SMP tree, the method that is based on the similarity between response messages takes a longer time. In the similarity-based heuristic method, the largest message is found first, then subsequent messages that have the greatest similarity with the first message will join a tc-SMP tree. Therefore, it is reasonable to expect that the similarity-based heuristic will have higher response time than the message size-based heuristic.

B) Maximum Optimality

This section presents an analysis of the network traffic reduction achieved by tc-SMP over SMP, multicast and unicast protocols in various message characteristic scenarios, to find the best variant of tc-SMP. The results presented in the previous section were obtained using a Zipf distribution of client requests. Here the behaviours of unicast, multicast, SMP and *incremental* tc-SMP for networks of different client request distributions are examined. The client request distribution is based on the overall similarity between all response messages ranging from 0.3 to 1 in this

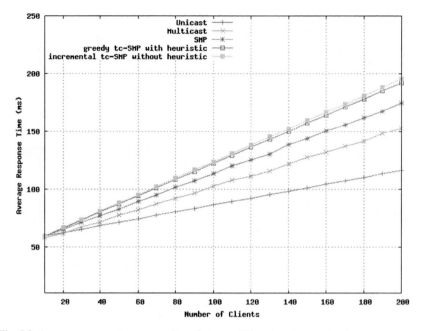

Fig. 5.8 Average response time comparisons between different routing protocols

experiment. Additionally, for simplicity and ease of comparisons, the size of all response messages is constant at 40Kb. The experiment was carried out for networks
of 10, 50, 100, 150 and 200 clients. The results for four protocols are depicted in
Figure 5.10(a).

According to the 3D graph in Figures 5.10 and 5.11, incremental tc-SMP outperforms other protocols consistently over various network sizes and message similarity scenarios. When the similarity between all response messages is 1, the performance of SMP and multicast is similar, but incremental tc-SMP gives a performance
gain of 25%. This reduction in traffic can be seen from the graph in Figure 5.11(b).

Figures 5.10(b) and 5.11(a) show the individual traffic results created by multicast and SMP respectively. It can be seen from these graphs that there is a trend
of lower total traffic when the similarity between all messages is higher. The same
trend also applies to incremental tc-SMP (see Figure 5.11(b)). However, with the
unicast method for the same network size (top graph in Figure 5.10(a)), the amount
of traffic generated is the same regardless of the similarity between the messages.

The best reduction in total network traffic, 80%, of tc-SMP over unicast is
achieved when all response messages are identical. In this scenario, multicast and
SMP produce only 70% reduction in traffic over unicast. When the similarity between all the response messages is low (0.3), the performance gain of tc-SMP over
unicast is 40% compared to 35% and 25% for SMP and multicast over unicast respectively.

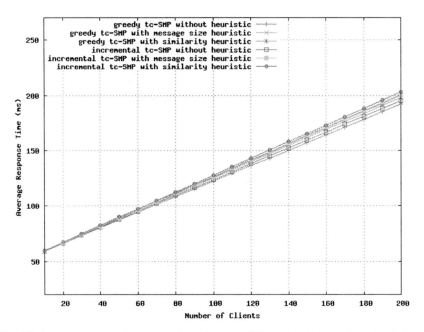

Fig. 5.9 Average response time comparisons between different heuristics and non-heuristic tc-SMP algorithms

5.7.3 Results Validation

The experimental results are validated here by comparing them with the analytical results. Only incremental tc-SMP is examined here because the incremental approach outperforms the greedy approach and similar analysis can be applied to the greedy approach without difficulty. In Section 5.6.1, the best case scenario for *incremental* tc-SMP over SMP in total traffic was examined. In that scenario, SMP becomes unicast since there is no shared link between paths spanning all clients. Therefore, the upper boundary for incremental tc-SMP's theoretical total traffic result is the difference between unicast's theoretical total traffic (see Equation 4.15) and the maximum limit of *Diff_Traffic{SMP, tc-SMP(incremental)}* (see Expression 5.8). From this observation and Expression 5.3, the theoretical limits of the total traffic result for incremental tc-SMP is shown by the following:

$$Total\_Traffic\{unicast\} - (hN + 1 - h - N)size_{msg} \leq Total\ Traffic\{tc\text{-}SMP(incremental)\}$$
$$\leq Total\_Traffic\{SMP\} \qquad (5.15)$$

From Equation 5.14, the upper and lower limits of the theoretical average response time for incremental tc-SMP can be given as follows:

$$Average\_Response\{SMP\} \leq Average\_Response\{tc\text{-}SMP\ (incremental)\}$$
$$\leq Average\_Response\{SMP\} + N \times n \times t_{path} \qquad (5.16)$$

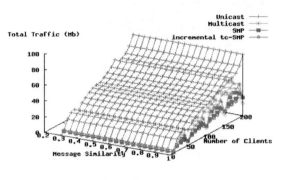

(a) All routing protocols

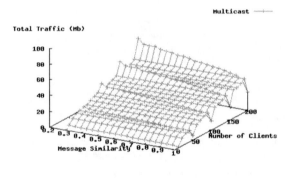

(b) Multicast

Fig. 5.10 Traffic comparison between different protocols

The experimental results of incremental tc-SMP are compared to its boundary values based on Expressions 5.15 and 5.16, and presented in Figures 5.12 and 5.13. Table 5.2 outlines the values of the key parameters used for obtaining the graphs.

Parameter	Value
$size_{msg}$	40Kb
t_{path}	0.001ms
n	$3 \times N$

Table 5.2 Assumptions of values used to obtain the theoretical boundaries in total traffic and average response time for the *incremental* tc-SMP algorithm

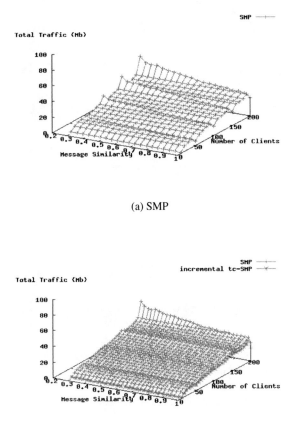

(a) SMP

(b) SMP vs. incremental tc-SMP

Fig. 5.11 Traffic comparison between different protocols

Variable t_{path} is the time it takes to determine if there exists a path from a node r to a client c and to compute the additional traffic introduced if c is added to a tree through r. One important point to note is that not all nodes in a network have paths connecting to all clients. If such a path exists, the process of computing the additional cost is also straightforward because the similarity between a new message and messages to existing clients in a tree is already known in advance by the server from the initial aggregation process. Therefore, the size of the new aggregated message with the inclusion of the new client can be computed easily. For this reason, the experiments assumed that $t_{path} = 0.001ms$. The total number of nodes in a network is denoted by n, which is set to be 3 times of the client number, as an approximation.

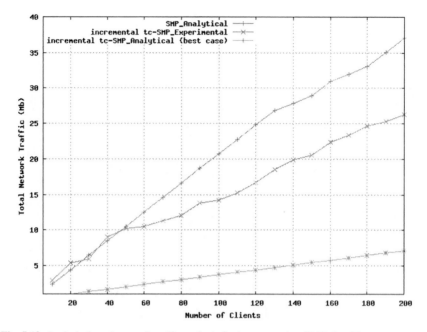

Fig. 5.12 Analytical total network traffic analysis for incremental tc-SMP algorithm

From Figures 5.12 and 5.13, it is obvious that experimental total traffic and average response time results (middle lines in both graphs) of the *incremental* tc-SMP algorithm are within their analytical boundaries. Therefore, the evaluation of tc-SMP is validated by both analytical and experimental studies.

5.8 Discussion

This section presents an analysis of the experimental results and discuss the advantages and disadvantages of tc-SMP over SMP.

Using tc-SMP, the traffic load is 4 or 5 times less than the traffic generated when individual original SOAP response messages are sent as unicasts. Tc-SMP reduces network bandwidth consumption of around 30% compared to SMP. A disadvantage of tc-SMP over SMP is that it requires additional time to build its own routing tree, which leads to an average response time increase of less than 10%.

As shown in Section 5.5, the tc-SMP routing algorithms perform in polynomial time, so the additional computation time is acceptable. The use of tc-SMP can be justified by traffic reduction whenever the increased response time is acceptable — from 3.5 up to 5 times reduction in traffic compared to under 2.5 times increase in average response time. Of course, results vary depending on network configurations.

This amount of delay is tolerable for many Web service applications, for example wireless communication among Intranet users, and personalised information retrieval over mobile networks. Tc-SMP represents a method for compressing size

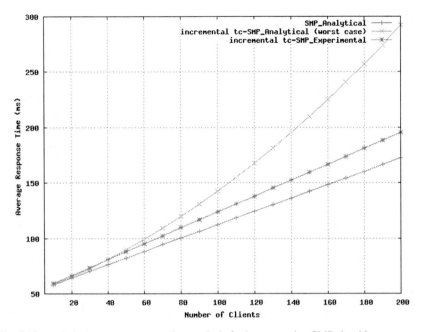

Fig. 5.13 Analytical average response time analysis for incremental tc-SMP algorithm

of messages in a network, thus it may be suitable for sensors network applications where bandwidth is limited and devices are constrained in power and battery life. Reducing the bandwidth consumption also benefits other applications by reducing traffic which is sent across those same links. The tc-SMP algorithm is particularly suitable in cases where the underlying networks are known to have multiple paths between nodes.

In addition, in high-speed wide-area networks, the link transmission delay is usually in microseconds, while the propagation delay may be close to milliseconds (much more greater) — so given a powerful processor, the trade-off in higher server processing overhead using tc-SMP over SMP is negligible. In wide-area networks propagation delay contributes the majority of the total delay.

5.9 Summary

This chapter of the book looked at the traffic-constrained SMP problem, where SMP messages are routed along paths that result in the least total network traffic. Two algorithms were proposed, both being extensions of the SMP algorithm presented in Chapter 4. Tc-SMP algorithms are an improvement over SMP for SOAP multicast traffic. They differ in the way that a source-routing algorithm (greedy or incremental approach) is used in tc-SMP for delivering aggregated messages along paths to introduce the minimal network traffic, instead of using the OSPF routing method which is used in SMP.

The `greedy` tc-SMP algorithm is the simpler approach of the two — every client is added to a tree along a path that introduces the least traffic. The `incremental` algorithm has similar objective, but it builds a tc-SMP tree gradually from a shortest path SMP tree — as such it can ensure that it outperforms or performs at least as well as SMP.

The problem of building a traffic-constrained similarity-based SOAP multicast tree is NP-complete. The proposed algorithms provide a good solution and operate in polynomial time with a complexity of $O(n(m + nlogn))$. On average, the incremental tc-SMP algorithm takes a little more time (less than 2% increase in average response time) time than the greedy algorithm, but provides a greater reduction (around 5%) in total traffic.

Simulations have shown that tc-SMP algorithms reduce further traffic generated over a network, by around 30%, when compared to SMP. The performance trade-off of tc-SMP over SMP is an increase in average response time of less than 10%. As the number of clients increases, the network traffic under tc-SMP is reduced even more than SMP, while the performance penalty is comparatively small. Two heuristic methods were also implemented for the tc-SMP algorithms. The heuristic based on the similarity between messages to new clients and messages to existing clients gives a gain of around 3% over tc-SMP without any heuristic. The heuristic based on message size achieves negligible performance gain.

Part II
Server Level Performance

Chapter 6
Scheduling for Heavy Traffic

> *"Everything is arranged so that it be this way, this is what is called culture."*
>
> *Jacques Derrida*

Previous chapters looked at SOAP performance through various optimisations, which included grouping messages (so to reduce the number of message) as well as smartly routing messages (so to reduce the routing path to destination). This chapter (as well as the next chapter) look at the performance of Web services on the server side. When messages are sent to the server (for the execution of operations, which called here *tasks*), specific improvements in the way tasks are executed on the server side is crucial. Indeed, when a server is overloaded (because of a huge number of submitted tasks for execution), this needs to be replicated to support the (heavy) load and therefore providing the needed Quality of Service (in terms of performance).

This chapter discusses some of the well-known *task assignment* policies that have been proposed to efficiently assign tasks in batch computing systems clusters. We consider both traditional and recent task assignment policies. We investigate the performance under realistic computer workloads that are represented using heavy-tailed distributions.

6.1 Motivation

Web services are running on platforms that are distributed by nature, and with back-ends based on cluster of servers (e.g. Web server farms) are widely being used by many organisations because these systems are scalable and cost effective. Such distributed systems typically consist of a central dispatcher and several loosely coupled hosts that offer mirrored services. Each arriving task, that is an execution of an operation of a Web service, is assigned to a host based on specific set of rules called the task assignment policy. The task assignment policy defines how the tasks are assigned to hosts and how they are processed at hosts. Task assignment policy may have a significant impact on the performance of the system.

The aim of this chapter is to investigate the performance of various task assignment that have been proposed to assign tasks in batch computing clusters. The hosts in a batch computing systems typically process tasks in a First-Come-First-Serve (FCFS) manner until completion or up to a predefined time limit. Tasks processed in batch computing systems have specific workload requirements. In most cases, tasks processed in batch computing systems are CPU bound and have very high memory requirements (64, 109).

Traditional task assignment policies such as Random and Round-Robin (127) are widely being used in distributed systems due their simplicity. These traditional task assignment policies, however, have serious performance drawbacks under realistic workload conditions which are best characterised by heavy-tailed distributions (13, 17)

Considerable efforts have been made over the years to develop novel task assignment policies that can efficiently schedule heavy-tailed workloads. Numerous new task assignment policies have been proposed (25, 26, 62, 64, 138, 156) and these policies have shown significant performance improvement over traditional task assignment policies (e.g. Random, Round-Robin) under heavy-tailed workloads. Most of these new policies are size-based policies and therefore process tasks with similar sizes at the same host. By processing tasks with similar sizes at the same host, these policies reduce the variance of task sizes in host queues. This results in an improvement in the overall system performance.

Existing task assignment policies can be categorised into many types depending on their numerous characteristics. In this chapter we focus on task assignment policies that can assign task with no prior knowledge about their processing requirements (task sizes), i.e., dynamic content (web service calls, database requests etc). Efficient scheduling of tasks with no prior knowledge about the actual task sizes (i.e. processing times) is a challenging research problem and which task assignment policy has the optimal performance is considered to be an open problem (25, 62, 64).

In this chapter we do not consider the task assignment polices that assume some prior knowledge about the actual processing times of tasks (62, 138, 156). Such policies are typically used to schedule static web content whose processing times can be estimated from file sizes prior to execution. Efficient scheduling of static web content is relatively easy and their exist numerous policies that can efficiently schedule these type of tasks. Existing solutions proposed for dynamic content are only optimal under specific conditions and further research is needed to improve the performance of these policies.

Figure 6.1 illustrates the distributed systems model we consider in this book. We consider a homogeneous cluster that consists of n number of hosts that are identical to each other in all respects. This model consists of a front-end dispatching device (e.g. router, switch), which receives the news tasks and directs these tasks to back-end hosts. The back-end hosts themselves have the ability to broadcast or multi-cast requests to different hosts. This architecture has become very popular in recent years due its cost effectiveness and scalability. This type of system can be constructed by networking a group of low cost commodity personal computer and capacity of the system can increased simply by adding more servers to the system.

We focus on virtual cluster where only one IP address (virtual IP address) is visible to the client. This virtual IP address can be considered as an IP address that is shared by each server. The other possibility is each server in the cluster to have a different IP address. The virtual cluster, has certain desirable properties that makes

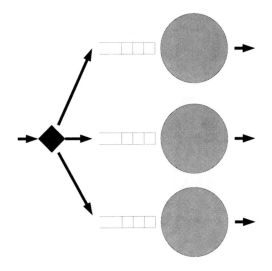

Fig. 6.1 A Cluster-based Distributed Computing System

it more attractive over the other model. In particular, it has a single IP address and hence single point of contact.

The rest of this chapter is organised as follows. Section 6.2 investigates in details the performance of traditional task assignment policies. Sections 6.3, 6.4, 6.5, 6.6 look the performance of four well-known (and recent) size-based task assignment policies.

6.2 Traditional Task Assignment Policies

The most commonly used traditional task assignment policies include Random, Round-Robin and Central-Queue. All the policies that we discuss in this section require no prior knowledge about actual task sizes, therefore these can be used for assigning dynamic content. Let us first consider the Random policy.

Let us consider again Figure 6.1 to illustrate the Random task assignment policy. Random dispatches news that tasks at the dispatcher into host with equal probability. The host processes task in a First-Come-First-Serve (FCFS) manner until completion. Let us now consider the expected waiting time in the system under Random. Let $E[W_i]$ and p_i be the expected waiting time of a task at host i and the probability that a task is dispatched to host i. Then expected waiting time in the system, $E[W]$ is given by the following formula:

$$E[W] = p_1 E[W_1] + p_2 E[W_2] + ... + p_n E[W_n] \qquad (6.1)$$

Since Random dispatches task with equal probability;

$$E[W] = \frac{1}{n}(E[W_1] + E[W_2] + ... + E[W_n]) \tag{6.2}$$

$E[W_i]$ is obtained using the Pollaczek-Khinchin formula (74);

$$E[W_i] = \frac{\lambda E[X^2]}{2(1 - \lambda_i E[X])} \tag{6.3}$$

where $E[X^2]$ and $E[X]$ represent 2nd moment and 1st moment of the service time distribution and λ_i denotes the average arrival rate into i^{th} host. The quantity $\lambda_i E[X]$ is typically referred to as the system load denoted by ρ_i

Since Random dispatches tasks with equal probability

$$\lambda_1 = \lambda_2 = ... = \lambda_n = \frac{1}{n} \tag{6.4}$$

Hence
$$E[W_1] = E[W_2] = ... = E[W_n] \tag{6.5}$$

Note that when Random is used, each host in the system sees the same service time distribution. Figure 6.2 shows the expected waiting for Random under Random under 3 different system loads. We notice that expected waiting time for Random depends on two factors, namely, the system load and α where α represents variability of task sizes. When α is fixed, the expected waiting time increases with the system load. For example, under the system loads of 0.7 and 0.3 when α equals 1.5 the expected waiting time under Random is equal to 117257 and 21537 respectively. Figure 6.3 illustrates the ratio between expected waiting times for three different scenarios, namely ratio between expected waiting time under the system load of 0.7 and 0.3, ratio between expected waiting time under the system load of 0.7 and 0.5 and ratio between expected waiting time under the system load of 0.5 and 0.3.

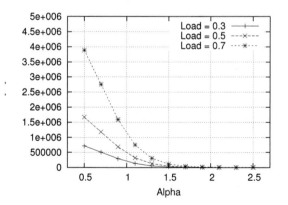

Fig. 6.2 3-host system

It is interesting to notice that the ratio between expected waiting time is constant and does not depend on α. Second, we notice from Figure 6.3 that the expected waiting time under Random is very much dependent on the variability of traffic (i.e. α). As the variability of traffic increases the expected waiting time increases and under very high variable traffic conditions (e.g. $\alpha = 0.5$), the performance of Random is very poor. For example, under the system load of 0.7, when $\alpha = 0.5$ the expected waiting time under Random is computed as 505477 while under the same system load when $\alpha = 2.5$ the expected waiting time is computed as 1142. As we notice from Equation 6.3 the expected waiting time is proportional to the second moment of the service time distribution which is very high for highly variable workload distributions.

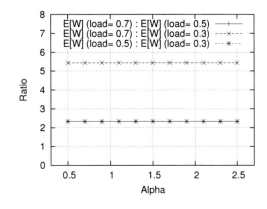

Fig. 6.3 3-host system

Round-Robin policy assigns tasks to hosts in a cyclical fashion. Both Random and Round-robin attempts to equalise the expected number of tasks at each server. The performance of Round-robin is very similar to Random and this has been discussed in (64). Variants of Random and Round-robin are Weighted-Random and Weighted-Round-Robin which have been designed to assign tasks in servers with different processing capacities, i.e. heterogeneous cluster. These policies assign different fraction of tasks to hosts.

Another task assignment policy that is used in cluster-based distributed systems is the Central-Queue. This policy holds tasks in a queue at the dispatcher until a host is idle. Once a host becomes idle the task in the head of the queue is assigned to that host. The task is processed in a FCFS manner until completion at that host. Central-Queue has shown the best performance under exponential service time distributions (142). However, it does not perform well under realistic computer workloads that are represented using heavy-tailed distributions.

6.3 TAGS Policy

TAGS (Task Assignment by Guessing Size) is one of the well-known policies. It was first introduced in (63), which appeared in 2000 and 2002, and another paper was published (64) on TAGS containing a more detailed and formal discussion on the TAGS policy. TAGS was proposed to assign tasks in batch computing systems. It assumes a homogeneous cluster with n number of hosts where each host has a task size range associated with it. The core functionality of TAGS is as follows. Each new task first arrives at the dispatcher and each task is assigned to Host 1 for processing. Host 1 processes the task up to the upper limit of its task size range in a FCFS manner. If the size of the task is less or equal to than the upper limit of the task size range the task departs the system. Otherwise the task is migrated to the next host. The next host processes the task from scratch up to its upper limit and so on. This process continues until the task is fully processed at which point the task departs the system. TAGS has been specially designed to assign tasks that exhibit high variability in their task sizes. TAGS can result in significant performance improvements over policies such Random, Round-robin and Central-queue under a wide range of such workload conditions. TAGS, however, can have poor performance under specific heavy-tailed workload conditions. We will look at this in detail later in this chapter.

Figure 6.4 illustrates the TAGS model where (s_{i-1}, s_i) denote the task size range associated with Host i and k and p represent smallest and largest task sizes in the service time distribution. The performance under TAGS depends on the variability of traffic, arrival rate and s_is. s_is are computed to optimise a certain performance criteria for a fixed variability (α) and arrival rate (λ).

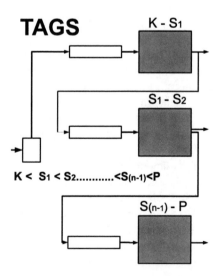

Fig. 6.4 The TAGS architecture

An Analysis of TAGS

The notation given in Table 6.1 is used to model the TAGS system.

n	Number of hosts in the system
$f(x)$	Service time distribution of tasks (i.e. $B(k, p, \alpha)$)
k	Lower bound of the task size distribution
p	Upper bound of the task size distribution
p_i	Fraction of tasks whose final destination is Host i
λ	Outside task arrival rate into system
ρ	System load
α	Heavy-tailed parameter
$E[X_j^l]$	l^{th} moment of the distribution of tasks whose final destination is host j
$E[X_{jv}]$	1st moment of tasks that visit host j
$E[X_{jv}^2]$	2nd moment of tasks that visit host j
$E[W_{jv}]$	Expected waiting time of a task that visits host j
$E[W_{if}]$	Expected waiting time of a task whose final destination is host i
$E[W]$	Expected waiting time in the system

Table 6.1 TAGS's notation

Let s_{i-1} and s_i be the lower and upper bounds of task size range assigned to host i and p_i be the probability that the service time of a task is between s_{i-1} and s_i. p_i is given by;

$$p_i = \int_{s_{i-1}}^{s_i} f(x)dx \tag{6.6}$$

where $f(x)$ is given by

$$f(x) = \frac{\alpha k^\alpha}{1 - (k/p)^\alpha} x^{-\alpha-1}, \quad k < x < p \tag{6.7}$$

The overall expected waiting time, i.e., the expected waiting time in the system depends on both the expected waiting time of a task that visits host j ($E[W_{jv}]$) and the expected waiting time of a tasks whose final destination is host i ($E[W_{if}]$). Let us first consider the $E[W_{jv}]$. An expression for $E[W_{jv}]$ can be derived using Pollaczek-Khinchin formula (74) as follows.

$$E[W_{jv}] = \frac{\lambda_j E[X_{jv}^2]}{(2(1 - \lambda_j(\sum_{k=j}^n p_k))E[X_{jv}])} \tag{6.8}$$

where λ_j denotes the arrival rate into a host j. λ_j is given by;

$$\lambda_j = \lambda \sum_{k=j}^n p_k \tag{6.9}$$

We note that $E[W_{jv}]$ is based on 1st and 2nd moments of tasks that visit host j. These are obtained as follows.

$$E[X_{jv}] = \frac{p_j}{\sum_{k=j}^n p_k} E[X_j] + \frac{\sum_{k=j+1}^n p_k}{\sum_{k=j}^n p_k} s_j \qquad (6.10)$$

$$E[X_{jv2}] = \frac{p_j}{\sum_{k=j}^n p_k} E[X_j^2] + \frac{\sum_{k=j+1}^n p_k}{\sum_{k=j}^n p_k} s_j^2 \qquad (6.11)$$

$E[X_j]$ and $E[X_j^2]$ in the above two equations denote 1st and 2nd moment of the distribution of tasks whose final destination is host j respectively. These are obtained as

$$E[X_j] = \int_{s_{j-1}}^{s_j} x f(x) dx \qquad (6.12)$$

$$E[X_j^2] = \int_{s_{j-1}}^{s_j} x^2 f(x) dx \qquad (6.13)$$

Let $E[W_{if}]$ be the expected waiting time of a task whose final destination is host i. $E[W_{if}]$ is given by the following formula.

$$E[W_{if}] = \sum_{j=1}^i E[W_{jv}] \qquad (6.14)$$

where $j \le i$. Finally, the expected waiting time in the system is computed as

$$E[W] = \sum_{i=1}^n E[W_{if}] p_i \qquad (6.15)$$

where $E[W]$ is a function of α, $s_1, s_2, .., s_{n-1}$ and λ_i. For a given set of α and λ_i, we compute $s_1, s_2, .., s_{n-1}$ so as to optimise the expected waiting time.

TAGS Performance Evaluation on 2-Hosts System

The performance of TAGS on a 2-host distributed system is investigated using the expected waiting time. Figure 6.5 depicts the performance of TAGS under three different system loads. Log scale for y axis is used. First we notice that under low (0.3) and moderate (0.5) system loads, there is an improvement in the expected waiting time with increasing α. For example, under the system load of 0.5, TAGS performs 7 times better when α equals 2.1 compared to when α equals to 0.5. As discussed earlier, the expected waiting time of a task in a FCFS queue is directly proportional to variance of tasks sizes. As α increases the variance, of task sizes in each host queue decreases leading to an improvement in the overall performance.

Second we notice that under the system load of 0.7, the expected waiting time of a task under the TAGS (64) decreases up to a certain α and then it begins to increase. Let this α be α_d. This behaviour of TAGS has not been discussed in (64) and (63) and reason for this as follows. Low α parameter indicates that there are very small number of tasks with very long processing requirements that constitutes to large fraction of the total workload. Under low α values, only a small fraction

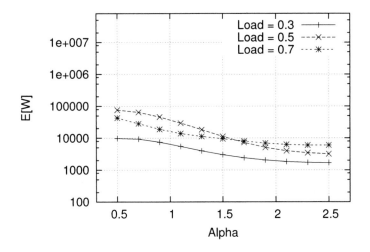

Fig. 6.5 TAGS performance under three different loads

of very large tasks are processed at Host 2. As α increases, very small number of tasks with a very long processing requirements (that make up large fraction of the workload) decreases. As a result, more tasks are needed to be migrated to Host 2 in order to ensure that Host 1 does not get overloaded. This means that as α increases, the number of tasks that needed to be restarted from starch at Host 2 increases. This results in excess load in the system to increase. The value of α_d is determined by both the system load and the number of hosts in the system. We will investigate the excess load under TAGS in detail later in Section 6.3.

It is worth mentioning that under low values TAGS significantly outperforms traditional task assignment policies. For example, under the system load of 0.7, when α equals 0.5, TAGS outperforms Random by a factor of 5. TAGS has the worst performance under very low task size variabilities and very high system loads. For example, under the same system load of 0.7, when $\alpha = 2.5$, Random outperforms TAGS by factor 14.

TAGS Performance Evaluation of TAGS on 3-Hosts System

The performance of TAGS on a 3-host distributed system is investigated. Figure 6.6 plots the expected waiting time under TAGS on a 3-host system. We note that for all three system load considered the expected waiting time decreases up to a certain value and then it begins to increase. As pointed out in Section 6.3, this happens due the variations in the excess load in the system which tends to increase with increasing α.

The main issue is to check whether TAGS performs better in a 3-host system compared to that of a 2-host system. The answer to the above problem depends on

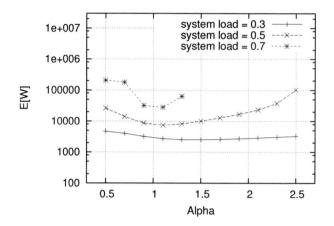

Fig. 6.6 3-host system

both the variability of traffic (α) and the system load. Figure 6.6 plots the expected waiting time for TAGS for the case of 3 and 2 hosts. We notice that if the task size variability is very high (when α is in the proximity of 0.4), TAGS performs better on a 3-host system compared to that of 2 host system. For example, under the system load of 0.5, when $\alpha = 0.5$, the performance of TAGS on a 3-host system is 1.6 better than that of a 2 host system. The reason for this is that 3-host system can offer higher overall reduction in the task size variance compared to that of 2 host system. We notice, as α increases, the factor of improvement decreases, since under low task size variabilities, the variance reduction of tasks sizes in host queues does not result in significant improvement on the performance. Second, under low task size variabilities, 3-host system generates significantly large amount of excesses load compared to that of 2 host system. Therefore, when α is greater than certain threshold value, 3-host TAGS system can no longer outperform 2-host TAGS system. Under the system load is 0.5, the turning point occurs when α at around 1.5. When the system load is 0.3, the turning point occurs at around 1.7. Under the system load of 0.5, when $\alpha = 2.5$ TAGS performs 17 times better in a 2-host system compared to that of 3-host system!

TAGS Excess Load

In this section the excess load for TAGS policy on 2/3-host systems is investigated. Recall that TAGS restarted the migrated tasks from scratch at destination hosts. This incurs an additional load in the system called the excess load.

Let ρ_i be true load on host i. We obtain:

$$\rho_i = \lambda \sum_{j=i}^{n} p_j E[X_{iv}] \qquad (6.16)$$

Note that $\lambda \sum_{j=i}^{n} p_j$ is the arrival arrival rate into the Host i and $E[X_{iv}]$ denotes expected waiting time of a task that visits Host i.

The excess load on the system is computed as

$$Excess_n = \lambda E[X] - \sum_{i=1}^{n} \rho_i \qquad (6.17)$$

$\lambda E[X]$ is expected load in the system. Let us now investigate the the excess load in the system for the case of 2 servers.

$$Excess_2 = \rho_1 + \rho_2$$
$$= \lambda \sum_{j=1}^{2} p_j E[X_{1v}] + \lambda \sum_{j=2}^{2} p_j E[X_{2v}]$$
$$= \lambda (p_1 + p_2)(\frac{p_1}{p_1 + p_2} E[X_1] + \frac{p_1 + p_2 - p_1}{p_1 + p2} s_1) + \lambda p_2(\frac{p_2}{p_2} E[X_2] + \frac{p_2 - p_2}{p_2}(p))$$
$$= \lambda (p_1 E[X_1] + (1 - p_1)s_1) + \lambda p_2 E[X_2]$$
$$= \lambda (\frac{p_1}{p_1} \int_k^{s_1} xf(x)dx + (1 - p_1)s_1 + \frac{1 - p_1}{1 - p_1} \int_{s_1}^{p} xf(x)dx)$$
$$= \lambda (\int_k^{s_1} xf(x)dx + (1 - p_1)s_1 + \int_{s_1}^{p} xf(x)dx$$
$$= \lambda (\int_k^{s_1} xf(x)dx + (1 - p_1)s_1 + \int_{s_1}^{p} xf(x)dx$$
$$= \lambda E[X] + (1 - p_1)s_1$$

$$(6.18)$$

$$Excess_n = (1 - p_1)s_1 \qquad (6.19)$$

From the above Equation we note that as s_1 (the upper limit of the task size range for Host 1) increases p_1 (Fraction of task whose final destination is Host 1) also increases and $(1 - p_1)$ decreases. This means that an increase in s_1 can lead $Excess_2$ to either increase or decrease.

Figure 6.7 plots the excess load generated under TAGS on 2 and 3 Host systems. Let us first concentrate on the excess load on 2-host TAGS system. We notice an increase in the excess load on the system with increasing system load. For example, the ratio between the excess loads, on the system under the system loads of 0.7 and 0.3 when α is equal to 0.5 is 3.8. The fraction of tasks migrated from Host 1 to Host 2 increases with increasing α in order to ensure that both Host 1 and Host 2 operate on steady state. The higher the fraction of tasks being migrated the higher the number of tasks killed and restarted from scratch resulting in higher excess load on the system. When α is in the proximity of 2.5, TAGS generates approximately 3 times more excess load on the system compared to when α in the proximity of 0.4 under all 3 system loads considered. For example, under the system load of 0.5,

TAGS generates 3.2 times more excess load on the system system compared that of when α is 2.5.

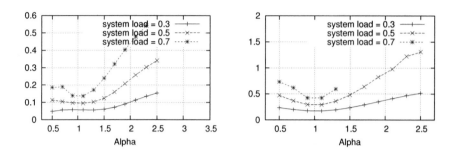

Fig. 6.7 Excess load on 2/3-host systems

Load on Hosts

As one can notice in the previous section, TAGS can result in significant performance improvements under a wide range of workload conditions. We also noticed that traditional policies outperforming TAGS under certain scenarios. In this section, we investigate how the load on individual hosts vary with the variability of traffic and system load. We consider distributed systems with 2/3-host systems.

Figures 6.8 and 6.18 plot the load on hosts for TAGS system consisting of 2/3-hosts. Let us first investigate the load on hosts on a 2-host TAGS system. We notice that when α is low the load on Host 2 is significantly higher than the load on Host 1. For example, under the system load of 0.5, when α equals 0.5 the load on Host 1 is 0.25 while under the same conditions the load on host 2 is 0.87. As α increases, the load on Host 1 increases whereas the load on Host 2 decreases. It is interesting to notice that when α is near 1 the load on both hosts are more or less the same for all three system loads considered.

The behaviour of host load in the case of 2-host is similar to the 3-host case. We notice relatively low load on Host 1, when α is low. As α increases the load on Host 1 increases. The load on Host 3 on the other hand is high when α is low and it decreases with increasing α. The load on Host 2 lies in between the load on Host 1 and Host 2.

Behaviour of Optimal Cutoffs

This section looks at the behaviour of optimal cutoffs of TAGS policy. Figures 6.10 and 6.11 plot the optimal cutoffs for the case of 2/3-host TAGS systems. Note that a 2-host TAGS system needs one cutoff (s_1) to be computed, while a 3-host system needs to 2 cutoffs (s_1, s_2). Let us first consider a 2-host system. Notice that under low α values the s_1 (first cutoff) is relatively high. As α increases, s_1 decreases. In

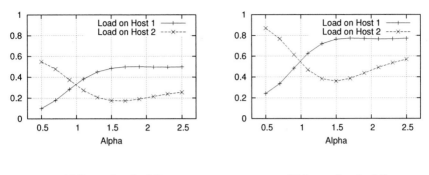

(a) System Load = 0.3   (b) System Load = 0.5

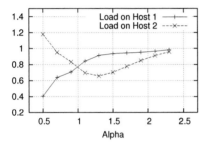

(c) System Load = 0.7

Fig. 6.8 Load for 2-host system

the case of 3-host system, the behaviour of s_1 is similar to that of a 2-host system. The behaviour of s_2 depends on the system load and under the system loads of 0.3 and 0.5, s_2 has a similar behaviour while under the system load of 0.7, there is a rapid increase in s_2 as α approaches 2.5.

6.4 TAGS-WC Policy

The TAGS policy does not support work-conserving migration. As such, tasks that have been migrated from one host another has been restarted from scratch at the destination hosts. This resulted in an additional load on the system which we called the excess load. The total amount of excess on the system was dependent on the variability of traffic, the arrival rate and number of hosts in the system. Furthermore, we noticed, that when all factors are constant the total excess on the system increased with increasing α.

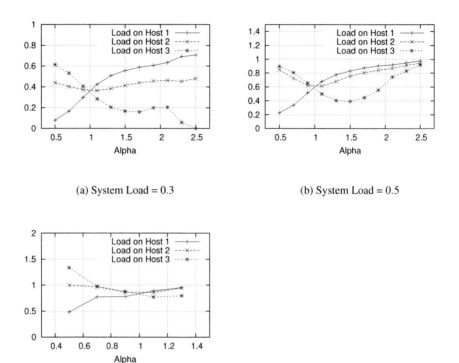

(a) System Load = 0.3   (b) System Load = 0.5

(c) System Load = 0.7

Fig. 6.9 Load for 3-host system

This section investigates a variant of TAGS, called TAGS-WC (Task Assignment by Guessing Size with Work-Conserving migration). The original version of TAGS (63, 64) did not support work-conserving migration which we discuss in this section. The aim of introducing work-conserving migration is to reduce the total excess load on the system. Systems that support work-conserving migration do not restart task from scratch rather they resume the execution of tasks at destination hosts. The main functionality of TAGS-WC is as follows. Each task arrives at the dispatcher is dispatched Host 1. Tasks are processed in a FCFS manner up to the designated time limit (upper limit of the task size range) associated with Host 1. If a size of a task is less than or equal to upper limit of the task size range task departs the system. Otherwise the task is migrated to the Host 2 in the system. Host 2 process the task in a similar manner and so on. This process continues until the task is fully processed.

The following notation is used to describe a TAGS-WC policy. Note that this similar is to the notation introduced in Table 7.3. However, it contains several new variables.

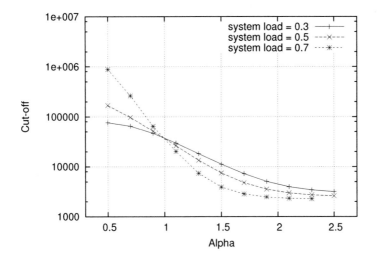

Fig. 6.10 Cutoff 2-host

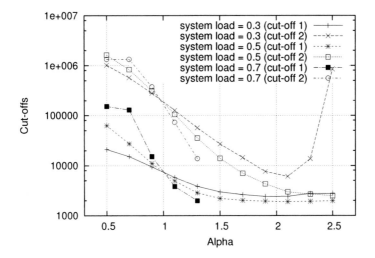

Fig. 6.11 Cutoff 3-host

n	Number of hosts in the system
$f(x)$	Service time distribution of tasks (i.e. $B(k, p, \alpha)$)
k	Lower bound of the task size distribution
p	Upper bound of the task size distribution
p_i	Fraction of tasks whose final destination is Host i
λ	Outside task arrival rate into system
ρ	System load
α	Heavy-tailed parameter
$E[X_j^l]$	l^{th} moment of the distribution of tasks whose final destination is host j
$E[X_{jv}]$	1st moment of tasks that visit host j
$E[X_{jv}^2]$	2nd moment of tasks that visit host j
$E[W_{jv}]$	Expected waiting time of a task that visits host j
$E[W_{if}]$	Expected waiting time of a task whose final destination is host i
$E[W]$	Expected waiting time in the system
γ_s	Fixed Migration cost at source host
γ_d	Fixed Migration cost at destination host
β_s	Proportional Migration cost at source host
β_d	Proportional Migration cost at destination host

Table 6.2 Notation for TAGS-WC

We investigate the performance of TAGS-WC under three different scenarios

- Zero Cost Migration
- Fixed Cost Migration
- Proportional Cost Migration

Analysis of TAGS-WC

Let us first consider the analysis TAGS-WC when the cost of migration is negligible. In this case the cost incurred on the source and destination node are minimal and can be equated to zero. Let s_i and s_{i-1} be the upper and lower limits of the task size range for Host i and p_i be the probability that the service time of a task is between s_{i-1} and s_i. p_i is given by;

$$p_i = \int_{s_{i-1}}^{s_i} f(x)dx \tag{6.20}$$

where $f(x)$ is given by

$$f(x) = \frac{\alpha k^\alpha}{1 - (k/p)^\alpha} \, x^{-\alpha-1}, \quad k < x < p \tag{6.21}$$

Let $E[W_{if}]$ be the expected waiting time of a task whose final destination is host i. $E[W_{if}]$ is given by;

$$E[W_{if}] = \sum_{j=1}^{i} E[W_{jv}] \tag{6.22}$$

where $E[W_{jv}]$ denotes the expected waiting time of a task that visits host j where $j \leq i$. $E[W_{jv}]$ is obtained using the Pollaczek-Khinchin formula (74);

$$E[W_{jv}] = \frac{\lambda_j E[X_{jv}^2]}{(2(1 - \lambda_j(\sum_{k=j}^n p_k))E[X_{jv}])} \tag{6.23}$$

where $E[X_{jv}]$ and $E[X_{jv}^2]$ denote the 1st and 2nd moments of tasks that visit host j. λ_j denotes the arrival rate into a host j. λ_j is given by;

$$\lambda_j = \lambda \sum_{k=j}^n p_k \tag{6.24}$$

$E[X_{jv}^l]$ can be obtained using the following formula.

$$E[X_{jv}^l] = \begin{cases} \frac{p_j}{\sum_{k=j}^n p_k} E[X_j^l] + \frac{\sum_{k=j+1}^n p_k}{\sum_{k=j}^n p_k}(s_j)^l & \text{if } j = 1, \\ \frac{p_j}{\sum_{k=j}^n p_k} E[X_j^l] + \frac{\sum_{k=j+1}^n p_k}{\sum_{k=j}^n p_k}(s_j - s_{j-1})^l & \text{if } j ¿ 1 \end{cases} \tag{6.25}$$

where $E[X_j^l]$ denotes the lth moment of the distribution of tasks whose final destination is host j. $E[X_j^l]$ is given by; Note that in Equation 3 we have taken into account the work already done, i.e., s_{j-1}.

$$E[X_j^l] = \begin{cases} \int_{s_{j-1}}^{s_j} x^l f(x)dx & \text{if } j = 1, \\ \int_{s_{j-1}}^{s_j} (x - s_{j-1})^l f(x)dx & \text{if } j > 1 \end{cases} \tag{6.26}$$

When we compute $E[X_j^l]$ we have conditioned on the distribution of task's reaming sizes.

Finally, the expected waiting time in the system is computed as

$$E[W] = \sum_{i=1}^n E[W_{if}]p_i \tag{6.27}$$

$E[W]$ is a function of α, $s_1, s_2, .., s_{n-1}$ and λ_i. For a given set of α and λ_i, we compute $s_1, s_2, .., s_{n-1}$ so as to optimise the expected waiting time.

TAGS-WC Performance Evaluation on 2/3-Hosts System

Recall that the key difference between TAGS and TAGS-WC conserving was that TAGS-WC facilitates work-conserving migration whereas TAGS does not. TAGS-WC, unlike TAGS does not restart a task that was migrated to another host from scratch at the destination hosts, rather it resumes the execution of migrated tasks at destination hosts. Figures 6.12 and 6.13 plot the expected waiting time vs α for TAGS-WC on 2 and 3 host systems respectively. Let us first have a look at the performance of TAGS-WC on a 2-host system in a bit more detail. We notice that the way in which the expected waiting time vary with α is not the same as TAGS particularly under high system loads (0.7). Under low and moderate system loads we notice an improvement in the expected waiting waiting time with α under both TAGS and TAGS-WC. Under high system loads, the expected waiting time under TAGS-WC decreases with α up to certain value and then it increases slightly and then it deceases again. This is different from TAGS in which the expected waiting time deceases up to a certain limit and it then continuously increases with α. We noticed in Figure 6.13 that under high system loads, when α is in the proximity of 2.5, TAGS has the worst performance. TAGS-WC, in contrast outperforms Random both under low and high α values. For example, under the system load of 0.7 when α is equal to 0.5, it outperforms Random by a factor of 30 and under the same system load when α equals 1.9, TAGS outperforms Random by a factor 1.1. Performance under TAGS-WC does not deteriorate as α increases since it does not restart tasks from scratch and as such it does not result in an excess load in the system.

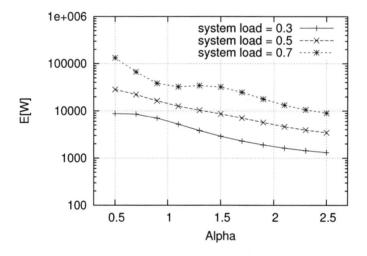

Fig. 6.12 Expected waiting time for TAGS-WC on 2-host system

Let us now investigate the expected waiting time for TAGS-WC on a 3-host system. Notice that the behaviour of expected waiting time with α for TAGS-WC on a 3 system is very similar to the case of 2 hosts. Unlike in TAGS (see Figures 6.14 and 6.15), the expected waiting time does not degrade under high system loads when α is close to 2.5. Moreover, we notice TAGS-WC having better performance on a 2-host system compared to that of 3-host system for all the scenarios considered. This is in contrast to the performance of TAGS on 2/3-host system where we noticed noticed an improvement only under specific conditions. Since the performance of TAGS-WC has improved for all the cases considered, we can conclude that it can scale well. TAGS, on the other hand is only scalable under specific workload conditions.

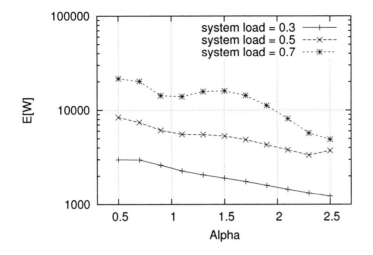

Fig. 6.13 Expected waiting time for TAGS-WC on 3-host system

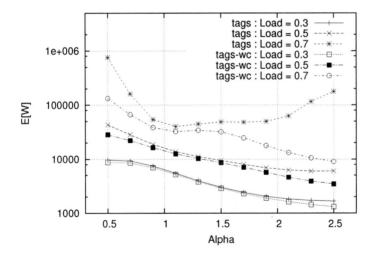

Fig. 6.14 Expected waiting time for TAGS and TAGS-WC on 2-host system

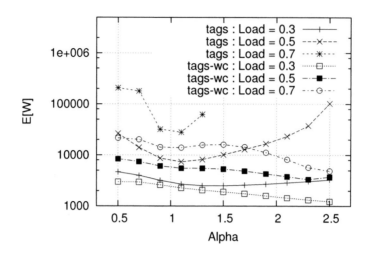

Fig. 6.15 Expected waiting time for TAGS and TAGS-WC on 3 Host system

Load unbalancing TAGS-WC

The load of TAGS on hosts does depend on the value of α as well as on system. It unbalances load on hosts for most of the scenarios. Here we look at the load on hosts for TAGS-WC. Let ρ_i be the average load on host i. We obtain:

$$\rho_i = \lambda \sum_{j=i}^{n} p_j E[X_{jv}] \tag{6.28}$$

Note that $\lambda \sum_{j=i}^{n} p_j$ is the arrival arrival rate into the Host i and $E[X_{jv}]$ denotes expected waiting time of a task that visits host i.

Since we are considering the case where there is no migration cost, the sum of individual loads on host must be equal to the system load, i.e., $\lambda E[X]$. We now prove this for the case of two hosts.

$$\rho_1 + \rho_2$$

$$= \lambda \sum_{j=1}^{2} p_j E[X_{1v}] + \lambda \sum_{j=2}^{2} p_j E[X_{2v}]$$

$$= \lambda(p_1 + p_2)(\frac{p_1}{p_1 + p_2}E[X_1] + \frac{p_1 + p_2 - p_1}{p_1 + p_2}s_1) + \lambda p_2(\frac{p_2}{p_2}E[X_2] + \frac{p_2 - p_2}{p_2}(p - s_1))$$

$$= \lambda(p_1 E[X_1] + (1 - p_1)s_1) + \lambda p_2 E[X_2]$$

$$= \lambda(\frac{p_1}{p_1}\int_k^{s_1} xf(x)dx + (1 - p_1)s_1 + \frac{1 - p_1}{1 - p_1}\int_{s_1}^{p}(x - s_1)f(x)dx)$$

$$= \lambda(\int_k^{s_1} xf(x)dx + (1 - p_1)s_1 + \int_{s_1}^{p} xf(x)dx - s_1\int_{s_1}^{p} f(x)dx)$$

$$= \lambda(\int_k^{s_1} xf(x)dx + (1 - p_1)s_1 + \int_{s_1}^{p} xf(x)dx - s_1(1 - p_1))$$

$$= \lambda E[X]$$

$$(6.29)$$

Figure 6.16 and 6.17 shows the load on Hosts for TAGS-WC on 2/3-host systems. We see that the way in which the load on hosts vary with α is similar to what was previously observed for TAGS-WC. If we consider the 2-host system, we notice that low α values, the load on host 2 is relatively higher than the load on host 1 and vice versa. For example, under the system load of 0.5, when α equals 0.5, the load on host 1 and host 2 are equal to 0.22 and 0.78 respectively. Under the same system load of 0.5, when α is equal to 2.5, the load on host 2 and host 1 are equal to 0.66 and 0.34 respectively. Notice that the sum of loads adds up to 1. We also notice that when α is near 1, the load on all host are approximately the same.

Analysis TAGS-WC : Fixed Cost Migration

Fixed cost migration incurs a fixed on the source and destination host. We denote the cost incurred on the source and destination nodes by γ_s and γ_d respectively. The analysis of TAGS-WC under fix-cost migration is similar to the analysis presented in Section 7.3 except that we need to redefine $E[X_j^l]$ and $E[X_{jv}^l]$ to cater for the fix-cost,

$$E[X_j^l] = \begin{cases} \int_{s_{j-1}}^{s_j}(x + \gamma_d)^l f(x)dx & \text{if } j = 1, \\ \int_{s_{j-1}}^{s_j}(x - s_{j-1} + \gamma_d)^l f(x)dx & \text{if } j > 1 \end{cases} \qquad (6.30)$$

$$E[X_{jv}^l] = \begin{cases} \frac{p_j}{\sum_{k=j}^{n} p_k}E[X_j^l] + \frac{\sum_{k=j+1}^{n} p_k}{\sum_{k=j}^{n} p_k}(s_j + \gamma_d + \gamma_s)^l & \text{if } j = 1, \\ \frac{p_j}{\sum_{k=j}^{n} p_k}E[X_j^l] + \frac{\sum_{k=j+1}^{n} p_k}{\sum_{k=j}^{n} p_k}(s_j - s_{j-1} + \gamma_d + \gamma_s)^l & \text{if } j > 1, \end{cases} \qquad (6.31)$$

The expected waiting time for TAGS-WC under fixed cost migration is not presented in this chapter and we leave for the reader as an exercise. Expected

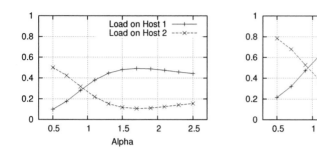

(a) System Load = 0.3   (b) System Load = 0.5

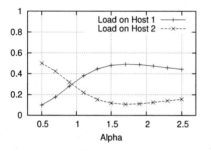

(c) System Load = 0.7

Fig. 6.16 TAGS-WC load on 2-host system

6.5 TAPTF Policy

Here we discuss another advanced task assignment policy, called TAPTF (Task Assignment based on Prioritising Traffic Flows). The TAPTF model first appeared in (26), and an extension to TAPTF that was based on work-conserving migration appeared in (25). This section focuses only on the TAPTF model to provide the important contribution and differences with previous policies. As TAGS generates a large amount of excess load on the system under certain scenarios, TAPTF model is to minimise this excess load on the system. TAPTF is based on a novel queueing architecture that utilise two queues for each host in the system.

The TATPF model is depicted in Figure 6.19. We can see that each host in TAPF (except Host 1) has two queues. These queues are called the ordinary queue (O queue) and the restart queue (R queue) respectively. The task in the O queue has priority of service over tasks in R queue. However, a task currently being served from the R queue cannot be pre-empted from service by the arrival of a task into the

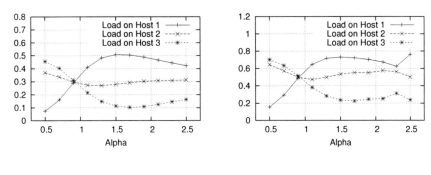

(a) System Load = 0.3   (b) System Load = 0.5

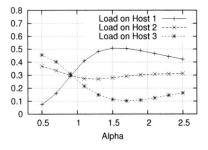

(c) System Load = 0.7

Fig. 6.17 TAGS-WC load on 3-host system

O queue. Host i's O queue deals only with tasks whose sizes are in the range $[k, s_i]$ while Host i's R queue deals only with tasks whose sizes are in the range $[s_{i-1}, s_i]$.

The basic functionality of TATPF is follows. New tasks arrive at the dispatcher following a Poisson process with the rate λ. The dispatcher assigns these tasks to one of the back-end hosts with probability q_i. These tasks are placed in the Ordinary Queue (O queue) and processed up to s_i. If the size of a task is less than or equal to s_i, the task depart the system. Otherwise the task is placed in the R queue of the next. At the next host task is restarted from scratch. This process continuous, until the task is fully serviced at which point the task depart the system.

Analysis of TAPTF

Table 6.3 shows the notation used in this section to describe TAPTF model.

Let p_i be the fraction of tasks whose final destination is host i. Then p_i is given by;

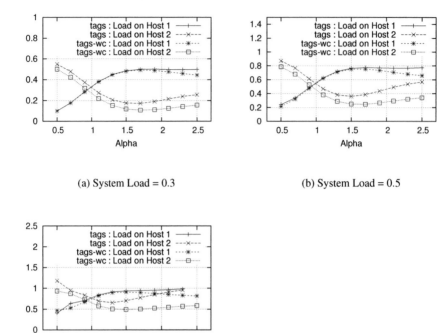

(a) System Load = 0.3

(b) System Load = 0.5

(c) System Load = 0.7

Fig. 6.18 TAGS and TAGS-WC on 2-host system

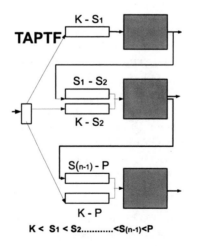

Fig. 6.19 TAPTF architecture

n	Number of hosts in the system
k	Lower bound of task size distribution
p	Upper bound of task size distribution
$f(x)$	Probability density function of service times
α	Heavy-tailed parameter
s_i	Task size cut-off for Host i
q_i	Fraction of tasks assigned to Host i
λ	Outside task arrival rate into system
ρ	System load
p_i	Fraction of tasks whose final destination is either Host i
$E[X_{jfO}^l]$	l^{th} moment of the distribution of tasks whose final destination is Host j's ordinary (O) queue
$E[X_{jfR}^l]$	l^{th} moment of the distribution of tasks whose final destination is Host j's ordinary (R) queue
$E[X_{jvO}^l]$	l^{th} moment of the distribution of tasks that spend time on (visit) Host j's ordinary (O) queue
$E[X_{jvR}^l]$	l^{th} moment of the distribution of tasks that spend time on (visit) Host j's ordinary (R) queue
$E(W_{ivO})$	Expected waiting time for a task at Host j's ordinary (O) queue
$E(W_{ivR})$	Expected waiting time for a task at Host j's ordinary (R) queue
$E(W_{ifO})$	Expected waiting time of a task whose final destination is Host i's ordinary (O) queue
$E(W_{ifR})$	Expected waiting time of a task whose final destination is Host i's ordinary (R) queue

Table 6.3 TAPTF notation

$$p_i = \int_{s_{i-1}}^{s_i} f(x)dx \tag{6.32}$$

Let $E[X_{jfO}^l]$ be the lth moment of the distribution of tasks whose final destination is Host j's ordinary (O) queue and $E[X_{jfR}^l]$ be the lth moment of the distribution of tasks whose final destination is Host j's ordinary (R) queue. Then

$$E[X_{jfO}^l] = \frac{1}{\sum_{i=1}^{j} p_i} \int_{s_k}^{s_j} x^l f(x)dx \tag{6.33}$$

$$E[X_{jfR}^l] = \frac{1}{p_i} \int_{s_{j-1}}^{s_j} x^l f(x)dx \tag{6.34}$$

We can now derive Equations for $E[X_{jvO}^l]$ (l^{th} moment of the distribution of tasks that spend time on (visit) Host j's ordinary (O) queue) and $E[X_{jvR}^l]$ (l^{th} moment of the distribution of tasks that spend time on (visit) Host j's ordinary (R) queue)

$$E[X_{jvO}^l] = \frac{q_j \sum_{i=1}^{j} p_i}{q_i} E[X_{jfO}^l] + \frac{(q_j - q_i \sum_{i=1}^{j} p_i)}{q_i} S_j^l \tag{6.35}$$

$$E[X_{jvR}^l] = \frac{(1-pj)p_j \sum_{i=1}^{j-1} q_i}{1 - \sum_{i=1}^{j-1} p_i \sum_{i=1}^{j-1} q_i} E[X_{jfO}^l]$$

$$+ \frac{(1 - \sum_{i=1}^{j-1} p_i \sum_{i=1}^{j-1} q_i) - ((1-pj)p_j \sum_{i=1}^{j-1} q_i)}{1 - \sum_{i=1}^{j-1} p_i \sum_{i=1}^{j-1} q_j} S_j^l \qquad (6.36)$$

$E(W_{ivO})$, i.e., Expected waiting time for a task at Host j's ordinary (O) queue and $E(W_{ivO})$, i.e., Expected waiting time for a task at Host j's ordinary (O) queue the expected waiting time for a task at Host j's ordinary (O) queue are then obtained by applying the classical result on non pre-emptive priority queue by Cobham in 1954 (36):

$$E(W_{ivO}) = \frac{\lambda q_i [E[X_{jvO}^l]}{(1 - \rho_i)} \qquad (6.37)$$

$$E(W_{ivO}) = \frac{\lambda (1 - \sum_{i=1}^{j-1} p_i \sum_{i=1}^{j-1} q_i) E[X_{jvO}^l]}{(1 - \rho_i)(1 - \rho_i')} \qquad (6.38)$$

where ρ_1 and ρ_2 are given by

$$\rho_i = \lambda q_i E[X_{jvO}^l] \qquad (6.39)$$

$$\rho_i' = \lambda q_i E[X_{jvO}^l] + \lambda (1 - \sum_{i=1}^{j-1} p_i \sum_{i=1}^{j-1} q_i) E[X_{jvR}^l])) \qquad (6.40)$$

We can now write an expressions for $E[X_{jfO}^l]$ and $E[X_{jfR}^l]$.

$$E[W_{ivO}] = q_i p_i E[X_{jvO}^l] \qquad < i < \qquad (6.41)$$

$$E[W_{ivR}] = p_j \sum_{i=1}^{j-1} \sum_{m=1}^{j-1} q_i (E[X_{mvO}^l] + \sum_{m=1+1}^{j} E[X_{mvR}^l]) \qquad (6.42)$$

The overall expected waiting time is then obtained as

$$E[W] = \sum_{i=1}^{n} E[W_{ivO}] + \sum_{i=2}^{n} E[W_{ivR}] \qquad (6.43)$$

For a given α and system load the cut-offs for hosts are computed such that the expected waiting time in the system is optimised.

TAPTF Performance Evaluation

The performance evaluation of TAPTF model is done by minimising the Equation 6.43. We will leave this as an exercise for the reader!

6.6 MTTMELL Policy

This policy consists of a central dispatcher and a set of homogeneous back-end hosts that offer mirrored services. We assume that the tasks can be migrated from one host to another and this migration is not work-conserving (any work done prior to migration is lost). We do not consider work-conserving migration as it can be expensive for certain tasks and it requires special algorithms.

MTTMEL (Multi-Tier Task Assignment with Minimum Excess Load) consists of multiple tiers that have one or more hosts. Each tier has a processing time limit assigned to it and the hosts in a particular tier only process tasks up to the time limit assigned to the tier. We assume that the arrival process into the system is Poisson and this is a reasonable assumption for many computer workloads (27). We assume that the arrival processes into all hosts are also Poisson. It is worth noting that the arrival processes into hosts in Tier 2,3,.. are less bursty than those of Poisson process. However, in this chapter, similar to much existing work, (25, 26, 64) we make this assumption. This assumption makes the proposed model analytically tractable, however, does not affect the accuracy of results significantly. This is justified by the fact that there are no significant differences in simulation results and analytical results.

A new task that arrives at the dispatcher is assigned to a host in the Tier 1 with equal probability. The task is processed up to the designated time limit of Tier 1 in a FCFS manner. If the service requirement (time) of the task is greater than the designated time limit assigned to Tier 1, the task is killed and migrated to a host in Tier 2. Otherwise the task departs system. The Tier 2 host processes the task from scratch in a similar manner and so on. This process continues until the task is fully serviced at which point the task departs the system. Let T be the number of tiers in the system. A host in Tier 1 dispatches each task to hosts in Tier 2 with equal probability and a host in Tier 2 dispatches each task to hosts in Tier 3 with equal probability. This process continuous until Tier $T - 2$ where $T > 2$. The time limits for tiers are computed to optimise expected waiting time. The number of hosts in Tier 1 is greater than the number of hosts in Tier 2 and the number of hosts in Tier 2 is greater than the number of hosts in Tier 3 and so on. The aim is to process tasks with relatively short processing requirements faster by assigning them to many hosts. The arrival rates into all the hosts in a particular tier are the same. Figures 6.20 and 6.21 illustrate MTTMEL systems with 3 and 6 hosts that satisfy these conditions. Another possible arrangement for a 6 host system is 5 host in Tier 1 and 1 host in Tier 2. The number of tiers that would result in the best performance, will depend on the factors such as variability of traffic and arrival rate into the system.

Analysis

This section provides a summary of the performance analysis of MTTMEL. The notation used for NTTMEL is given below in Table 7.11.

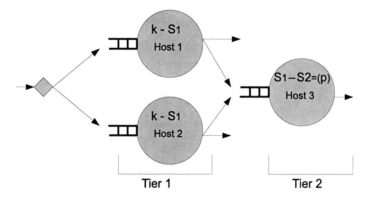

Fig. 6.20 3-host system

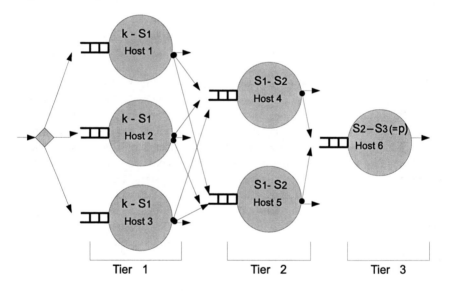

Fig. 6.21 6 Host system

Let s_i be the designated time limit assigned Tier i and p_i be the probability that the service time of a task is between s_{i-1} and s_i. p_i is given by;

$$p_i = \int_{s_{i-1}}^{s_i} f(x)dx \qquad (6.44)$$

where $f(x)$ is given by Equation (1).

Let $E[W_{if}]$ be the expected waiting time of a task whose final destination is a host in Tier i. $E[W_{if}]$ is given by;

n	Number of hosts in the system
s_i	designated time limit assigned Tier i
$f(x)$	Service time distribution of tasks (i.e. $B(k, p, \alpha)$)
k	Lower bound of the task size distribution
p	Upper bound of the task size distribution
p_i	Probability that the service time of a task is between s_{i-1} and s_i
λ	Outside task arrival rate into system
ρ	System load
α	Heavy-tailed parameter
$E[X_j^l]$	l^{th} moment of the distribution of tasks whose final destination is a host in Tier j.
$E[X_{jv}]$	1st moment of tasks that visit a host in Tier j
$E[X_{jv}^2]$	2nd moment of tasks that visit a host in Tier j
$E[W_{jv}]$	Expected waiting time of a task that visits a host in Tier j
$E[W_{if}]$	Expected waiting time of a task whose final destination is a host in Tier i
$E[W]$	Expected waiting time in the system

Table 6.4 Notation: MTTMEL

$$E[W_{if}] = \sum_{j=1}^{i} E[W_{jv}] \tag{6.45}$$

where $E[W_{jv}]$ denotes the expected waiting time of a task that visits a host in Tier j. $E[W_{jv}]$ is obtained using the Pollaczek-Khinchin formula (74);

$$E[W_{jv}] = \frac{\lambda_j E[X_{jv}^2]}{(2(1 - \lambda_j(\sum_{k=j}^{T} p_k))E[X_{jv}])} \tag{6.46}$$

where $E[X_{jv}]$ and $E[X_{jv}^2]$ denote the 1st and 2nd moments of tasks that visit a host in Tier j. λ_j denotes the arrival rate into a Tier j host and T denotes the number of tiers in the system. In Section V we discuss how to compute λ_j for distributed systems with different number of hosts. $E[X_{jv}^l]$ can be obtained using the following formula.

$$E[X_{jv}^l] = \frac{p_j}{\sum_{k=j}^{T} p_k} E[X_j^l] + \frac{\sum_{k=j+1}^{T} p_k}{\sum_{k=j}^{T} p_k} s_j^l \tag{6.47}$$

where $E[X_j^l]$ denotes the lth moment of the distribution of tasks whose final destination is a host in Tier j. $E[X_j^l]$ is given by;

$$E[X_j^l] = \int_{s_{j-1}}^{s_j} x^l f(x) dx \tag{6.48}$$

Finally, the expected waiting time in the system is computed as;

$$E[W] = \sum_{i=1}^{T} E[W_{if}] p_i \tag{6.49}$$

Note that the expected waiting time of a task is the same for all hosts in a given tier since all hosts in the tier receive tasks from the same distribution and with the same arrival rate. $E[W]$ is a function of α, $s_1, s_2, .., s_{n-1}$ and λ_i. For a given set of α and λ_i, we compute $s_1, s_2, .., s_{n-1}$ so as to optimise the expected waiting time.

Performance Evaluation on 3/6-Hosts System

The performance analysis of MTTMEL is provided for 3 and 6 host systems. Similar analysis can be carried out for different number of hosts as well. In order to vary the system load, we vary the outside arrival rate (λ) into the system. The performance of policies both analytically and experimentally is given here.

For a system consisting of n number of hosts, the arrival rate is given by the following formula

$$\lambda = \frac{\rho * n}{E[X]} \tag{6.50}$$

where ρ is the system load and $E[X]$ is equal to 3000 (refer to Background). Since the MTTMEL restarts certain tasks from scratch the true load in the system is higher than the system load discussed above. We will consider this in detail in Section V-A. We evaluate the performance of MTTMEL against performance of two well known policies namely, RANDOM (127) and TAGS (64). RANDOM assigns tasks to hosts with equal probability while TAGS assigns all incoming tasks to host 1. Host 1 processes tasks up to a designated time limit in a First-Come-First-Serve manner. If the processing time of a task is greater than the designated time limit, the task is killed and restarted from scratch at the next host. Otherwise the task departs the system. This process continues until the task is fully processed. The time limits for TAGS are computed to optimise a certain performance criteria such as the expected waiting time or slowdown. As pointed out, in this chapter we use the expected waiting time.

Let us first consider a 3-host system with two tiers. For a 3-host system λ_1 and λ_2 are computer as follows

$$\lambda_1 = \frac{\lambda}{2}$$
$$\lambda_2 = \lambda p_2 \tag{6.51}$$

Note that λ and p_2 are previously defined. Figure 6.22 illustrates the performance of MTTMEL under a 3-host system. First we note that, except when α is very high, RANDOM has the worst performance under all the system loads considered. MTTMEL outperforms RANDOM under a wide range of α values and the factor of improvement is highly significant when α lies in the range 0.7-1.5. For example, under the system load of 0.5, when α equals 1.1, MTTMEL outperforms RANDOM by a factor of 23. Second we notice that MTTMEL outperforms TAGS under a range of α. For example, under the system load of 0.7, when α equals 1.3, MTTMEL outperforms TAGS by a factor of 2.6.

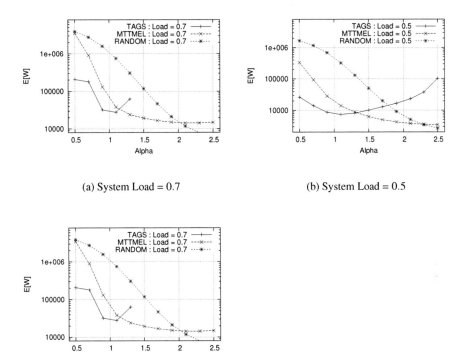

(a) System Load = 0.7   (b) System Load = 0.5

(c) System Load = 0.7

Fig. 6.22 3-host system for MTTMEL

Note that under high system loads (i.e. 0.7) TAGS fail to operate in steady state, if α is greater than 1.3. This means that we cannot find cut-offs for hosts (designated time limits) such that load on each host is less than 1. MTTMEL, however, does not suffer from this problem and it can function in steady state throughout the entire range of α values considered.

We also note that under the system load of 0.5, the TAGS's performance deteriorates considerably if α exceeds a certain value. This means that in a 3-host system TAGS can only perform well if α is low. Finally, notice that TAGS outperforms MTTMEL when α approaches 0.5 and the factor of improvement is significant for low α values. However, as the number of hosts increases the factor of improvement becomes less significant.

Let us now concentrate on a 6 host system with three tiers. For such a system, λ_1, λ_2 and λ_3 are given by the following formula.

$$\lambda_1 = \frac{\lambda}{3}$$

$$\lambda_2 = \frac{\lambda}{2}(p_2 + p_3) \qquad (6.52)$$

$$\lambda_3 = \lambda p_3$$

Note that λ, p_2 and p_3 are previously defined.

Figure 6.23 illustrates the performance of the policies considered under a 6 host system.

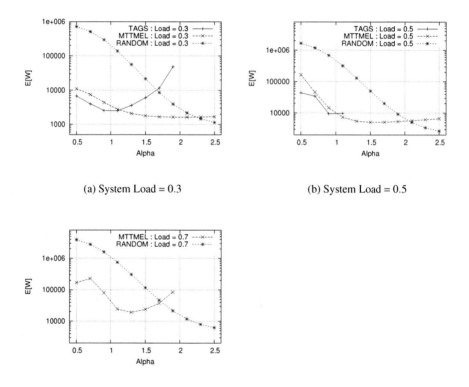

(a) System Load = 0.3   (b) System Load = 0.5

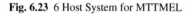

(c) System Load = 0.7

Fig. 6.23 6 Host System for MTTMEL

First notice that the factor of improvement in TAGS over MTTMEL is not significant under low α values. Second notice that under moderate (0.5) system loads, TAGS can operate in steady state only if α is low. This means that for a wide range of α values we cannot find cut-offs so that load on each host is less than one. When the system load is high (0.7), TAGS cannot operate in steady state at all. MTTMEL performs consistently well in steady state in both 3 and 6 host systems for almost all the scenarios considered. This indicates that it is scalable.

Analysis of Excess Load

In this section we investigate the excess load generated by the TAGS and MTTMEL. Let Z_i be the true load on a host in Tier i, where

$$Z_i = \lambda_i E[X_{iv}] \tag{6.53}$$

Let L_{sum} be the true sum of loads in the system;

$$L_{sum} = \sum_{i=1}^{T} Z_i T_i \tag{6.54}$$

where T_i denotes the number of hosts in Tier i. The excess load in the system is the difference between the true sum of loads and expected sum of loads.

$$Excess = L_{sum} - \lambda E[X] \tag{6.55}$$

Figure 6.24 depicts the excess load of TAGS and MTTMEL in a 3 and 6 host systems. Under each system load considered, we note that MTTMEL has significantly less excess compared to that of TAGS. The reason for this is as follows. In a heavy-tailed distribution a small fraction of large tasks contribute to more than 50% of the workload. Under the TAGS large tasks are killed and restarted from scratch many times whereas in a MTTMEL large tasks are killed and restarted from scratch only a few times. For example, a TAGS system with 6 hosts may kill and restart large tasks up to 5 times while in a 6 host MLTMEL very large tasks may be killed and restarted only up to 2 times. MTTMEL, therefore, generates less excess compared to that of TAGS.

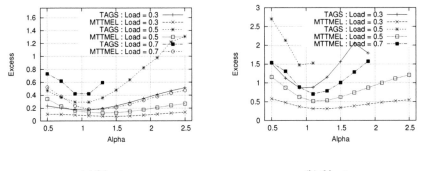

(a) 3 hosts   (b) 6 hosts

Fig. 6.24 MTTMEL Excess Load

The ratio between TAGS excess and MTTMEL excess increases as α increases. For example, in a 3-host system under the system load of 0.5, when α equals 0.5, this ratio is 1.3 and under the same system load, when α equals 2.1, the ratio is 4.6. We also notice that the excess under TAGS increases with increasing α. In the case of MTTMEL there is a slight decrease in excess up to a certain α and then there is a slight increase.

It is possible that under high system loads when the number of hosts are also high (e.g. 10), MTTMEL may no longer operate in steady state for certain α values. This issue can be resolved by increasing the number of hosts in the tiers that are close to the dispatcher. This may result in less number of tiers in the system. For example, under high system loads, a MTTMEL system with 10 hosts may have 5 hosts in Tier 1, 4 host in Tier 2 and just 1 host in Tier 3 rather than 4 hosts in Tier 1, 3 hosts in Tier 2, 2 hosts in Tier 3 and 1 host in Tier 4. If the variability of traffic itself changes over time (this means that the variance of the distribution changes over time), an adaptive version of MTTMEL (Adapt-MTTMEL) can be developed. Adapt-MTTMEL will utilise features such as on line traffic monitoring and traffic prediction models. Based on predicted traffic, the best configuration and the parameters for the best configuration, i.e., optimal number of hosts in each tier and their cut-offs can be determined.

6.7 Summary

It is true that there has been so much work over two decades in the area of performance in distributed systems and networking, which produced a substantial body of knowledge. However such a work was based on assumptions that are not consistent anymore with various traffic characteristics (such as Internet traffic). As detailed in this chapter, it is shown that task size in the Internet traffic does follow a different distribution (i.e. Pareto distribution/s), which makes the traditional load balancing approaches not relevant to Web services. This chapter first described one of the well-known task assignments, TAGS (Task Assignment by Guessing Size), and later we have shown the various extensions of TAGS to deal with excess load and high variance of task size (in server queues). A few policies were presented and these include: TAGS-WS, TAPTF, and MTTMEL. These have shown substantial performance improvement over TAGS.

Chapter 7
Scheduling with Time Sharing

> *"A guilty conscience needs to confess. A work of art is a*
> *confession."*
>
> *Albert Camus*

This last chapter also looks at the performance of Web services at the server side, but with a special focus on specific aspects that can improve performance (like time sharing). The performance of various task assignment policies will be discussed in the context of time sharing computing systems clusters. Both traditional and recent task assignment policies are investigated. Realistic computer workloads (using heavy-tailed distributions) will be considered in the benchmarking of the various policies.

We consider both simple models and advanced time sharing models. The main focus is to investigate the performance of more advanced time sharing model in detail. The previous chapter looked at the performance of task assignment policies in batch computing systems. These policies processed tasks according to the First-Come-First-Serve (FCFS) policy until completion or up to predefined time limits. Many modern computer systems are time sharing systems, which are based on policies such round-robin, multi-level time sharing. Multi-level time sharing policy (MLTP) policy has recently gained considerable attention because of its ability perform well under task size heavy-tailed distributions (e.g. Pareto) that have the property of decreasing failure rate (120, 152) and its ability process tasks with unknown sizes. MLTP policy has been used for scheduling flows in a bottleneck routers, scheduling jobs in operating systems and in many other situations (49, 119). This chapter looks at the performance of multi-level time sharing on cluster based web systems (i.e. web server farms).

The analysis of time sharing policies are more difficult compared to those policies that process tasks using FCFS until completion or up to predefined time limits because the modelling of time sharing systems require us to model the behaviour of partially completed tasks that are fed back to the system together with the new tasks that arrive at the system.

The distributed systems model that we consider is a cluster-based system that consists of several back-end hosts and a single central dispatcher. The back-end hosts in the cluster host identical content and therefore offer mirrored services. More details about this distributed computing model reader may refer to the previous chapter. We investigate the performance of these policies under realistic computer workloads that are represented using heavy-tailed distributions. We use Bounded Pareto Distributions to represent heavy-tailed workloads. We consider advanced time sharing policies that supports work-conserving migration and non work-conserving migration. Details about Heavy-tailed distributions, Bounded Pareto distributions and types of migrations can be found in the previous chapter.

7.1 Simple Models

Two scheduling policies, which are utilised on cluster-based distributed system, are discussed here. The distributed systems model we consider in this chapter is shown in Figure 7.1.

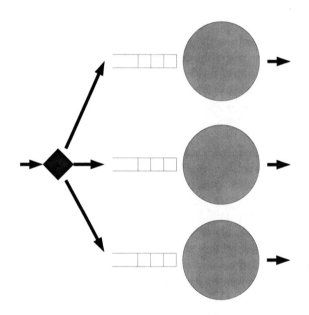

Fig. 7.1 Distributed System Model

Note that this is same distributed model we considered in the previous chapter. The traditional task assignment policies used in cluster-based distributed systems include Random, Round-Robin and Central Queue. Random assigns tasks to hosts with equal probability while Round-robin assigns tasks to hosts in a cyclic fashion. In central queue policy, an incoming tasks are first placed in queue located at the dispatcher. Whenever a host becomes idle, the task at the head of the queue is assigned to that host. The detail description of tradition models can be found in the previous chapter.

It is important to understand that main difference between the batch and time sharing task assignment policies is not in manner in which task are assigned to hosts but in the manner how these tasks are processed at hosts. For example, tasks cab be assigned to hosts with equal probability and processed according to the First-Come-First-Serve policy until completion or process according the round-robin scheduling policy. The former is considered as batch task assignment while the later is time sharing task assignment. We now discuss two scheduling policies that can utilised on time sharing hosts namely, Round-robin and Foreground-background. Note that Round-robin scheduling policy we will discuss next has no relationship between the Round-robin task assignment policy that assigns tasks to hosts in cyclic fashion.

Round-Robin

The most simplest type of time sharing policy is the conventional Round-Robin policy in which a task is allocated at most a quantum of resource time (e.g. CPU time) and if the job requires more service it is be put back at the end of the queue where the it waits in a FCFS manner for more service. The expected waiting time under Round-robin policy for general service time distributions have been obtained assuming that the quantum approaches zero. This special case of round-robin policy is called the processor sharing. There exist analytical results for the expected waiting time for the case of positive quantum. However, these models assume that both the inter-arrival times and service times follow exponential service time distributions. In this chapter since we consider heavy-tailed service time distributions we cannot use these results. The expected waiting time under Round-robin when the the quantum approaches zero is given by

$$E[W] = \frac{\lambda E[X]}{1 - \lambda E[X]} \qquad (7.1)$$

where λ represents the average arrival rate into the system and $E[X]$ represents the mean of the service time distribution. We note that the expected waiting time does not depend on $E[X^2]$, the second moment of the service time distribution indicating that variance of the service time distribution has no impact on the expected waiting time (Note : the higher variance the higher second moment). The reason for is that Equation 7.1 has obtained under the assumption of infinitely small quantum. In real systems the quantum is not infinitely small and it is positive constant whose value is determined by various factors such as context switch overhead. Therefore, in real systems, the variance of the service time distribution does have an impact on the expected waiting time.

Foreground-background (FB)

Another scheduling policy used time sharing hosts is the Foreground-background (FB) policy. FB gives gives priority to the task with the least amount of service. FB is a preemptive task assignment policy. Let us explain the behaviour of FB using two tasks. Let us assume that the task 1 is currently being serviced. While it is being serviced task 2 arrives at the system. When task 2 arrives at the system task 1 has received x amount of service. Upon the arrival of task 2, task 1 is preempted from the service and task 2 processed up to x. Once it receives x amount of service both tasks are serviced simultaneously until completion.

The expected waiting time of a task of size x under FB is given by the following formula.

$$EW(x) = \frac{1}{1 - \lambda \int_0^x \overline{F(t)}dt} + \frac{\lambda \int_0^x t\overline{F(t)}dt}{x(1 - \lambda \int_0^x \overline{F(t)}dt)^2} \tag{7.2}$$

Expected waiting in the system is obtained by multiplying the $EW(x)$ by the probability density function and then integrating it over k and p with respective to x (note that k and p are the smallest and the largest task sizes in the distribution).

$$EW = \int_k^p EW(x)f(x)dx \tag{7.3}$$

FB can be inefficient because each time a new task arrives, the task currently being processed have to be preempted. Under high arrival rates this can be very inefficient and costly. Further more, FB can difficult to implement in a typical time sharing system. Time sharing systems are quantum-based systems that process tasks up to a fixed amount of time (quantum).

7.2 Multi-level Time Sharing Policy

Figure 7.2 illustrates the basic model that is of interest to us. The multi-level time sharing model consists of N queues. A newly arriving task is first placed in the lowest level (queue) where it is serviced in FCFS manner up to a maximum of T_1 amount of service. If the task's service time is less than or equal to T_1, it departs system. Otherwise it will join the queue above and wait until it receives at most T_2 amount of service. The task propagates through the system of queues until the total processing time the task has so far received is equal to its service time at which point the task depart the system.

Most of discussion on time sharing policies are based on the assumption that infinitely small quanta and infinite number of queueing levels. In this chapter we consider multi-level time sharing policy which have non-zero quanta and finite number of queueing levels because such a policy is more practical to implement on real computer systems.

L. E. Schrage is one of the few researchers who analysed the model like the above under an arbitrary (general) service time distribution (126). He derived the expected time in the system conditioned on the size of a task. We now derive the final result obtained Schrage's, the expected time in the system including and up to i^{th} simple processing time in a more detail manner. The aim is to get an in-dept understanding of the behaviour of a multi-level time sharing policy.

We use the following notation to describe the system. The following notation is the same as the notation used in Scharge's (126) paper.

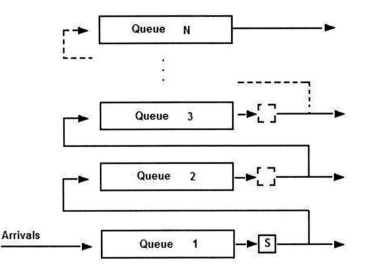

Fig. 7.2 Multi-level Time Sharing Model

λ	arrival rate into 1st queue
T_i	i^{th} simple processing; the length of processing time which a task on i^{th} queue receives
$F(t)$	Cumulative distribution function (CDF) of service time distribution
$F_i(t)$	$P[T_i \leq t]$ CDF of ith simple processing time
$L_F(i,s)$	$\int_0^\infty e^{-st} F_i(t)$; the L.S.T of $F_i(t)$
S_i	$T_1 + T_2 + ... + T_i$ given that the job returns to the system at least i times
$D_i(t)$	$P[S_i \leq t]$
$L_D(i,s)$	$\int_0^\infty e^{-st} D_i(t)$
U_i	S_i if the job returns to the system at least $i - 1$ times
U_i	$T_1 + T_2 + ... + T_k$ if the job returns the system only $k - 1$ times, $k < i$
$G_i(t)$	$P[U_i \leq t]$
N	number of queues (levels)
Λ_k	$\lambda(1 - \int_0^{S_i} dF(t))$
FT_i	time in the system up to and including i^{th} simple processing time
W_i	waiting time in the system up to i^{th} level. This time does not include i simple processing times (i.e. $T_1, T2, , , T_i$)

Table 7.1 Notation borrowed from (126)

The expected time in the system up to and including i^{th} simple processing time by investigating the behaviour of a random arrival to the system at time T_i.

The time in the system including and up to i^{th} simple processing time is composed of the following three components.

FT_i = time required to process the backlog

    + time required to process i simple processing times   (7.4)

    + time required to process any jobs that arrive during $FT_i - T_i$

The time required to process the backlog, T_{bi}, at time T_i is defined as the time to complete the kth simple processing time ($1 \leq k \leq N$) being processed plus the time to process all the tasks in the first i queues. Therefore we write,

T_{bi} at time T_i = time required to complete the kth simple processing time

        being processed + time required to process all the tasks   (7.5)

        in the first i queues

The 3rd component of Equation 7.4, the time to process any additional tasks that arrive during $FT_i - T_i$, is generated by the task that arrive during the processing of the backlog plus the tasks that arrive during the processing of $i - 1$ simple processing times. Let the time required to process any additional tasks that arrive during T_i be T_{bi}^*, and the time required to process any additional tasks that arrive during S_{i-1} be S_{i-1}^*. It is not difficult to see that the two additional delays (processing times), have the form of U_{i-1} busy periods. If there are $n1$ and $n2$ arrivals during S_{i-1} and T_{bi} the $T_{bi}^* + S_{i-1}^*$ have the form of $n1 + n2$ independent busy periods which are generated by the independent processing times having the distribution of $G_{i-1}(t)$.

    Let $T_{additional}$ be the time required to process any additional tasks that arrive during $FT_i - T_i$. Then

$T_{additional}$ = time required to process any

        additional tasks that arrive during T_{bi} $(=T_{bi}^*)$

    + time required to process any   (7.6)

        additional tasks that arrive during S_{i-1} $(=S_{i-1}^*)$

From above equations we get

FT_i = time required to process the backlog $(= T_{bi})$

    + time required to process any additional tasks that arrive during $T_{bi} (= T_{bi}^*)$

    + time required to process $i - 1$ simple processing times $(= S_{i-1})$

    + time required to process any additional tasks that arrive during $S_{i-1} (= S_{i-1}^*)$

    + time required to process the ith simple processing time $(= T_i)$

$FT_i = T_{bi} + T_{bi}^* + S_{i-1} + S_{i-1}^* + T_i$

                                           (7.7)

In Equation 7.7, we have written S_i as a sum of $S_{i-1} + T_i$. The reason for this would become clear as we progress with our analysis. Let T_{bi}^{total} be the sum of T_{bi} and U_{i-1} busy periods initiated by T_{bi}. Let S_{i-1}^{total} be the sum of S_{i-1} and U_{i-1} busy periods initiated by S_{i-1}.

We can now write the time in the system including and up to i^{th} simple processing time as follows.

$$FT_i = T_{bi}^{total} + S_{i-1}^{total} + T_i \tag{7.8}$$

Since T_{bi}^{total}, S_{i-1}^{total} and T_i are random variables which are independent of each other

$$E[FT_i] = E[T_{bi}^{total}] + E[S_{i-1}^{total}] + E[T_i] \tag{7.9}$$

We will now derive the expressions for $E[T_{bi}^{total}]$ and $E[S_{i-1}^{total}]$. Let $H_i^*(t)$ be the cumulative distribution function of T_{bi}^{total} and $L_H^*(i,s)$ be the L.S.T of $H_i^*(t)$

$$H_i^*(t) = P[T_{bi}^{total} \leq t] \tag{7.10}$$

$$L_H * (i,s) = \int_0^\infty e^{-st} dH_i^*(t) \tag{7.11}$$

Let $H_i(t)$ be the cumulative distribution function of T_{bi} and $L_H(i,s)$ be the L.S.T of $H_i(t)$.

$$H_i(t) = P[T_{bi} \leq t] \tag{7.12}$$

$$L_H(i,s) = \int_0^\infty e^{-st} dH_i(t) \tag{7.13}$$

It has been shown in [10] that

$$L_H(i,s) = \frac{(1-\rho)s + \sum_{k=i+1}^{N} \Lambda_k [1 - L_F(k,s)]}{L_D(i,s) - \lambda + s} \tag{7.14}$$

where Λ_k denotes the arrival rate onto the ith level, which can be calculated by multiplying arrival rate onto the first queue, λ, by the the probability of jobs having i or more processing times.

$$\Lambda_k = \lambda \left(1 - \int_0^{S_i} dF(t)\right) \tag{7.15}$$

Finally, let $A_i(t)$ be the cumulative distribution function of type U_{i-1} busy periods and $L_A(i,s)$ be the L.S.T of $A_i(t)$

$$A_i(t) = P[B_i \leq t] \tag{7.16}$$

$$L_A(i,s) = \int_0^\infty e^{-st} dA_i^*(t) \tag{7.17}$$

The following relationship exists between $L_A(i,s)$ and $L_G(i-1,s)$. The proof of this is relatively easy and can be found in [Donald Gross].

$$L_A(i,s) = L_G(i-1,s+\lambda - \lambda L_A(i,s)) \tag{7.18}$$

$H_i^*(t)$ is obtained as follows

$$H_i^*(t) = [\sum_{j=0}^{\infty} \int_0^t \frac{e^{-\lambda y}(\lambda y)^j}{j!} dH_i(y)] * A_i^{(j)}(t) \tag{7.19}$$

$A_i^{(j)}(t)$ represents i-fold (iterated) convolution of $A_i(t)$
By taking the Laplace transform of both sides we obtain

$$L_{H*}(i,s) = L_H(i-1, s+\lambda - \lambda L_A(i,s)) \tag{7.20}$$

Let $D^*(t)$ be the cumulative distribution function of S_{i-1}^{total} and $L_{D*}(i,s)$ be the L.S.T of $D^*(t)$. Then

$$L_{D*}(i,s) = L_D(i-1, s+\lambda - \lambda L_A(i,s)) \tag{7.21}$$

Lets now derive $E(S_{i-1}^{total})$

$$\begin{aligned}
E(S_{i-1}^{total}) &= -\frac{dL_D^*(i,s)}{ds}|_{s=0} \\
&= -\frac{dL_D(i-1, s+\lambda - \lambda L_A(i,s))}{ds}|_{s=0} \\
&= -L_D'(i-1, s+\lambda - \lambda L_A(i,s))(1 - \lambda L_A'(i,s))|_{s=0} \\
&= -L_D'(i-1, \lambda - \lambda L_A(i,0))(1 - \lambda L_A'(i,0)) \\
&= -L_D'(i-1,0)(1 - \lambda L_A'(i,0)); L_A(i,0) = 1
\end{aligned} \tag{7.22}$$

$$\begin{aligned}
L_A'(i,0) &= \frac{L_G(i-1, s+\lambda - \lambda L_A(i,s))}{ds}|_s = 0 \\
&= L_G'(i-1, s+\lambda - \lambda L_A(i,s))(1 - L_A'(i,s))|_s = 0 \\
&= L_G'(i-1, \lambda - \lambda L_A(i,0))(1 - \lambda L_A'(i,0)) \\
&= L_G'(i-1,0)(1 - \lambda L_A'(i,0)) \\
&= \frac{L_G'(i-1,0)}{1 + \lambda L_G'(i-1,0)}
\end{aligned} \tag{7.23}$$

By substituting 7.23 into 7.22

$$E(S_{i-1}^{total}) = -L_D'(i-1,0)(1 - \frac{\lambda L_G'(i-1,0)}{1 + \lambda L_G'(i-1,0)}) \tag{7.24}$$

$$-L_D'(i-1,0) = E[S_{i-1}] \tag{7.25}$$

$$-L_G'(i-1,0) = E[U_{i-1}] \tag{7.26}$$

Hence

$$E(S_{i-1}^{total}) = -\frac{dL_D^*(i,s)}{ds}\Big|_{s=0} = \frac{E(S_{i-1})}{1 - \lambda E[U_{i-1}]} \tag{7.27}$$

Lets now obtain an expression for $E(T_{bi}^{total})$ through a similar process

$$
\begin{aligned}
E(T_{bi}^{total}) &= -\frac{dL_D^*(i,s)}{ds}\Big|_{s=0} \\
&= -\frac{dL_H(i-1, s + \lambda - \lambda L_A(i,s))}{ds}\Big|_{s=0} \\
&= -L_H'(i-1, s + \lambda - \lambda L_A(i,s))(1 - \lambda L_A'(i,s))|_{s=0} \\
&= -L_H'(i-1, \lambda - \lambda L_A(i,0))(1 - \lambda L_A'(i,0)) \\
&= -L_H'(i-1,0)(1 - \lambda L_A'(i,0)); L_A(i,0) = 1
\end{aligned}
\tag{7.28}
$$

$$-L_H'(i-1,0) = \frac{\lambda E[U_i^2] + \sum_{k=i+1}^N \Lambda_k E[T_k^2]}{2(1 - \lambda E[U_{i-1}])} \tag{7.29}$$

$$E(T_{bi}^{total}) = \frac{\lambda E[U_i^2] + \sum_{k=i+1}^N \Lambda_k E[T_k^2]}{2(1 - \lambda E[U_{i-1}])(1 - \lambda E[U_i])} \tag{7.30}$$

The expected time the system up to and including i^{th} simple processing time is thus given by

$$E[FT_i] = \frac{\lambda E[U_i^2] + \sum_{k=i+1}^N \Lambda_k E[T_k^2]}{2(1 - \lambda E[U_{i-1}])(1 - \lambda E[U_i])} + \frac{E[S_{i-1}]}{(1 - \lambda E[U_{i-1}])} + T[i] \tag{7.31}$$

7.3 MLTP Policy

The task assignment policies we will be discussing in the chapter are based on the multi-level time sharing policy. MLTP (Multi-level Time Sharing) is considered under more general setting where a amount of time service time (quantum) allocated on levels using a random variable. In this section we discuss quantum-based MLTP policy. Figure 7.3 illustrates the multi-level multi-server task assignment policy. In the rest of chapter we only concentrate on quantum-based multi-level time sharing policy which we simply called the multi-level time sharing policy (MLTP).

We use the notation in Table 7.2 to describe MLTP policy.

MLTP consists of N levels/queues (we use the terms levels and queues interchangeably). Each level under MLTP has a designated time limit (cut-off) associated with it. Let Q_i be the cut-off of the ith level. Q_i is defined as maximum amount of service a task waiting in the ith queue can receive plus the total amount of service that the task has so far received (on previous $i - 1$ levels). New tasks/jobs (Note that the tasks and jobs refer to the same entity) to a MLTP system is immediately dispatched to lowest level queue. These tasks are processed in a First-Come-First-Serve (FCFS)

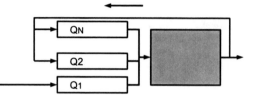

Fig. 7.3 Multi-level time sharing model (MLTP)

N	Number of levels
λ	Arrival rate into the system
q_i	i^{th} quantum
Q_i	i^{th} cut-off point ($= q_1 + q_2 + ... + q_i$)
T_i	The length of processing time that a task in i^{th} queue receives
$E[T_i]$	First moment of the distribution of T_i
$E[T_i^2]$	Second moment of the distribution of T_i
U_i	$= T_1 + T_2 + ... + T_i$ if the job returns to the system at least $i - 1$ times; $=$ $T_1 + T_2 + ... + T_k$ if the job returns to the system $k - 1$ times, $k < i$
G_i	Probability distribution function of U_i
$E[U_i^k]$	k^{th} moment of G_i
$E[EW_i]$	Expected time of a task in i^{th} queue

Table 7.2 Notation for MLTP

manner up to a maximum of Q_1. Tasks with service requirements higher than Q_1 are pre-empted from service and placed at the back of the second queue while the tasks with service times less than or equal to Q_1 depart the system. When tasks receive more service on the second level their execution is resumed (note that MLTP does not restart jobs from scratch). This process continues until tasks are fully serviced. The tasks waiting in the ith queue have the priority of service over those tasks that are waiting in the $i + 1^{th}$ queue. This means that a task waiting in the $i + 1$ queue will only be serviced if there are no tasks waiting in lower level queues (there are i such queues). However, a task currently being serviced cannot be interrupted by the new arrival to system. Indeed it is not practical to pre-empt the task currently being executed each time a new task arrives. This will increase the number of context switches and the expected waiting time of certain tasks. We assume that the context switch time is negligible and could be equated to zero. In the case where there are such overheads MLTP can be easily modified to cater for such variations.

Analysis of MLTP

We now present the equation that we use to compute the expected waiting time of tasks waiting in i^{th} queue. Let λ and Λ_i be the outside arrival rate into the system and arrival rate into i^{th} queue respectively. Λ_i given by

$$\Lambda_i = (1 - \int_0^{Q_{i-1}} f(x)dx) \tag{7.32}$$

where $f(x)$ denote the service time distribution of tasks. Let T_i be the processing time that a task in i^{th} queue receives and $F_i(t)$ be the distribution of T_i. The expected waiting time of a task whose size is higher than Q_{i-1} and less than Q_i is given by the following formula:

$$E[W_i] = \frac{\lambda E[U_i^2] + \sum_{k=i+1}^{N} \Lambda_k E[T_k^2]}{2(1 - \lambda E[U_{i-1}])(1 - \lambda E[U_i])} + \frac{Q_{i-1}}{(1 - \lambda E[U_{i-1}])} - Q_{i-1} \tag{7.33}$$

The above equation is obtained by taking into consideration the total delay experienced by a random arrival to the system as the sum of independent delay components. Further details of on the derivation of the above formula can be found in (98?). Note that $E[T_i]$ and $E[T_i^2]$ are 1st and 2nd moments of $F_i(t)$ respectively. $E[U_i]$ and $E[U_i^2]$ are first and second moments of $G_i(t)$ where $G_i(t)$ is the distribution of $T_1 + T_2 + .. + T_i$. $E[U_i^k]$ and $E[T_i^k]$ are obtained as follows.

$$E[U_i^k] = \int_0^{Q_i} x^k dF(x) + Q_n^k (1 - F(Q_i)) \tag{7.34}$$

$$E[T_i^k] = \frac{1}{(1 - F(Q_{i-1}))} (\int_{Q_{i-1}}^{Q_i} (x - Q_{i-1})^k dF(x) + (Q_n - Q_{n-1})^k (1 - F(Q_i))) \tag{7.35}$$

Finally the overall expected waiting time is obtained by multiplying $E[W_i]$ by the probability that service requirement is within the interval $[Q_{i-1}, Q_i], i = 1, ..., N (Q_0 = 0)$ and then taking the sum of each product term.

$$E[W] = \sum_{k=1}^{N} E[W_k] \int_{Q_{k-1}}^{Q_k} f(x)dx \tag{7.36}$$

Q_i's is computed to optimise expected waiting time.

Load in Queues

Modelling the load variation in queues is important, especially with α under different system loads. We compute the load on i^{th} level by multiplying the arrival rate into i^{th} level by $E[T_i]$, where $E[T_i]$ is the expected value of ith simple processing time. $Load_i$ represents the load on i^{th} level:

$$load_i = \Lambda_i * E[Ti] \tag{7.37}$$

Once the load is computed as above, the sum of loads on levels are equal the system load.

$$load = load_1 + load_2 + ... + load_N \tag{7.38}$$

We give below the proof of equation for the case of 2 levels.

$$load(\lambda E[X]) = load_1 + load_2$$
$$load_1 + load_2 = \Lambda_1 E[T_1] + \Lambda_2 E[T_2]$$
$$load_1 + load_2 = \lambda \left(\frac{1}{(1-F(Q_0))} (\int_{Q_0}^{Q_1} (x-Q_0)dF(x) + Q_1(1-F(Q_1))) \right.$$
$$\left. + (1-F(Q_1)) \frac{1}{(1-F(Q_1))} (\int_{Q_1}^{Q_2} (x-Q_1)dF(x) + (Q_2-Q_1)(1-F(Q_2))))) \right)$$
$$= \lambda(\int_{Q_0}^{Q_1} xdF(x) + \int_{Q_1}^{Q_2} xdF(x) + Q_1(1-F(Q_1)) - Q_1(F(Q_2)-F(Q1)))$$
$$= \lambda E[X]$$

$$(7.39)$$

We define $load_i$ as the load on level 1. Let us first consider the variations in load on levels with α on a MLTP system. Figures 7.4 and 7.5 plot how $load_i$ varies with α on a MLTP based on 2 and 3 levels.

We notice that under low and moderate system loads the shape of the load curves are very similar. Note that MLTP improves the performance by unbalancing the load among the 2 levels and as α increases the $load_1 - load_2$ increases. For example, when the system load is 0.3 and α is 0.4 the ratio between $load_1$ and $load_2$ is equal to 2 while under the same system load with α equal to 1.1 the ratio between $load_1$ and $load_2$ is 16. Second, we notice that as the system load changes from moderate to high the shape of the load curves for MLTP has changed significantly. We also notice that as α increases $load_1$ increases and $load_2$ decreases. We see that under high system loads when α is low, $load_1$ is lower than $load_2$ and under high system loads when α is high, $load_1$ is higher than $load_2$. For example, when system load is 0.9 and α equals 0.4, the ratio between $load_1$ and $load_2$ is equal to 0.05 whereas under the same system load, with α equals 0.4 this ratio equals 8.

Let us now look at load on hosts when the number of levels on MLTP is equal to 3. Figure 7.5 plot in how $load_i$ varies with α when the number of levels in MLTP 3. First, we see that the variations in load with α on a MLTP based on 2 levels have certain similarities with that of MLTP with 3 levels. Notice that $load_2$ and $load_3$ has a similar behaviour with α while $load_1$ has different behaviour from $load_2$ and $load_3$. Clearly MLTP, improves the performance by unbalancing the load.

The impact of quanta on the performance for the case of 2 levels

This section looks at how the expected time vary with the quanta for a range of system workloads and α values. We show that the optimal quanta are unique for a given task size variability and system load for both performance metrics. However, for some system loads, there may be another set of quanta that would result in near optimal performance. In such cases the system designer has the option of using either set of quanta. However, if the system designer is not certain about the exact quanta to be used it is recommended that he/she uses the one that is least sen-

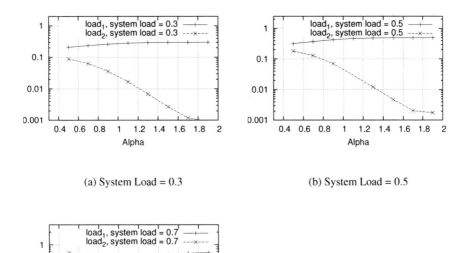

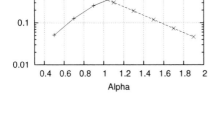

(c) System Load = 0.7

Fig. 7.4 Queue load variation on 2 levels

sitive to the performance. We investigate the consequences of overestimating and underestimating the optimal quanta.

We now transform the quantum based multi-level time sharing system previously discussed into a cut-offs (cut-off points) based multi-level time sharing system by partitioning the domain $[0, p]$ of a Pareto's distribution into a series of cutoff points $p_1, p_2, ..., p_N$. We assume that the upper bound, p, of the Bounded Pareto Distribution is 10^7. The high value of p will ensure that the Bounded Pareto distribution will represent a realistic heavy-tailed workload.

We represent the cut-off (cut-off point), p_i, corresponding to the minimal overall expected slowdown and flow time using $p_{i\_sd\_opt}$ and $p_{i\_ft\_opt}$ respectively. Figures 7.6 illustrates how the overall expected waiting time in the system and the overall expected slowdown vary with p_1. First, we consider the effect of p_1 on the overall expected time in the system. We note that when the system load is constant an increase in α will result in $p_{i\_ft\_opt}$ to decrease. For example, under the system load of 0.3, when α increases from 0.4 to 1.8, $p_{i\_ft\_opt}$ decreases approximately

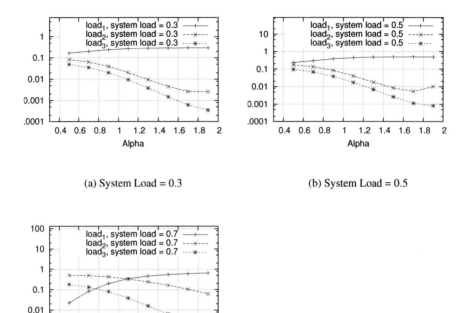

(a) System Load = 0.3

(b) System Load = 0.5

(c) System Load = 0.7

Fig. 7.5 Queue load variation on 3 levels

from 2.0 x 10^6 to 3 x 10^5. When the system load is 0.9, as α increases from 0.4 to 1.8, $p_{i\_ft\_opt}$ decreases approximately from 1.5 x 10^4 to 10^4. As α increases the fraction of small tasks contributing to system load increases and therefore, 2-LOQTP increases the degree of preferential treatment given to small tasks.

Second, we note from Figure 7.6 that $p_{i\_ft\_opt}$ under low and average system loads is significantly higher than $p_{i\_ft\_opt}$ under high system loads (0.7 and 0.9). This relates to one of our earlier observations that is when the system load changes from moderate to high the shape of the load curves changed dramatically.

Third, we note that the overall expected waiting time curves have 2 minima for most of the system loads and α values considered. Moreover, for some system loads (e.g. 0.5) these two minima are very close to each other. In this case the policy designer may use either set of quanta as they both result in the similar performance. Moreover, when there are two such sets of quanta we find that one set of quanta always performs better than the other, therefore for a given system load and task size variability optimal p_1 is unique for overall expected waiting time.

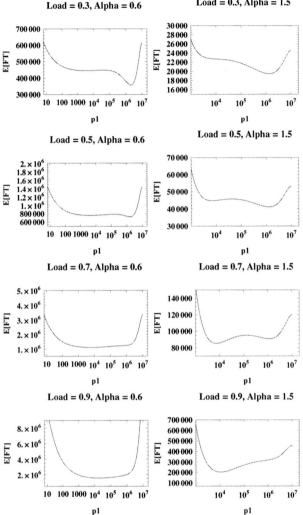

Fig. 7.6 Impact of p_1 on overall expected flow time (N=2)

The last plot of Figure 7.6 illustrates the behaviour of $p_{i\_ft\_opt}$ (in a 2-level policy) varies with the system. We find that there is sudden drop in $p_{i\_ft\_opt}$ which occurs between the system loads of 0.6 and 0.7. The first 4 plots indicated that when system load increases from 0.5 to 0.7 a rapid decrease in $p_{i\_ft\_opt}$. The sudden drop in figure 10 corresponds to this.

Finally, let us consider the case where there are 2 minima that have roughly the same performance. In this scenario the minimum on the left is highly sensitive to the overall expected waiting time compared to the minimum on the right. In such cases the if the designer is not certain about the exact quanta to be used it is recommended that he uses the quanta on the right. This will minimise the performance degradation by slightly overestimating or underestimating the optimal quanta.

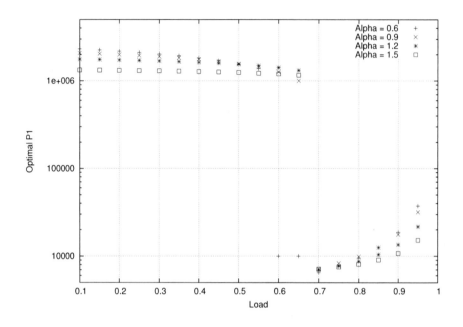

Fig. 7.7 Behaviour of Optimal p_i

The Impact of Quanta on the Performance for the case of 3 levels

In this section we investigate the impact cut-offs on the performance of MLTP consisting of 3-levels. Figures 7.8 and 7.9 illustrate the effect of cut-offs (i.e. p_1 and p_2) on the performance. We see from the figures that for each metric there is minimum which corresponds to optimal cut-offs. As we saw before, optimal p_1 is small compared to the largest task, p (=10^7), in the service time distribution. In this chapter we do not investigate the uniqueness of quanta under 3-level policy. However, as we saw before we see that there is a sudden drop in optimal p_1 and optimal p_2 of overall expected flow time (see Figure 7.8). We noticed that if the objective function consists of two minima, Mathematica did not always return the global minimum. And this happened very frequently when the two minima are close to each other. One way to resolve this problem is to specify the range of the global minimum as a constraint in the Mathematica optimisation function. The range of the global minimum can be identified by making plot of objective function. As the number of levels increase, finding the optimal cut-offs becomes more difficult. Graphical representations such as Figures 7.8 and 7.9 will allow us to identify the ranges of the optimal cut-offs approximately. However, such plots are only possible for the case of 2 and 3 levels.

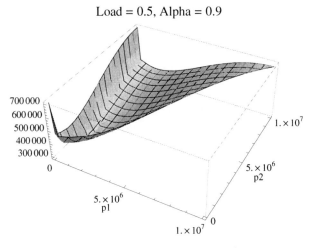

Fig. 7.8 Overall expected Flowtime

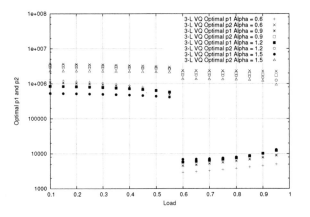

Fig. 7.9 Behaviour of Optimal p_i

Fraction of tasks served on levels

This section investigates the fraction of tasks completed at levels using a 2-Level policy. We compute the fraction of tasks completed at levels using the cumulative distribution function of the Bounded Pareto Distribution. The cumulative distribution function of Bounded Pareto Distribution is given by the following formula.

$$F(x) = \int_k^x \frac{\alpha k^\alpha}{1 - (k/p)^\alpha} \, x^{-\alpha-1}, \quad k < x < p$$

$$= -\frac{k^\alpha}{1 - (k/p)^\alpha} (x^{-\alpha} - k^{-\alpha}) \tag{7.40}$$

We compute the fraction of tasks completed at 1st and 2nd levels as follows.

$$Frac\_L1\_ft = F(p_{1\_ft\_opt})$$
$$Frac\_L2\_ft = 1 - F(p_{1\_ft\_opt}) \tag{7.41}$$

We can see from Figure 7.10 that more than 95% of tasks are completed at the first level for the range of workloads considered. Under low and moderate system loads, the fraction of tasks completed at level 1 is very high (0.999). Previously, we noticed high $p_{1\_ft\_opt}$ under low and moderate workloads indicating a large fraction of jobs being completed at 1st level. As the system load increases, the fraction of tasks completed at 1st level decreases by a small amount (0.05). As the system load increases, the policy improves the overall expected flow time by increasing the degree of preferential treatment given to small tasks.

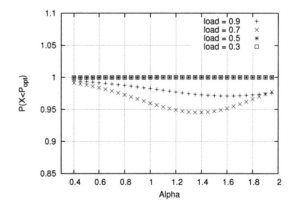

Fig. 7.10 $Frac\_L1\_ft$ (N=2)

7.4 MLMS Policy

This section discusses the MLMS (Multi-level Multi-server Load Distribution Policy) policy. Figure 7.11 depicts the MLMS policy. MLMS consists of a central dispatcher (this can be a switch or a router) and n number of back-end hosts that offer mirrored services. The central dispatcher receives new tasks and distributes them among back-end hosts with equal probability. Note that MLMS attempts to improve the performance by reducing the variability of tasks in queues and at the same time by giving preferential treatment to small jobs. Each host under MLMS processes tasks from the full Bounded Pareto Distribution (i.e. $B(k, p, \alpha)$).

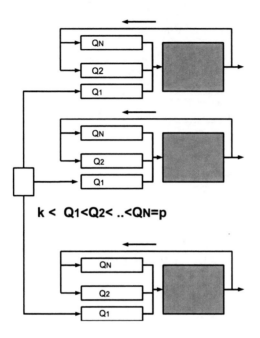

Fig. 7.11 MLMS architecture

Analysis of MLMS

Let us now consider the analysis of MLMS. For MLMS the expected waiting time of tasks at each host is the same because the dispatcher distributes tasks with equal probability. Therefore, the expected waiting time in the system is simply equal to expected waiting time under MLTP on a single host. (This follows the assumption that each host has the same number of levels). The notation given in Table 7.3 is used to describe the MLMS system.

Let λ_d be the arrival rate of tasks at the dispatcher. The arrival rate of task into a back-end host, λ, is simply $\frac{\lambda_d}{n}$. Let Λ_i be the arrival rate into the ith queue. Λ_i is the product of λ and $(1 - \int_0^{Q_{i-1}} f(x)dx)$ where $f(x)$ denotes the probability density function of the task size distribution. The expected waiting time of a task whose size is higher than Q_{i-1} and less than Q_i is given by the following formula.

N	Number of levels
$B(k,p,\alpha)$	Bounded Pareto task size distribution
λ_d	Outside task arrival rate into system
λ	Arrival rate into a back-end host
Q_i	i^{th} cut-off point
T_i	The length of processing time that a task in i^{th} queue receives
$E[T_i]$	First moment of the distribution of T_i
$E[T_i^2]$	Second moment of the distribution of T_i
U_i	$= T_1 + T_2 + ... + T_i$ if the job returns to the system at least $i-1$ times; $=$ $T_1 + T_2 + ... + T_k$ if the job returns to the system $k-1$ times, $k < i$
G_i	Probability distribution function of U_i
$E[U_i^k]$	k^{th} moment of G_i
$E[W_i]$	Expected waiting time of tasks in i^{th} queue
$E[W]_{MLMS}$	Expected waiting time in the system

Table 7.3 MLMS notation

$$E[W_i] = \frac{\lambda E[U_i^2] + \sum_{k=i+1}^{N} \Lambda_k E[T_k^2]}{2(1 - \lambda E[U_{i-1}])(1 - \lambda E[U_i])} + \frac{Q_{i-1}}{(1 - \lambda E[U_{i-1}])} - Q_{i-1} \qquad (7.42)$$

The above equation is obtained by taking into consideration the total delay experienced by a random arrival to the system as the sum of independent delay components (126). $E[T_i^m]$ is given by the following formula.

$$E[T_i^m] = \frac{1}{(1 - F(Q_{i-1}))} \left(\int_{Q_{i-1}}^{Q_i} (x - Q_{i-1})^m f(x)dx + (Q_i - Q_{i-1})^m (1 - F(Q_i)) \right) \tag{7.43}$$

$E[U_i^m]$ is given by

$$E[U_i^m] = \int_0^{Q_i} x^m f(x)dx + Q_i^m (1 - F(Q_i)) \tag{7.44}$$

The expected waiting time in the system is obtained by multiplying $E[W_i]$ by the probability that service requirement is within the interval $[Q_{i-1}, Q_i], i = 1,2,,,,,N(Q_0 = 0)$ and then taking the sum of each product term;

$$E[W]_{MLMS} = \sum_{k=1}^{N} E[W_k] \int_{Q_{k-1}}^{Q_k} f(x)dx \tag{7.45}$$

We derive $E[W]_{MLMS}$ for a Bounded Pareto distribution described in Section ??. When the variability of traffic (α), the system load ($\lambda E[X]$) and the number of levels (N) are fixed, $E[W]_{MLMS}$ is a function of $Q_1, Q_2, ...Q_N$ where $k < Q_1 < Q_2 < ... < Q_N = p$. We compute Q_i to optimise the expected waiting time defined by Equation 7.

The performance evaluation of MLMS

The evaluation of the performance of MLMS (and MLMS-M) is performed by comparing the performance of MLMS with TAGS policy (64). TAGS similar to MLMS (and MLMS-M) has n back-end hosts that offer mirrored services. It dispatches all the incoming tasks to the first host. Each host processes tasks in a FCFS manner up to a fixed time limit. Tasks whose sizes are greater than the time limit of a host are killed and restarted from scratch at the next host (the next host has a higher time limit). These time limits (cut-offs) are computed to optimise expected waiting time. We do not consider the processor sharing hosts since processor sharing assumes infinitely small quanta ($q \to 0$) which is not a realistic assumption. Figures 7.12 illustrates the performance of MLMS and TAGS policy. In this analysis only MLMS policy up to 20 levels (queues) is considered.

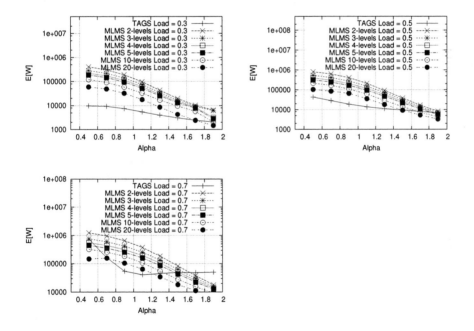

Fig. 7.12 Expected Waiting time for MLMS

First notice that under a system load of 0.3, TAGS outperforms MLMS for almost all the variabilities (i.e. all α values considered). As the system load increases, MLMS begins to outperform TAGS for certain α values. For example, when the system load is 0.5 and α is between 1.5 and 2.0, MLMS with 20 levels outperforms TAGS. As the system load increases from 0.5 to 0.7, MLMS outperforms TAGS for a wider range of α values. Notice that under a system load of 0.7 MLMS outperforms TAGS in two different α ranges. For a MLMS policy with 20 levels these two ranges are $0.4 - 0.7$ and $1.3 - 2.0$.

Finally notice that an increase in the number levels results in an improvement in the performance. In (98), we showed that if the amount of service allocated to tasks on levels are equal (equal quantum time sharing), the relationship between the performance (i.e. expected waiting time or slowdown) and the number of levels has a form of a power curve where the coefficients of the curve are determined by the arrival rate and the variability of traffic. Although MLMS does not have equal quanta, here we notice a similar behaviour.

In conclusion MLMS is be more efficient under moderate to high system loads. MLMS may require a large number of levels if MLMS is to outperform TAGS. For example under a system load of 0.7 and $\alpha = 0.5$, MLMS with 20 levels outperforms TAGS by 500% while under the same conditions, TAGS outperforms MLMS with 2 levels by 150%.

The advantage of MLMS is that hosts do not need task migration facilities. Moreover, MLMS does not kill task and restart those from scratch. As such, it does not generate wasted processing.

Note that an increase/decrease in the number of hosts does not affect the distribution of tasks seen by hosts. Therefore, the number of hosts has no impact on the performance of MLMS. This follows the assumption that α, the system load and the number of levels are constant.

7.5 MLMS-M Policy

This section discusses the MLMS-M (Multi-level Multi-server Load Distribution Policy with Task Migration) policy. Figure 7.13 depicts MLMS-M. A new task to the system is immediately dispatched to the host 1. The task is processed at the first host up to a designated time limit (cut-off) using MLTP. If the service requirement of the task exceeds the cut-off of the first host the task is killed and migrated to the next host (second host) in the system. The second host processes the task in a similar manner. This process continues until the task is fully serviced, at which point the task departs the system.

Analysis of MLMS-M

We use the notation given in Table 7.5 to describe the MLMS-M. Note that the hosts do not necessarily have to have equal number of levels. However, in this chapter we assume this is the case.

To obtain the expected waiting time of tasks in the system, we need to first consider the expected waiting time of tasks that spend time at host i (i.e. $E[W_i]$). To obtain $E[W_i]$ we multiply expected waiting time of tasks in the ith host's j^{th} queue (i.e. $E[W_{(i,j)}]$) by the probability that the service time of tasks is between $Q_{(i,j-1)}$ and $Q_{(i,j)}$ (refer to Equation 7.68). Note that the size of tasks processed in the ith queue lies between $Q_{(i,j-1)}$ and $Q_{(i,j)}$. The expected waiting time in the system (overall expected waiting time) is then obtained using Equation 7.54. Here we have conditioned on the final destination of tasks. When the variability of traffic, the system

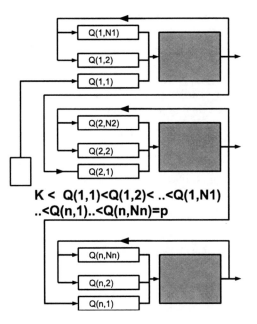

Fig. 7.13 MLMS-M architecture

n	Number of hosts in the system
N_i	Number of levels at i^{th} host
$f(x)$	Service time distribution of tasks (i.e. $B(k, p, \alpha)$)
k	Lower bound of the task size distribution
p	Upper bound of the task size distribution
p_i	Fraction of tasks whose final destination is host i
$P_{(i,j)}$	Fraction of tasks whose final destination is host i's j^{th} queue
λ	Outside task arrival rate into system
ρ	System load
α	Heavy-tailed parameter
$Q_{(i,j)}$	i^{th} host's j^{th} cut-off
$T_{(i,j)}$	i^{th} host's j^{th} simple processing time; the length of processing time that a task in the ith host's j^{th} queue receives
$E[T_{(i,j)}]$	First moment of the distribution of $T_{(i,j)}$
$E[T_{(i,j)}^2]$	Second moment of the distribution of $T_{(i,j)}$
$U_{(i,j)}$	$= T_{(i,1)} + T_{(i,2)} + \ldots + T_{(i,j)}$ if the job returns to the system at least $j-1$ times; $= T_{(i,1)} + T_{(i,2)} + \ldots + T_{(i,k)}$ if the job returns to the system $k-1$ times, $k < j$
$G_{(i,j)}$	Probability distribution function of $U_{(i,j)}$
$E[U_{(i,j)}^k]$	k^{th} moment of $G_{(i,j)}$
$E[W_i]$	Expected waiting time of tasks that spend time at host i
$E[W]$	Expected waiting time in the system

Table 7.4 MLMS-M Notation

load and the number of levels are fixed, $E[W]_{MLMS-M}$ (Equation 7.54) is a function of $Q_{(1,1)}, Q_{(1,2)}, ..., Q_{(n,N_n)}$ where $k < Q_{(1,1)} < Q_{(1,2)} < ... < Q_{(n,N_n)} = p$. We compute these cut-offs to optimise the expected waiting time. The full analysis of MLMS-M is given below

Let $f(x)$ be the probability distribution function of task sizes (i.e. $B(k, p, \alpha)$) and let $F(x)$ be the cumulative distribution function of $f(x)$ respectively. Let $p_{(i,j)}$ be the probability that the service time of task is between $Q_{(i,j-1)}$ and $Q_{(i,j)}$. We obtain;

$$P_{(i,j)} = \int_{Q_{(i,j-1)}}^{Q_{(i,j)}} f(x)dx \qquad (7.46)$$

Let p_i be the fraction of tasks whose final destination is host i;

$$p_i = \int_{Q_{(i-1,N_{i-1})}}^{Q_{(i,N_i)}} f(x)dx \qquad (7.47)$$

Let $E[W_{(i,j)}]$ be expected waiting time of tasks in i^{th} host's j^{th} queue. We obtain:

$$E[W_{(i,j)}] = \frac{\lambda_{(i,1)}E[U_{(i,j)}^2] + \sum_{k=j+1}^{N_i} \Lambda_{(i,k)}E[T_{(i,k)}^2]}{2(1 - \lambda_{(i,1)}E[U_{(i,j-1)}])(1 - \lambda_{(i,1)}E[U_{(i,j)}])}$$

$$= +\frac{Q_{(i,j-1)}}{(1 - \lambda_{(i,1)}E[U_{(i,j-1)}])} - Q_{(i,j-1)} \qquad (7.48)$$

In equation 7.63, $E[T_{(i,j)}]$ represents expected length of processing time that a task in i^{th} host's j^{th} queue receives.

The terms $\lambda_{(i,1)}$ and $\Lambda_{(i,j)}$ in Equation 7.63 denote the arrival rate into the ith host's 1st queue and the ith host's j^{th} queue respectively. We obtain these as follows.

$$\lambda_{(i,1)} = \lambda(1 - \int_k^{Q_{(i-1,N_{i-1})}} f(x)dx) \qquad (7.49)$$

$$\Lambda_{(i,j)} = \lambda(1 - \int_k^{Q_{(i,j-1)}} f(x)dx); j > 1 \qquad (7.50)$$

$E[U_{(i,j)}^m]$ and $E[T_{(i,j)}^m]$ are obtained as follows.

$$E[U_{(i,j)}^m] = \frac{\int_{Q_{(i-1,N_{i-1})}}^{Q_{(i,j)}} x^m f(x)dx}{(1 - F(Q_{(i-1,N_{i-1})}))} + \frac{Q_{(i,j)}^m(1 - F(Q_{(i,j)}))}{(1 - F(Q_{(i-1,N_{i-1})}))} \qquad (7.51)$$

When we compute $E[U_{(i,j)}^m]$ we have to condition on the tasks with sizes greater than $Q_{(i-1,N_{i-1})}$. Hence the term $\frac{1}{(1-F(Q_{(i-1,N_{i-1})}))}$.

$$E[T^m_{(i,j)}] = \frac{\int_{Q_{(i,j-1)}}^{Q_{(i,j)}} (x - Q_{(i,j-1)})^m f(x)dx}{(1 - F(Q_{(i,j-1)}))} + \frac{(Q_{(i,j)} - Q_{(i,j-1)})^m (1 - F(Q_{(i,j)}))}{(1 - F(Q_{(i,j-1)}))}$$

(7.52)

Let $E[W_i]$ be the waiting of tasks at host i. We have:

$$E[W_i] = \sum_{j=1}^{N_i} E[W_{(i,j)}] \frac{p_{(i,j)}}{p_i}$$

(7.53)

We can now write an expression for the expected waiting time of the system (i.e. overall expected waiting time). Let n be the number of hosts in system and let $E[W]$ be the expected waiting time in the system. $E[W]$ is given by

$$E[W] = E[W_1]p_1 + (E[W_1] + E[W_2])p_2$$
$$+ \dots + (E[W_1] + \dots + E[W_n])p_n$$

(7.54)

The performance evaluation of MLMS-M for the case of 2 hosts

The performance evaluation of MLMS-M under a 2 host system is provided here. Figure 7.14 illustrates the expected waiting time for the MLMS-M (refer to the 3 figures on the left) and the effect of number of levels on the expected waiting time (refer to the 3 figures on the right). First notice that MLMS-M outperforms TAGS for almost all the cases considered. The highest improvement in the performance is seen under high workloads and very high task sizes variabilities (i.e. low α values). For example, when the system load is 0.7 and α is 0.5 MLMS-M with 2 levels outperforms TAGS by 270%. Under the same conditions, MLMS-M with 5 levels outperforms TAGS by 675%. As the number of levels increases, we notice an improvement in the performance of MLMS-M. The explanation for this is as follows. Recall that MLMS-M serves tasks on each level in a FCFS manner. The expected waiting time in a FCFS queue is proportional to the variability of tasks in the queue. As the number of levels increases, the variability of tasks in queues decreases. This results in an improvement in the overall performance.

Second we note that the improvement in the performance with the number of levels is not linear (Note that we have used log scale for Y axis). Moreover, as the number of levels increases, the rate at which the performance improves decreases. For example, when $\alpha = 0.5$ and $load = 0.7$, MLMS-M with 3 levels outperforms MLMS-M with 2 levels by a factor of 1.5 while under the same conditions MLMS-M with 4 levels outperforms MLMS-M with 3 levels only by a factor of 1.3. Further experiments indicate that as the number of levels approaches infinity the expected waiting time approaches a constant value. The value of this constant depends on a number of factors which include the number of hosts in the system, the variability of traffic and the system load.

Finally, notice that under a fixed system load the expected waiting time does not always decrease with increasing α. This behaviour becomes more apparent under moderate to high system loads with higher number of levels. As α increases the

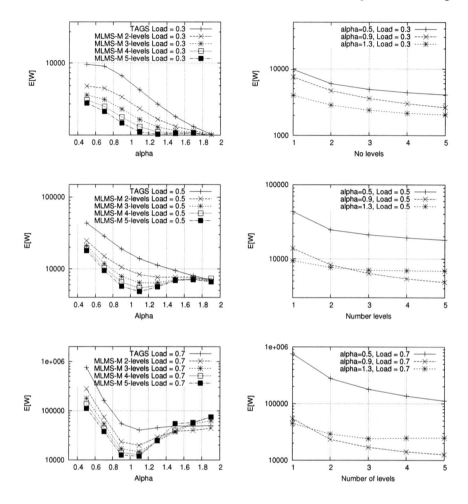

Fig. 7.14 Expected Waiting time for MLMS-M

expected waiting time decreases up to a certain value and then it starts to increase. The excess load generated due to restarting jobs from scratch results in the expected waiting time to increase. This means that after certain α improvement in the performance due to having different time limits for hosts becomes less significant. We find that for a given number of levels and system load there may exist a unique α that produces the best waiting time. For example, when system load is equal to 0.7 and the number of levels are 5 the value of this α lies between 1 and 1.2.

If the task migration is work-conserving (this type of policies do not restart jobs from scratch rather resume the execution) performance always improves with increasing α provided that the cost migration is negligible.

7.6 MLMS-M* Policy

In the previous section we noticed that the performance of MLMS-M improving with the number of hosts for certain α values. We also noticed that as the number of hosts increases, the performance under MLMS-M deteriorate for a range of α values. When the number of hosts in the system is increased beyond three, the performance of MLMS-M becomes even worse for high α values due to large amount of excess load generated. Under very low α values, on the other hand, MLMS-M will continue to perform well even if the number of hosts in the system is high.

MLMS-M* has been designed to perform well under high α values on relatively larger clusters. MLMS-M is an extension of our previous MTTMEL (97) model which was proposed for a batch computing system. MLMS-M* generates significantly less amount of excess load under high α values compared to its counterpart MLMS-M and therefore, it maintains satisfactory performance under high α values. It does so via its multi-tier architecture that consists of one or more hosts in tiers. Hosts in a particular tier has the same cut-offs (designated time limits). $Q(i, j)$, therefore, denotes the ith tiers's j^{th} cut-off.

- Unlike MLMS-M, MLMS-M* does not assign all incoming tasks to the Host 1 in the system, rather it assigns an incoming task to a Host in tier 1 with equal probability.
- A new task is processed at a tier 1 Host using MLTP (refer to Section III-C) up to the designated time of tier 1, i.e. $Q_{(1,N_1)}$
- If the task's processing requirement exceeds $Q_{(1,N_1)}$ the task is migrated to a Host in tier 2 with equal probability. Otherwise the task departs the system.
- This process continues until the task is fully processed at which point the task departs the system.

Tier 1 has more hosts than tier 2 and tier 2 has more hosts than tier 3 and so on. The aim is to process small tasks faster by assigning them to many hosts and to minimise the total excess load by minimising the number of task migrations. The architecture for MLMS-M* for the case of 3 hosts (MLMS-M* requires at least 3 hosts) is shown in Figure 7.15.

Similar models can be devised for higher number of hosts as well. For example, one possible configuration for a system with 6 hosts is 3 hosts in tier 1, 2 hosts in tier 2 and 1 host in tier 3.

Analysis of MLMS-M*

This section presents the performance analysis of MLMS-M*. The expected waiting time under MLMS-M* can be derived from Equation 14 that we obtained in Section V-A. Let T denotes the number of tiers in the system and let $E[W]_{MLMS-M*}$ be the expected waiting time under MLMS-M*. Notice that MLMS-M (Section V) can be considered as a special case of MLMS-M* where $T = n$ and n denotes the number of hosts in the system. Each tier in MLMS-M, therefore, has only 1 host.

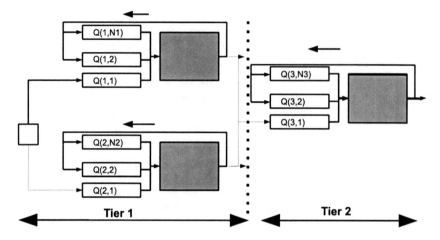

Fig. 7.15 MLMS-M* in a 3 host system

What we consider in this section is the case of $T < n$. We note that the expected waiting time of a task under hosts in a given tier are equal because all hosts in a particular tier have same set of parameters (i.e. arrival rates, cut-offs, etc). Therefore, the overall expected waiting time of a task in a particular tier is equal to the expected waiting time of a task under any given host in that tier. Therefore, we can consider MLMS-M* as a MLMS-M having T number of hosts. $E[W]_{MLMS-M*}$ is hence given by

$$E[W]_{MLMS-M*} = [E[W]_{MLMS}]_{n=T} \tag{7.55}$$

where n denotes the number of hosts in a MLMS-M system (Equation 14). The above computation can be carried out using the same equations obtained in Section V-A except the Equations 11 and 12 that deal with the arrival rates into hosts and individuals levels. We provide more details about these two equations in Section V-C. Finally, the time limits for tiers are computed such that the expected waiting time is optimised. The notation that was previously introduced in Table II is used to describe MLMS-M*.

Analysis of Excess load

Let T_i and $L^*excess$ be the number of hosts in tier i and excess load generated under MLMS-M* system. Then;

$$L^*_{excess} = \sum_{i=1}^{T} T_i \lambda_{(i,1)} E[U_i] - \lambda E[X] \tag{7.56}$$

$\lambda_{(i,1)}$ denotes the arrival rate into a Host in tier i's 1st queue. $E[U_i]$ is given by Equation 16 and λ and $E[X]$ denote the arrival rate into the system and the mean of the service time distribution respectively.

Performance Evaluation of MLMS-M* for 3-Hosts System

This section provides the performance evaluation of the MLMS-M* system illustrated in Figure 7.16. First let us obtain the arrival rates into hosts. Since MLMS-M* distributes tasks with equal probability and all hosts in a particular tier has the same task size range, the arrival rates of tasks into hosts in a given tier are the same. In the case of a 3 host system, there are 2 tiers in the system, i.e, 2 hosts in tier 1 and 1 host in tier 2. $\lambda_{(1,j)}$, $\lambda_{(2,j)}$, $\Lambda_{(1,j)}$ and $\Lambda_{(2,j)}$ are obtained as follows.

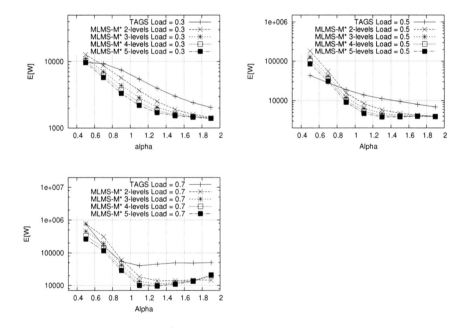

Fig. 7.16 MLMS-M vs MLMS-M*

$$\lambda_{(1,1)} = \frac{\lambda}{2} \tag{7.57}$$

$$\lambda_{(2,1)} = \lambda\left(1 - \int_{k}^{Q_{(1,N_1)}} f(x)dx\right) \tag{7.58}$$

$$\Lambda_{(1,j)} = \frac{\lambda}{2}\left(1 - \int_{k}^{Q_{(1,j-1)}} f(x)dx\right) \quad j > 1 \tag{7.59}$$

$$\Lambda_{(2,j)} = \lambda \left(1 - \int_{k}^{Q_{(2,j-1)}} f(x)dx\right) \quad j > 1 \tag{7.60}$$

Using the above arrival rates, the cut-off for MLMS-M* and the expected waiting time are computed by optimising Equation 19.

Figure 7.16 depicts the expected waiting time for MLMS-M* and TAGS, in a 3 host system. First, notice that MLMS-M* maintains satisfactory performance under high α values. Unlike MLMS-M there is no significant performance degradations under high α values for all three system loads considered. As pointed out earlier, this is due the less excess load generated by MLMS-M*. Figure 7.17 compares the excess load between MLMS-M and MLMS-M* on a 3 host system. We note that under high α values MLMS-M* generates significantly small amount excess compared to that of MLMS-M. For example, under the system load of 0.5, when α 1.7, MLMS-M generates approximately 300% more excess than MLMS-M*. Under these workload conditions, a 2-level MLMS-M* system outperforms 2-level MLMS-M by a factor of 2.5. Under very low α values, however, MLMS-M* generates more excess load than MLMS-M (this behaviour further discussed later in this section). For example, under the system load of 0.5, when α equals 0.9, MLMS-M generates 160% more excess than MLMS-M. Under these conditions a MLMS-M with 2-levels outperforms MLMS-M by a factor of 2.7.

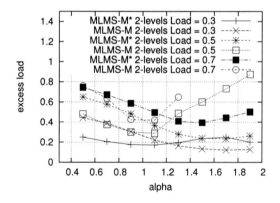

Fig. 7.17 Comparison of Excess Load : MLMS-M and MLMS-M*

7.7 MLMS-WC-M Policy

This section presents an extension of MLMS policy, called MLMS-WC-M (Multi-Level-Multi-Server Task Assignment Policy with Work-Conserving Migration). MLMS-WC-M is designed to distribute tasks in a cluster-based system that supports time sharing and work-conserving migration.

Cluster-based systems support two types of task migration, namely, non-work-conserving migration and work-conserving migration. Non-work-conserving migration does not require any state information to be transferred from the source host to the destination host and as a result cost of migration is minimal. The drawback of non-work-conserving migration is that it requires a task being migrated to be restarted from scratch at the destination node. This type of migration is typically accomplished via a remote invocation. Under the work-conserving migration the state information of the task is transferred from the source node to the destination node and the destination host resumes the execution of the task.

The functionality is as follows MLMS-WC-M (see Figure 7.18). Each has a designated time limit assigned to it. The designated time limit of ith Host is given by $Q_{(i,Ni)}$.

- Each newly arriving task, arrive at the dispatcher, and it is immediately dispatched to Host 1.
- Host 1 processes the task according to the multi-level time sharing policy (MLTP) described in section II-b.
- If the size of the task exceeds the designated time limit assigned to Host 1, i.e., $Q_{(1,N1)}$, the task is migrated to the next host. Otherwise the task departs the system from Host 1.
- Host 2 resumes the execution of the task and processes it in a similar manner using the MLTP.
- This process continues until the task is fully serviced, at which point the task departs the system.

We focus on negligible cost work-conserving migration where the tasks possess minimal state information. We assume that the arrival process into the system is Poisson. This is a reasonable assumption for many computer workloads (27). For modelling purposes, we assume that the arrival process from Host i to Host $i+1$ is Poisson. Much previous work is based on this assumption (25, 26, 64).

Analysis of MLMS-WC-M

Let us now consider the analysis of MLMS-WC-M. We use the notation given in Table 7.5 to describe the MLMS-WC-M. The aim is to obtain an expression for the expected waiting time in the system.

Obtaining the expected waiting time in the system (i.e. overall expected waiting time) involves, $E[W_i]$, the expected time of a task that spends time at Host i. $E[W_i]$ is computed by multiplying the expected waiting time of a task in the ith Host's j^{th} queue (i.e. $E[W_{(i,j)}]$) by the probability that the service time of a task is between $Q_{(i,j-1)}$ and $Q_{(i,j)}$, i.e, the fraction of tasks whose final destination is Host i's j^{th} queue.

Let $p_{(i,j)}$ be the fraction of tasks whose final destination is Host i's j^{th} queue. We obtain

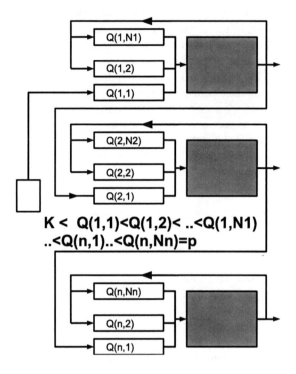

Fig. 7.18 MLMS-WC-M architecture

$$P_{(i,j)} = \int_{Q_{(i,j-1)}}^{Q_{(i,j)}} f(x)dx \qquad (7.61)$$

Let p_i be the fraction of tasks whose final destination is Host i. We obtain:

$$p_i = \int_{Q_{(i-1,N_{i-1})}}^{Q_{(i,N_i)}} f(x)dx \qquad (7.62)$$

Let $E[W_{(i,j)}]$ be expected waiting time of a task in i^{th} Host's j^{th} queue. We obtain

$$E[FT_{(i,j)}] = \frac{\lambda_{(i,1)}E[U_{(i,j)}^2] + \sum_{k=j+1}^{N_i}\Lambda_{(i,k)}E[T_{(i,k)}^2]}{2(1-\lambda_{(i,1)}E[U_{(i,j-1)}])(1-\lambda_{(i,1)}E[U_{(i,j)}])} + \frac{Q_{(i,j-1)}}{(1-\lambda_{(i,1)}E[U_{(i,j-1)}])} - Q_{(i,j-1)}$$

$$(7.63)$$

Note that $Q_{(i,j-1)}$ and $E[T_{(i,j)}]$ denote the total processing time up to i^{th} host's $j-1$ level and the expected processing time at i^{th} host's j^{th} level. $\lambda_{(i,1)}$ and $\Lambda_{(i,j)}$ in Equation 5 denote the arrival rate into i^{th} Host's 1st queue and i^{th} Host's j^{th} queue respectively. We obtain these as follows:

n	Number of hosts in the system
N_i	Number of levels at i^{th} Host
$f(x)$	Service time distribution of tasks (i.e. $B(k, p, \alpha)$)
k	Lower bound of the task size distribution
p	Upper bound of the task size distribution
p_i	Fraction of tasks whose final destination is Host i
$P_{(i,j)}$	Fraction of tasks whose final destination is Host i's j^{th} queue
λ	Outside task arrival rate into system
ρ	System load
α	Heavy-tailed parameter
$Q_{(i,j)}$	i^{th} Host's j^{th} cut-off
$T_{(i,j)}$	i^{th} Host's j^{th} simple processing time; the length of processing time that a task in the ith Host's j^{th} queue receives
$E[T_{(i,j)}]$	First moment of the distribution of $T_{(i,j)}$
$E[T_{(i,j)}^2]$	Second moment of the distribution of $T_{(i,j)}$
$U_{(i,j)}$	$= T_{(i,1)} + T_{(i,2)} + ... + T_{(i,j)}$ if the job returns to the system at least $j-1$ times; $= T_{(i,1)} + T_{(i,2)} + ... + T_{(i,k)}$ if the job returns to the system $k-1$ times, $k < j$
$G_{(i,j)}$	Probability distribution function of $U_{(i,j)}$
$E[U_{(i,j)}^k]$	k^{th} moment of $G_{(i,j)}$
$E[FT_{(i,j)}]$	expected flow-time of a task in i^{th} Host's j^{th} queue
$E[W_{(i,j)}]$	expected waiting time of a task in i^{th} Host's j^{th} queue
$E[W_i]$	Expected waiting time of a task that spends time at Host i
$E[W]$	Expected waiting time in the system

Table 7.5 MLMS-WC-M notation

$$\lambda_{(i,1)} = \lambda \left(1 - \int_k^{Q_{(i-1,N_{i-1})}} f(x)dx\right) \tag{7.64}$$

$$\Lambda_{(i,j)} = \lambda \left(1 - \int_k^{Q_{(i,j-1)}} f(x)dx\right) \quad j > 1 \tag{7.65}$$

$E[U_i^m]$ is given by

$$E[U_{(i,j)}^m] = \frac{\int_{Q_{(i-1,N_{i-1})}}^{Q_{(i,j)}} (x - Q_{(i-1,N_{i-1})})^m f(x)dx}{(1 - F(Q_{(i-1,N_{i-1})}))} + \frac{(Q_{(i,j)} - Q_{(i-1,N_{i-1})})^m (1 - F(Q_{(i,j)}))}{(1 - F(Q_{(i-1,N_{i-1})}))} \tag{7.66}$$

$E[U_i^m]$ conditions on the distribution of task's remaining size by considering the work already done, i.e, $Q_{(i-1,N_{i-1})}$.

Similarly, $E[T_{(i,j)}^m]$ given by

$$E[T_{(i,j)}^m] = \frac{\int_{Q_{(i,j-1)}}^{Q_{(i,j)}} (x - Q_{(i,j-1)})^m f(x)dx}{(1 - F(Q_{(i,j-1)}))} + \frac{(Q_{(i,j)} - Q_{(i,j-1)})^m (1 - F(Q_{(i,j)}))}{(1 - F(Q_{(i,j-1)}))} \tag{7.67}$$

Let $E[W_i]$ be the waiting of a task at Host i. We have:

$$E[W_i] = \sum_{j=1}^{N_i} E[W_{(i,j)}] \frac{p_{(i,j)}}{p_i} \tag{7.68}$$

We can now write an expression for the expected waiting time in the system (i.e. overall expected waiting time). Let n be the number of hosts in system and let $E[W]$ be the expected waiting time. $E[W]$ is given by

$$\begin{aligned} E[W] &= E[W_1]p_1 + (E[W_1] + E[W_2])p_2) \\ &\quad + \ldots + (E[W_1] + \ldots + E[W_n])p_n \end{aligned} \tag{7.69}$$

In this calculation, we have conditioned on the final destination of tasks. When the variability of processing requirements, the system load and the number of levels are fixed, $E[W]$ (Equation 7.69) is a function of $Q_{(1,1)}, Q_{(1,2)}, \ldots, Q_{(n,N_n)}$ where $k < Q_{(1,1)} < Q_{(1,2)} < \ldots < Q_{(n,N_n)} = p$. We compute these cut-offs so as to optimise the expected waiting time.

Performance Evaluation

The performance evaluation of MLMS-WC-M policy against the performance of four other task assignment policies is given here.

- TAGS (64) : Under the TAGS (64) an incoming task is immediately dispatched to the Host 1 in the system. The task is processed according the First-Come-First-Serve (FCFS) policy up to a maximum amount of time. If the task's processing requirement exceeds the time limit of Host 1, the task is killed and redirected to the Host 2. Otherwise the task departs the system from Host 1. The Host 2 restarts the task from scratch and processes it up the its maximum time limit. This process continues until the task is fully serviced, at which point the task departs the system. The expected waiting time under TAGS (64) is a function of number of hosts in the system (n), system load, cut-offs and variability in processing requirements (α). The cut-offs are computed so as to optimise the expected waiting time for a given system load, α and n. Note that it makes no sense to compare the performance of TAGS with MLMS-WC-M as TAGS it is a non-work conserving task assignment policy. It has been included here for different purposes.
- TAGS-WC (25, 64) : TAGS-WC is the work-conserving version of the TAGS. The original TAGS did not facilitate work-conserving migration. To make it comparable with MLMS-WC-M we introduce this special version of TAGS. As was done for TAGS, cut-offs for TAGS-WC are computed to optimise the expected waiting time for a given system load, α and n.
- Processor-Sharing (127) : This policy assigns tasks to hosts with an equal probability. Each host in the system processes task according to the processor sharing policy (PS). The expected waiting time of a task under processor sharing ($E[W]_{PS}$) is given by

$$E[W]_{PS} = \frac{E[X]}{1 - \lambda E[X]} \tag{7.70}$$

where $E[X]$ and λ denote the mean of the service time distribution and the arrival rate into a back-end host respectively. Since tasks are distributed with an equal probability, the arrival rates of tasks into back-end hosts are the same so are the expected waiting times.

- MLMS (98, 126): This policy assigns tasks to host with equal probability and each host processes tasks according to the MLTP. Cut-offs for MLTP are computed to optimise the expected waiting time. Since the arrival rates into all hosts are the same, all hosts have identical cut-offs (Note: We assume that the hosts have equal number of levels). In a MLTP system, the expected waiting time of a task waiting in i^{th} queue, $E[W_i]$, given by the following formula.

$$E[W_i] = E[FT_i] - E[T_i] - Q_{i-1} \tag{7.71}$$

where $E[FT_i]$ is the expected flow-time in i^{th} queue. $E[FT_i]$ is obtained using Equation 2 (Section II-b). To obtain the expected waiting of a task in the system, we simply multiply the expected waiting time in i^{th} queue by the probability that the task is processed at i^{th} level and then take the sum of these product terms.

$$E[W]_{MLTP} = \sum_{k=1}^{N} E[W_k] \int_{Q_{k-1}}^{Q_k} f(x)dx \tag{7.72}$$

Let $E[W]_{MLMS}$ be the expected waiting time of a task under MLMS. Since all hosts have equal number of levels and experience the same arrival rate;

$$E[W]_{MLMS} = E[W]_{MLTP} \tag{7.73}$$

Performance Evaluation for 2-Hosts System

This section provides an analytical comparison of MLMS-WC-M and the policies discussed in the previous section in a two host distributed system. It is worth noting that all the expected waiting time plots are presented on a log scale for the y-axis. Figure 7.19 depicts the results under the system loads of 0.3 (low), 0.5 (moderate) and 0.7 (high). The notation POLICY-N-x-L-y is used to describe a policy with x (e.g. 4) number of levels and y (e.g. 0.3) denotes the system load.

As we expected, the performance of all policies degrade as the system load increases. We note that under constant system load, the performance of policies tend to improve with increasing α. However, there is one exception to this, i.e, the TAGS. Notice that under the system load of 0.7, the expected waiting time of a task under the TAGS (64) decreases up to a certain α and then it begins to increase. Let this α be α_d. This behaviour of the TAGS can be explained as follows. Low α parameter indicates that there are very small number of tasks with very long processing requirements that constitutes to large fraction of the total workload. Under low α values only a small fraction of very large tasks are processed at Host 2. As α increases,

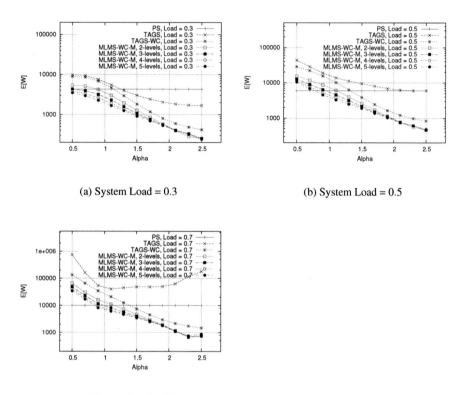

(a) System Load = 0.3   (b) System Load = 0.5

(c) System Load = 0.7

Fig. 7.19 Performance of MLMS-WC-M under various loads

very small number of tasks with very long processing requirements (that make up large fraction of the workload) decreases. As a result, more tasks are needed to be migrated to Host 2 in order to ensure that Host 1 does not get overloaded. This means that as α increases, the number of tasks that needed to be restarted from starch at Host 2 increases. This results in the load on Host 2 to increase and as a result expected waiting time increases. The value of α_d is determined by both the system load and the number of hosts in the system.

Note that the expected waiting time under Processor-Sharing does not depend on α. The expected waiting time of Processor-Sharing is only a function of the arrival rate/system load. We notice that under low system loads (0.3), the TAGS outperforms Processor-Sharing for a range of α values. However, under moderate and high system loads, the TAGS does not outperform the Processor-Sharing. The TAGS-WC, on the other hand, outperforms Processor-Sharing under all system loads for a range of α values. We note that the line representing Processor-Sharing intersects the line representing TAGS-WC when α is between 1 and 1.5. As the system load increases, there is a slight movement of this intersection point to the right direction.

Let us now consider the expected waiting time of a task under MLMS-WC-M. First, notice that it does not suffer from the problem that TAGS suffered, i.e, its performance does not degrade after certain α. Second, we note that MLMS-WC-M outperforms Processor-Sharing for a wide range α values. For example, under the system load of 0.5, when α equals 1.1 MLMS-WC-M (with 5 levels) outperforms Processor-Sharing by a factor of 2 while under the same system load, when α equals 2.5 MLMS-WC-M (with 5 levels) outperforms Processor-Sharing by a factor of 12. Processor-Sharing outperforms MLMS-WC-M only if α is very small.

Note that MLMS-WC-M outperforms TAGS-WC for all the scenarios considered. The highest improvement in the performance is obtained under high system loads and low α values. For example, under the system load of 0.7 when α equals 0.5, MLMS-WC-M (with 5 levels) outperforms TAGS-WC by a factor of 4. Under low α values, MLMS-WC-M performs significantly better than TAGS-WC even under low system loads. For example, under the system load of 0.3, when α equals 0.5 MLMS-WC-M outperforms TAGS-WC by a factor of 2.3. The factor of improvement in the expected waiting time for the MLMS-WC-M over TAGS-WC is minimal if α is close to 2.5.

Impact of levels

Figure 7.20 depicts the effect of number of levels on the expected waiting time. Similar behaviour is observed under low and high system loads. We note that the performance of MLMS-WC-M improves with increasing number of levels. For example, under the system load of 0.5, when α is equal to 0.5, MLMS-WC-M with 5 levels outperforms MLMS-WC-M with 2 levels by a factor of 1.5.

As we increase the number of levels, the variance of tasks' processing requirements decreases for each queue. This results in an improvement of expected waiting time of tasks with relatively small processing requirements leading to an improvement in the overall performance (Note: heavy-tailed distribution has many small tasks). However, the improvement in the performance is significant only between lower levels.

MLMS vs MLMS-WC-M

This section compares the performance of the MLMS with MLMS-WC-M. MLMS processes tasks according to MLTP policy at individual hosts. It does not support task migration between hosts. Figure 7.21 compares the performance of MLMS and MLMS-WC-M. We have considered a MLMS policy up to 10 levels and MLMS-WC-M up to 5 levels.

We note that MLMS-WC-M significantly outperforms MLMS for all the system loads considered. Even with large number of levels, MLMS does not outperform MLMS-WC-M. For example, under the system load of 0.5 when $\alpha = 0.5$, MLMS-WC-M with 2 levels outperforms MLMS with 10 levels by a factor of 24. Under

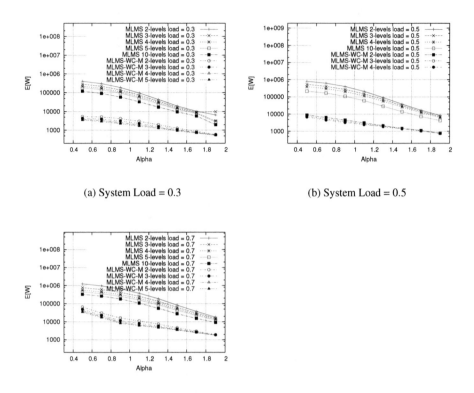

(a) System Load = 0.3   (b) System Load = 0.5

(c) System Load = 0.7

Fig. 7.20 MLMS-WC-M

the same conditions, MLMS-WC-M with 4 levels outperforms MLMS with 10 levels by a factor of 42. Clearly, the 2-level variance reduction model has resulted in significant performance improvements.

Performance Evaluation for 3-Hosts System

This section compares the performance of MLMS-WC-M in 2 and 3 host systems. For the sake of brevity, we fix the number of levels at 5. The figure plots the performance of MLMS-WC-M under the system loads of 0.5. Note that due to space limitations results under other workloads are not presented. We note that MLMS-WC-M performs better in a 3 host system compared to that of a 2 host system (assuming that the system load is fixed). The reason for this is as follows. When we increase the number of hosts from 2 to 3, both $E[W_1]$ and $E[W_2]$ tend to improve because the variability of processing requirements decreases at Host 1 and Host 2 (Note : $E[W_i]$ denote the expected waiting time of a task that spends time at Host i). This implies that tasks with relatively short processing requirements are processed faster in a 3

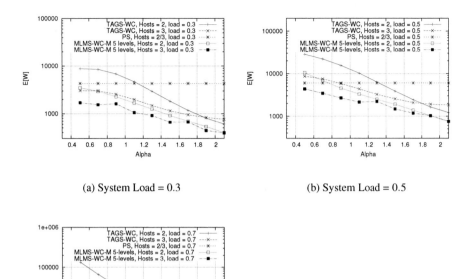

(a) System Load = 0.3   (b) System Load = 0.5

(c) System Load = 0.7

Fig. 7.21 2/3-Hosts System

host system compared to that of a 2 host system. In heavy-tailed distributions, there are many tasks with short processing requirements and improving waiting time of these short tasks improves the overall performance. The highest improvement in the performance is obtained under low α values and high system loads. For example, under the system load of 0.7 when α equals 0.5, MLMS-WC-M performs 2.5 times better in a 3 host system compared to that of a 2 host system. Under low and moderate system loads there is significant improvement in the performance if α is not very high (i.e. close to 2.5).

In section IV-A we noted that in a 2 host system, Processor-Sharing outperformed MLMS-WC-M under the system loads of 0.5 and 0.7 for very low α values. We note that in a 3 host system MLMS-WC-M outperforming Processor-Sharing under the system load of 0.5 even under very low α values. For example, under the system load of 0.5, when α equals 0.5 MLMS-WC-M with 5 levels outperforms Processor-Sharing by a factor of 1.3. The magnitude of this performance improvement grows as α approaches 2.5.

More than 3 Hosts

This section briefly investigates the performance of MLMS-WC-M for more than 3 hosts. Figure 7.22 illustrates the performance of MLMS-WC-M under the system load of 0.5 in 2, 3 and 4 host system. Clearly, an increase in the number of hosts has resulted in an improvement in the performance. The reason for this improvement is explained in the previous section. The highest improvement in the performance is obtained under low α values. As α increases, the improvement in the performance decreases. Moreover, as the number of hosts increases, the rate at which the performance improves decreases. For example, under the system load of 0.5 when α equals 0.5, MLMS-WC-M (with 5 levels) performs 2.5 times better in a 3 host system compared to that of a 2 host system. Under the same conditions, MLMW-WC-M (with 5 levels) performs only 1.5 times better in a 4 host system compared to that of a 3 host system.

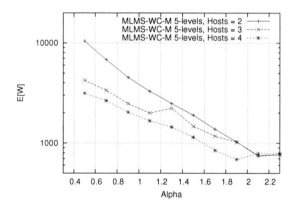

Fig. 7.22 Impact of hosts

7.8 Conclusion

This chapter provided a detailed performance analysis of time sharing task assignment policies. Our analysis assumed heavy-tailed workload distributions because heavy-tailed distributions have been proven to represent many realistic computer workloads. We considered traditional task assignment models and advanced task assignment models. The advanced task assignment models were based on MLTP policy. Multi-level time sharing was used due to two reasons. First it has the ability improve the performance under distributions with the property of decreasing failure rate. Second it can schedule tasks with unknown processing requirements. MLMS outperformed TAGS under certain traffic conditions while MLMS-M outperformed TAGS for the all the scenarios considered. Similarly MLMS-WC-M outperformed

TAGS-WC for the all the scenarios considered. The most significant performance improvement is seen under high task size variabilities and workloads. The factor of improvement in MLMS-M/MLMS-WC-M over TAGS/TAGS-WC depends on the variability of traffic, the system load, the number of levels MLTP has and the number of hosts. MLMS-M* was a variant of MLMS-M and it outperformed MLMS-M and TAGS under specific workload conditions. When all other factors are constant, an increase in the number of levels results in an improvement in the performance (for all policies considered). However, the rate at which the performance improves, decreases with the number of levels. In the case of MLMS-M an increase in the number of hosts does not always improve the performance. However, in MLMS-WC-M the performance always improved with the number of hosts.

Chapter 8
Conclusion

"I paint objects as I think them, not as I see them."

Pablo Picasso

Web Services are quickly becoming a strategic technology in organisations of all sizes, thanks to Web Services's promise of interoperability between technologies and platforms, and ease of development and deployment. As organisations spend more time and money investigating how best to leverage Web Services and its enabling technologies, they should be aware of the strengths and limitations of the technology specifically those related to performance and scalability, interoperability, and security.

This book looked at performance of Web services from a *holistic* perspective, where it addressed both the communication (e.g. transmission of requests through SOAP) and the execution (e.g. scheduling of of operations at the server side) aspects. From the SOAP perspective, improving its performance is important to allow the widespread deployment of Web services in different environments, especially in low bandwidth networks. To cope with the high network traffic created by SOAP messages and low bandwidth availability, new techniques must be used to reduce the amount of traffic so that SOAP can perform well in limited bandwidth environments. This book described a similarity-based SOAP multicast protocol to reduce network traffic. An alternative SOAP-over-UDP binding was also examined.

From the server perspective, this book looked at scalability by replicating the sever so better performance can be obtained for the execution of operations. Both heavy load and the variation of the task size are the major issues when attempting to improve performance. Classical assumptions for task size (e.g. exponential distribution) are not applicable for Web Services, as Internet traffic is proven to be heavy tail (for the task sizes). This therefore makes scheduling traditional approaches, like RR-Round Robbin, out of date. New approaches need to take into account the specific nature of Internet traffic. Task-based assignment policies smartly assign task so to reduce the various in the queues of servers, therefore reducing the waiting time of tasks.

What was presented in this book?

This book described advanced solutions that deal with the optimising of both SOAP engine and sever task allocation. Here is a summary:

- SOAP Binding Benchmark. Firstly, a benchmark suite of SOAP bindings in wireless environments was proposed and implemented. The experimental results reveal that HTTP binding, which is the most often used in Web service applications, exposes high protocol overhead in wireless environments due to the slow start, connection establishments and packet acknowledgements. On the other hand, UDP binding has lower overhead, hence reduces response time and increases total throughput. Experimental results show that UDP binding can reduce message size by between 30% to 50% compared to HTTP binding. Such reduction leads to a huge saving in transmission cost (50%–75%) and a significant increase in throughput (40%–78%).
- Similarity-based SOAP Multicast Protocol. The SOAP multicast technique, called SMP, exploits on the similarity of SOAP messages to efficiently multicast SOAP messages to a large number of clients requesting similar operations of the same service. SMP takes advantage of the similarity of SOAP messages' data structures and combines messages of similar content in one message. In this way, common data structures or values are not repeated and are sent only once, resulting in reduced network traffic. While previous studies utilised this feature of SOAP to improve the processing time of serialisation and de-serialisation, those results were noticeable only at the server or client side and did not affect the network. Through experiments, it was found that the total traffic over a network can be reduced by 35% to 70% if SMP is used instead of unicast.

  A model was also presented to measure the similarity of outgoing SOAP messages, so that the server can determine if messages have enough common XML structure or payload values to compensate the cost required to process SMP aggregated messages. In addition, the SOAP indexing technique enables fast merging and splitting of SMP messages. Instead of a full SOAP message, an indexed version of the message, which is composed of data type IDs referenced back to the WSDL document, positions of each node in the SOAP message and the node values, is sent. SOAP messages' index representation further reduces the message size because of the omission of full XML tag names. The index representation also improves the grouping of common and distinctive data in SMP messages.
- SOAP Multicast Protocol to Minimize SOAP Network Traffic. This book described routing algorithms for traffic-constrained SMP (called tc-SMP), so that the network traffic can be minimised. Two algorithms, greedy and incremental, are described and extended from SMP to solve the tc-SMP problem. Tc-SMP algorithms offer better performance than SMP for SOAP multicast traffic. Tc-SMP differs from SMP in the way that a source-routing algorithm is used under tc-SMP for delivering aggregated messages instead of OSPF. Test results show that tc-SMP outperforms SMP by 10–25% further reduction in network traffic.

The greedy tc-SMP approach aims to minimise the total traffic in a tc-SMP tree every time a new client is added to the tree. However, this approach does not guarantee that the greedy tc-SMP always perform better than the original SMP. The incremental approach firstly establishes an SMP tree and iteratively improves this SMP tree. Using this approach, incremental tc-SMP never under-performs SMP. Experiments show that incremental tc-SMP is better than greedy tc-SMP in general but there is a small cost in response time. Two heuristics were also described for the tc-SMP algorithms: one is based on message size and the other is based on similarity with previous messages. The heuristic based on the similarity between messages to new clients and messages to existing clients gives a gain of around 3 percent over tc-SMP without any heuristic. The message size-based heuristic achieves negligible performance gain.

- A series of advanced task assignment policies: TAGS (Task Assignment by Guessing Size), TAGS-WC (TAGS with Work Conserving), TAPTF (Task Assignment based on Prioritising Traffic Flows), TAPTF-WC (TAPTF with Work Conserving), and MTTMELL (Multi-Tier Task Assignment with Minimum Excess Load) Policy. Some of these policies were designed as extensions of TAGS to address various issues, including reduction of excess load as well as the reduction of the variance in the queues. By avoiding restarting tasks, the new policies do reduce the excess load. Also by introducing priority queues for the re-started tasks, the variance of task size can be reduced in the queues; and therefore better performance could be obtained.

- Multi-level Time Sharing (MLTP) Policy. This book investigated time sharing under more general setting where a amount of time service time (quantum) allocated on levels using a random variable. Each level under MLTP has a designated time limit (cut-off) associated with it. A good optimisation of the quanta for the various queues does provide substantial performance results. Detailed comparison with size-based approaches (like TAGS) is provided and discussed.

How good are the solutions described?

Through extensive experiments for the section related to SOAP benchmarking, it is shown that using HTTP or TCP binding for SOAP leads to significantly higher overhead than using the UDP binding. For a large number of requests of small to medium size messages, SOAP-over-UDP is about 4–5 times faster than SOAP-over-HTTP and around 3–3.5 times faster than SOAP-over-TCP. Specifically, the throughput of UDP binding is approximately 6 times higher for small messages, and 3 times higher for large messages, than the HTTP binding.

Detailed mathematical models of unicast, traditional IP multicast, SMP and tc-SMP were discussed. These models provide an insight into the properties of different routing protocols, and enable accurate comparisons to be made between them according to important measurement metrics such as total network traffic and average response time. Experimental evaluations have also been carried out to verify the accuracy of the theoretical models. The results obtained from the experiments fall into the boundaries of the analytical models, therefore the correctness of the models is confirmed.

SMP's main advantage is that it reduces the traffic generated over a network by 50–70% compared to unicast in large networks (over 100 clients) with large message payload (over 100Kb) at a cost of small increase in response time. There is a 3 time reduction in traffic compared to 1.5 time increase in response time — which is acceptable in Web service applications that handle a large amount of data in limited bandwidth environments, such as wireless networks, and do not have strong constraints on end-to-end delay.

The traffic-constrained similarity-based SOAP multicast problem is known to be NP-hard. The proposed greedy and incremental tc-SMP algorithms provide a good solution and operate in polynomial time with a complexity of $O(n(m+nlogn))$ where n is the number of nodes and m is the number of links in a network. Experiments have shown that tc-SMP algorithms outperform SMP, a reduction of around 30% in traffic compared to SMP, at a cost of 10% increase in response time. As the network size increases, the reduction in network traffic under tc-SMP increases even more than under SMP, while the performance penalty still remains comparatively small. On average, the incremental tc-SMP algorithm provides a greater reduction (around 5 percent) in total traffic, but takes a little more time (less than 2 percent increase in average response time) time than the greedy algorithm.

For the server side performance, the various extensions of TAGS (i.e. TAGS-WC, TAPTF, APTF-WC, MTTMELL) have lead to substantial performance improvement. By avoiding re-starting the tasks from scratch, TAGS-WC can make improvement up to 10% because of the reduction in excess load of TAGS. TAPTF goes further than TAGS-WS and introduces prioritisation in the traffic by distinguishing between two classes of tasks: restarted tasks and originals task (i.e those that came from dispatcher). This induces a reduction of task variance in the queues, and therefore substantially improving the waiting time of tasks. MTTMEL extends TAPTF by introducing multiple tiers that have one or more hosts, where each tier has a processing time limit assigned to it and the hosts in a particular tier only process tasks up to the time limit assigned to the tier. The last chapter added the process sharing feature to the scheduling and clearly illustrated how a proper setting of quanta can further improve performance in each server. Finally these various extensions of TAGS demonstrated the importance of dealing with server side optimisation, and also showed the substantial improvements in the execution of TAGS requests.

What could be done next?

Even though this book provided a good inside of the issue of performance in Web services, more work still needs to done on SMP, tc-SMP, an MTTMEL.

An experiment on the use of UDP binding for SMP or tc-SMP protocol will be an interesting study. The low protocol overhead of UDP binding which is due to the absence of connection establish and tear-down processes and of strict flow control mechanism offers a promise to accelerate the overall processing time in SMP and tc-SMP. However, real experiments are needed to validate this theory. Future work will involve researching better heuristic algorithms to further improve performance. Considerations of other quality of service parameters (such as delay bounds and bandwidth requirements) for each client may also be incorporated into the tc-SMP routing algorithm.

Another important work is the extension SMP and tc-SMP to support communication from different servers. Currently SMP or tc-SMP only supports aggregations of SOAP messages generated from the same service provider. Messages created from the same service have the same set of data type definitions in the WSDL service description, therefore merging and splitting of these messages are easier than doing the same process on messages that have different schemas. It is a challenge to find the syntactic similarity of messages from various providers. However if this can be done, and intermediate routers that are equipped with SMP layer can integrate messages from different sources together and sent only the union of those (all repeated sections are avoided), the network traffic will be considerably reduced. SOAP will become more dominantly viable to many business applications.

When a service provider can provide different SOAP frameworks, conventional SOAP, SMP, tc-SMP, UDP binding and reliable UDP binding, a negotiation mechanism can be developed to allow clients to negotiate with the server their preferred SOAP representation depending on their performance requirements. For example, client applications that have a strict delay requirement and no specific constraint on bandwidth or reliability can request to use SOAP implementation that uses UDP binding. Applications that are constrained on low total network traffic and no requirement in response time could use SMP or tc-SMP in their communications. The negotiation uses a conventional SOAP message, so that two endpoints can revert to the SOAP message based Web Service communication, if they fail to negotiate.

The server side optimisation has highlighted the importance of taking into account the realistic assumptions of Internet traffic. Different policies were described to deal with the server queue/s (so to reduce the variance). However still a lot of work needs also to be done at the dispatcher so to complement the processing efforts done at the queues. The dispatcher could, for example, build up profiles on the various tasks so more precise information can be built (e.g. task size, frequency). The dispatcher can them smartly allocate tasks by their profiles.

References

[1] ADT: A Little Action on Java-ready Phones. Application Development Trends, 2005. http://www.adtmag.com/article.asp?id=11017.

[2] Abu-Ghazaleh, N., Lewis, M.: Differential Deserialization for Optimized SOAP Performance. Proceedings of International Conference for High Performance Computing, Networking, and Storage, pp. 21-31, 2005.

[3] Abu-Ghazaleh, N., Lewis, M., Govindaraju, M.: Differential Serialization for Optimized SOAP Performance. Proceedings of the 13th IEEE International Symposium on High Performance Distributed Computing, pp. 55–64, 2004.

[4] Abu-Ghazaleh, N., Lewis, M.: Differential Deserialization for Optimized SOAP Performance. Proceedings of the 2005 ACM/IEEE Conference on Super-Computing, pp. 21–31, 2005.

[5] Abu-Ghazaleh, N., Govindaraju, M., Lewis, M.: Optimizing Performance of Web Services with Chunk-Overlaying and Pipelined-Send. Proceedings of the International Conference on Internet Computing, pp. 482–485, 2004.

[6] Allman, M., Paxson, V., Stevens, W.: TCP Congestion Control. RFC 2581 Internet EngineeringTask Force (IETF). http://tools.ietf.org/html/rfc2581, 1999.

[7] Alonso, G., Casati, F., Kuno, H., Machiraju, V.: Web Services: Concepts, Architecture and Applications. Springer Verlag, 2004.

[8] Andras Varga, A.: OMNet++ Discrete Event Simulation System. http://www.omnetpp.org, 2006.

[9] Angelen. R: gSOAP: C/C++ Web Services and Clients. http://www.cs.fsu.edu/~engelen/soap.html, 2003.

[10] Apache Software Foundation: Web Services Axis. http://ws.apache.org/axis, 2007.

[11] Apache Software Foundation: Apache Tomcat. http://tomcat.apache.org/, 2007.

[12] Apte, N., Deutsch, K., Jain, R.: Wireless SOAP: Optimizations for Mobile Wireless Web Services. Proceedings of the 14th International Conference on World Wide Web (WWW), pp. 1178–1179, 2005.

[13] Arlitt, M.F., Williamson, C.L.: Web Server Workload Characterization: the Search for Invariants. IEEE/ACM Transactions on Networking, 5(5):631-645, 1997.

[14] Awduche, D., Chiu, A., Elwalid, A., Widjaja, I., Xiao, X.: Overview and Principles of Internet Traffic Engineering. Internet Engineering Task Force, RFC 3272, 2002. http://www.ietf.org/rfc/rfc3272.txt.

[15] Bansal, V., Dalton, A.: A Performance Analysis of Web Services on Wireless PDA. Technical Report, Duke University (Department of Computer Science), 2002. http://www.cs.duke.edu/vkb/advnw/project/PDAWebServices.pdf.

[16] Barford , P., Bestavros, A., Bradley, A., Crovella, M.: Changes in Web Client Access Patterns: Characteristics and Caching Implications. Kluwer International Journal on World Wide Web, 2 (1-2): 15–28, 1999.

[17] Barford, P., Bestavros, A., Bradley, A., Crovella, M.E.: Changes in Web Client Access Patterns: Characteristics and Caching Implications. International Journal on World Wide Web, Special Issue on "Characterization and Performance Evaluation", 2:15-28, 1999.

[18] BEA Systems Inc., Lexmark and Microsoft Corporation Inc., Ricoh: SOAP-over-UDP Specification. `http://ftpna2.bea.com/pub/downloads/SOAP-over-UDP.pdf`, 2004.

[19] Bellman, R.: On a Routing Problem. Quarterly of Applied Mathematics, 16(1): 87–90, 1958.

[20] Bilorusets, R., Box, D., Cabrera, L.F, Davis, D., Ferguson, D.: Web Services Reliable Messaging Protocol (WS-ReliableMessaging). `http://msdn.microsoft.com/library/en-us/dnglobspec/html/WS-ReliableMessaging.pdf`, 2005.

[21] Boivie, R., Feldman, N., Metz, C.: Small Group Multicast: A New Solution for Multicasting on the Internet. IEEE Internet Computing, 4(3): 75–79, 2000.

[22] Boudani, A., Guitton, A., Cousin, B.: GXcast: Generalized Explicit Multicast Routing Protocol. Proceedings of the 9th International Symposium on Computers and Communications, pp. 1012–1017, 2004.

[23] Boudani, A., Cousin, B.: SEM: A New Small Group Multicast Routing Protocol. Proceedings of the 10th International Conference on Telecommunications, 1:450–455, 2003.

[24] Breslau, L., Cao, C., Fan, L., Phillips, G., Shenker, S.: Web Caching and Zipf-like Distributions: Evidence and Implications. Proceedings of the IEEE Conference on Computer 1:126–134, 1999.

[25] Broberg, J., Tari, Z., Zeephongsekul, P.: Task Assignment with Work-Conserving Migration. Elsevier Journal on Parallel and Distributed Computing (JPDC), 32(11-12):808–830, 2006.

[26] Broberg, J., Tari, Z., Zeephongsekul, P.: Task Assignment based on Prioritising Traffic Flows. Proceedings of the International Conference on Principles of Distributed Systems, pp. 15-17, 2004.

[27] Cao, J., Cleveland, W.S., Lin, D., Sun, D.X.: On the Nonstationarity of Internet Traffic. Proceedings ACM SIGMETRICS International Conference on Measurement and Modeling of Computer Systems, pp. 102-112, 2001.

[28] Chakraborty, C., Chakraborty, G., Pornavalai, C., Shiratori, N.: Optimal Routing for Dynamic Multipoint Connection. European Transactions on Telecommunication, 10(2):183–189, 1999.

[29] Chen, L., Nath, R.: A Framework for Mobile Business Applications. International Journal of Mobile Communications, 2(4):368–381, 2004.

[30] Chen, M., Zhang, D., Zhou, L.: Providing Web Services to Mobile Users: the Architecture Design of an M-Service Portal. International Journal of Mobile Communications, 3(1):1–18, 2005.

[31] Chen, S., Nahrstedt, K.: An Overview of Quality-of-Service Routing for the Next Generation High-speed Networks: Problems and Solutions. IEEE Networks Magazine, Special Issue on Transmission and Distribution of Digital Video, 12(6):64–79, 1998.

[32] Chen, S., Nahrstedt, K.: A Distributed Quality-of-Service Routing in Ad-Hoc Networks. IEEE Journal on Selected Areas in Communications, 17(8):1488–1505, 1999.

[33] Chen, S., Nahrstedt, K.: A Distributed Quality-of-Service Routing in Ad-Hoc Networks. IEEE Journal on Selected Areas in Communications, 17(8):1488–1505, 1999.

[34] Chakraborty, D., Chakraborty, G., Shiratori, N.: A Dynamic Multicast Routing Satisfying Multiple QoS Constraints. International Journal of Network Management, John Wiley & Sons, Inc., 13(5):321–335, 2003.

[35] Chiu, K., and Govindaraju, M., Bramley, R.: Investigating the Limits of SOAP Performance for Scientific Computing. Proceedings of the 11th IEEE International Symposium on High Performance Distributed Computing (HPDC), pp. 246–255, 2002.

[36] Cobham, A.: Priority Assignment in Waiting Line Problems. Journal of Operational Research Society American, 2:7076, 1954.

[37] Cormen, T.H., Leiserson, C.E., Rivest, R.L., Stein, C.: Introduction to Algorithms. MIT Press and McGraw-Hill, 2:595–601, 2001.

[38] Damiani, E., et al.: The APPROXML Tool Demonstration. Proceedings of the 8th International Conference on Extending Database Technology (EDBT), 753–755, 3002.

[39] Davis, A., Zhang, D.: A Comparative Study of DCOM and SOAP. Proceedings of the 4th IEEE International Symposium on Multimedia Software Engineering, 48–56, 2002,

[40] Davis, D., Parashar, M.: Latency Performance of SOAP Implementations. Proceedings of the 2nd IEEE/ACM International Symposium on Cluster Computing and the Grid, pp. 407–413, 2002.

[41] Devaram, K., Andresen, D.: SOAP Optimization via Parameterized Client-Side Caching. Proceedings of the 2nd IEEE/ACM International Symposium on Cluster Computing and the Grid, pp. 439–312, May 2002.

[42] Dewey, M.: Dewey Decimal Classification. In: A Classification and Subject Index for Cataloguing and Arranging the Books and Pamphlets of a Library. Kingsport Press, 2004. http:www.gutenberg.org/etext/12513.

[43] Doar M., Leslie, I.: How Bad is Naive Multicast Routing? Proceedings of the 12th Annual Joint Conference of the IEEE Computer and Communications Societies, Networking: Foundation for the Future, 1:82–89, 1993.

[44] Dorneles, C., et al.: Measuring Similarity Between Collection of Values. Proceedings of the 6th ACM Annual International Workshop on Web information and Data Management, 56–63, 2004.

[45] Englander, R.: Java and SOAP. Chapter 4 (RPC-Style Services), O'Reilly and Associates, 2002.

[46] Eppstein, D.: Finding the k Shortest Paths. SIAM Journal on Computing, 28(2):652-673, 1998.

[47] Fell, S: PocketSOAP. http://www.pocketsoap.com/, 2004.

[48] Feng, G., Makki, K., Pissinou, N.: Efficient Implementations of Bounded Shortest Multicast Algorithm. Proceedings of the 11th International Conference on Computer Communications and Networks, pp. 312–317, 2002.

[49] Feng, H., Misra, V.: Mixed Scheduling Disciplines for Network Flows. ACM SIGMETRICS Performance Evaluation Review, 31(2):36-39, 2003.

[50] Fenner, W.: RFC 2236 Internet Group Management Protocol, Version 2. Internet EngineeringTask Force (IETF). `ftp://ftp.isi.edu/in-notes/rfc2236.txt`, 1997.

[51] Fernandez, M., Malhotra, A., Marsh, J., Nagy, M., Walsh, M.: XQuery 1.0 and XPath 2.0 Data Model (XDM). World Wide Web Consortium (W3C), January 2007. `http://www.w3.org/TR/xpath-datamodel/`.

[52] Ferris C. and Williams S.: SOAP Underlying Protocol Binding. `http://www.w3.org/2000/xp/Group/1/10/12/Binding_Framework_Proposal`, 2001.

[53] Fox, G., Pallickara, S.: JMS Compliance in the Narada Event Brokering System. Proceedings of the 2002 International Conference on Internet Computing, 2:391–397, 2002.

[54] Ganesan, P., Garcia-Molina, H., Widom, J.: Exploiting Hierarchical Domain Structure to Compute Similarity. ACM Transactions on Information Systems, 21(1):64-93, 2003.

[55] Gisolfi, D.: Web Services Architecture, Part 3 −− Is Web services the reincarnation of CORBA? IBM, 2001. `http://www.ibm.com/developerworks/webservices/library/ws-arc3/`.

[56] Gryazin, E.A., Seppala, O.: SOAP and CORBA Productivity Comparison for Resource-Limited Mobile Devices. Proceedings of the IASTED International Conference Software Engineering, pp. 707–712, 2004.

[57] Guido, G., Ralf, B.: Performance of mobile Web Service Access using the Wireless Application Protocol (WAP). Proceedings of the 5th World Wireless Congress, pp. 427–432, 2004.

[58] Gudgin, M., Hadley, M., Mendelsohn, N., Moreau, J-J., Nielsen, H.F.: SOAP Version 1.2 Part 1: Messaging Framework. World Wide Web Consortium (W3C), April 2007. `http://www.w3.org/TR/soap12-part1/`.

[59] Gudgin, M., Mendelsohn, N., Nottingham, M., Ruellan, H.: SOAP Message Transmission Optimization Mechanism. World Wide Web Consortium (W3C), 2005. `http://www.w3.org/TR/soap12-mtom/`.

[60] Gudgin, M., Mendelsohn, N., Nottingham, M., Ruellan, H.: XML-binary Optimized Packaging. World Wide Web Consortium (W3C), 2005. `http://www.w3.org/TR/xop10/`.

[61] Han, B., Jia , W., Shen, J., Man-Ching Yuen, M.-C.: Context-Awareness in Mobile Web Services. Proceedings of Parallel and Distributed Processing and Applications, Springer, pp. 519–528, 2004.

[62] Harchol-Balter, M., Crovella, M.E., Murta, C.D.: On Choosing a Task Assignment Policy for a Distributed Server System. Journal of Parallel Distributed Computing (JPDC), 59(2):204-228, 1999.

[63] Harchol-Balter, M.: Task Assignment with Unknown Duration. Proceedings of the The 20th International Conference on Distributed Computing Systems (ICDCS), pp. 214-223, 2000.

[64] Harchol-Balter, M.: Task Assignment with Unknown Duration. Journal of the ACM, 49(2):260–288, 2002.

[65] Harchol-Balter, M., Crovella, M.E., Murt, C.D: On Choosing a Task Assignment Policy for a Distributed Server System. Proceedings of the 10th International Conference on Modelling Techniques and Tools, pp. 231-242, 1998.

[66] Haustein, S., Seigel, J.: kSOAP: An open source SOAP for the kVM. http://ksoap2.sourceforge.net/, 2003.

[67] Haustein, S.: kXML. http://kxml.sourceforge.net/, 2005.

[68] Head, M., Govindaraju, M., Slominski, A., et al.:A Benchmark Suite for SOAP-based Communication in Grid Web Services. Proceedings of International Conference for High Performance Computing, Networking, and Storage, 19–31, 2005.

[69] Horstmann, M., Kirtland, M.: DCOM Architecture. Microsoft Corporation Inc, 1997. urlhttp://msdn2.microsoft.com/en-us/library/ms809311.aspx.

[70] Hwang, F.K., Richards, D.S, Winter, P.: The Steiner Tree Problem. Elsevier, North-Holland, 1992.

[71] Jaccard, P.: Jaccard Index. Bulletin del la Société Vaudoisedes Sciences Naturelles, 37:241–272, 1901.

[72] Kendall, D.G.: Stochastic Processes Occurring in the Theory of Queues and their Analysis by the Method of the Imbedded Markov Chain. Journal of the Annals of Mathematical Statistics, 24(3):338–354,1953.

[73] Kohlhoff, C., Steele, R.: Evaluating SOAP for High Performance Business Applications: Real-Time Trading Systems. Proceedings of World Wide Web (WWW), pp. 262-270, 2003.

[74] Kleinrock, L.: Queuing Systems Volume 11. John Wiley and Sons, 1976.

[75] Khintchine, A.Y.: Mathematical Theory of a Stationary Queue.. Matematicheskii Sbornik 39 (4): 7384, 1932.

[76] Kompella, V., Pasquale, J., Polyzos, G.: Two Distributed Algorithms for Multicasting Multimedia Information. Proceedings of the 2nd International Conference on Computer Communications and Networks, pp. 343–349, 1993.

[77] Laux, A., Martin, L.: XUpdate Working Draft. http://xmldb-org.sourceforge.net/xupdate/xupdate-wd.html, 2000.

[78] Lee, S., Fox, G.: Wireless Reliable Messaging Protocol for Web Services (WS-WRM. Proceedings of the IEEE International Conference on Web Services, pp. 350–357, 2004,

[79] Levenshtein, V.I.: Binary Codes Capable of Correcting Deletions, Insertions and Reversals. Journal on Cybernetics and Control Theory, 10(8): 707–710, 1966.

[80] Lu, W., Chiu, K., Gannon, D.: Building a Generic SOAP Framework over Binary XML. Proceedings of the 15th IEEE International Symposium on High Performance Distributed Computing (HPDC), pp. 195–203, 2006.

[81] Ma, Y., Chbeir, R.: Content and Structure Based Approach For XML Similarity. Proceedings of the 5th International Conference on Computer and Information Technology, pp. 136–140, 2005.

[82] Marshak, D.S.: Sun Java System Platform and Architecture and Java Web Services Infrastructure Enables Easy Access to Government Services. Sun Microsystems Inc., February 2004. http://www.sun.com/service/about/success/gta_p2.html.

[83] Microsoft Corporation Inc: Thomson Financial: Cutting-Edge Financial Software Puts Asset Managers in Control. http://www.microsoft.com/casestudies/casestudy.aspx?casestudyid=200352, November 2006.

[84] Microsoft Corporation Inc: Danske Bank: Danish Bank Uses Visual Studio .NET, Web Services to Generate New Revenue Sources. http://www.microsoft.com/casestudies/search.aspx?keywords=danske, February 2003.

[85] Mitra, N., et al.: SOAP Version 1.2 Part 0: Primer. World Wide Web Consortium (W3C), April 2007. http://www.w3.org/TR/soap12-part0/.

[86] Mokbel, M., Elhaweet, W., Elderini, M.: An Efficient Algorithm for Shortest Path Multicast Routing Under Delay and Delay Variation Constraints. Proceedings of the Symposium on Performance Evaluation of Computer and Telecommunication Systems (SPECTS), pp. 190–196, 2000.

[87] Mouat, A.: XML Diff and Patch Utilities. http://diffxml.sourceforge.net/docs/docs.html, 2002.

[88] Object Management Group (OMG): IIOP - OMG's Internet Inter-ORB Protocol - A Brief Description. http://www.omg.org/news/whitepapers/iiop.htm, 2007.

[89] Oh, S., Fox, G.: HHFR: A new architecture for Mobile Web Services: Principle and Implementations. Technical Report, Indiana University, Community Grids Laboratory, 2005. http://grids.ucs.indiana.edu/ptliupages/publications/HHFR_ohsangy.pdf.

[90] Papazoglou, M.P.: Web Services: Principles and Technology. Prentice Hall, 207.

[91] Pendarakis, D., Shi, S., Verma, D., Waldvogel M.: ALMI: An Application Level Multicast Infrastructure. Proceedings of the 3rd USENIX Symposium on Internet Technologies and Systems, pp. 49–60, 2001.

[92] Perepletchikov, M., Ryan, C.: A Controlled Experiment for Evaluating the Impact of Coupling on the Maintainability of Service-Oriented Software. IEEE Transactions on Software Engineering (TSE), 37(4):449 - 465, 2010.

[93] Perepletchikov, M., Ryan, C., Tari, Z.: The Impact of Service Cohesion on the Analysability of Service-Oriented Software. IEEE Transactions on Services Computing (TSC), pp. 89-103, April, 2010.

[94] Pollaczek, F.: ber eine Aufgabe der Wahrscheinlichkeitstheorie. Mathematische Zeitschrift, 32: 64100, 1930.

[95] Prim, R.: Shortest Connection Networks and Some Generalizations. Bell System Technical Journal, 36:1389–1401, 1957.

[96] Maedche, A., Staab, S.: Comparing Ontologies — Similarity Measures and a Comparison Study. Internal Report No. 408, Institute AIFB, University of Karlsruhe (Germany), 2001.

[97] Jayasinghe, M., Tari, Z., Zeephongsekul, P.: A Scalable Multi-tier Task Assignment Policy With Minimum Excess Load. Proceedings of International Conference on Computers and Communications (ISCC), pp. 913-918, 2010.

[98] Jayasinghe, M., Tari, Z., Zeephongsekul, P.: Performance Analysis of Multi-level Time Sharing Task Assignment Policies on Cluster-based Systems. IEEE International Conference on Cluster Computing (IEEE Cluster), 2010.

[99] Levitin, A: Introduction to the Design and Analysis of Algorithms. Addison Wesley, 2nd Edition, 2007.

[100] Liang, W., Yokota, H.: A Path-sequence Based Discrimination for Subtree Matching in Approximate XML Joins. Proceedings of the 22nd IEEE International Conference on Data Engineering (ICDE) Workshops, pp. 116-123, 2006.

[101] Liang, W., Yokota, H.: LAX: An Efficient Approximate XML Join Based on Clustered Leaf Nodes for XML Data Integration. In: Database: Enterprise, Skills and Innovation, Springer, 3567: 82–97, 2005.

[102] Liu, X., Deters, R.: An Efficient Dual Caching Strategy for Web Service-enabled PDAs. Proceedings of the 22nd Annual ACM Symposium on Applied Computing, pp. 788-794, 2007.

[103] Lu, J., Ling, T.W., Chan, C.Y, Chen, T.: From Region Encoding to Extended Dewey: on Efficient Processing of XML Twig Pattern Matching. Proceedings of the 31st International Conference on Very Large Databases (VLDB), pp. 193–204, 2005.

[104] Makino, S., Tatsubori, M., Tamura, K. Yuichi, N.: Improving WS-Security Performance with a Template-Based Approach. Proceedings of the IEEE International Conference on Web Services, pp. 581–588, 2005.

[105] Makino, S., Tatsubori, M., Tamura, K., Nakamura, Y.: Improving WS-Security Performance with a Template-Based Approach. Proceedings of the IEEE International Conference on Web Services, pp. 581–588, 2005.

[106] McCarthy, J.: Reap the Benefits of Document Style Web Services. http://www.ibm.com/developerworks/webservices/library/ws-docstyle.html, 2002.

[107] Microsoft Corporation: .NET Compact Framework. http://msdn2.microsoft.com/en-us/netframework/aa497273.aspx, 2007.

[108] Microsoft Corporation: Web Service Enhancement. http://msdn2.microsoft.com/en-us/webservices/aa740663.aspx

[109] Milojicic, D.S., Douglis, F., Paindaveine, Y., Wheeler, R., Zhou, S.: Process Migration. ACM Comput. Survey, 32(3):241–299, 2000.

[110] Mitchell, R.: Web Services on Mobile Devices. http://itmanagement.earthweb.com/entdev/article.php/3612721, June 2006.

[111] Ng, A., Chen, S., Greenfield, P.: An Evaluation of Contemporary Commercial SOAP Implementations. Proceedings of the 5th Australasian Workshop on Software and System Architectures (AWSA), pp. 64–71, 2003.

[112] Oh, S., Lee, D., Kumara, S.: Web Service Planner (WSPR): An Effective and Scalable Web Service Composition Algorithm. International Journal of Web Services Research, 4(1):1-23, 2007.

[113] Oliveira, C., Pardalos, P., Resende, M.: Optimization Problems in Multicast Tree Construction. Handbook of Optimization in Telecommunications, Kluwer, 2005.

[114] Organization for the Advancement of Structured Information Standards (OASIS): UDDI. http://www.uddi.org/, 2006.

[115] Organization for the Advancement of Structured Information Standards (OASIS): Web Services Reliable Messaging TC: WS-Reliability 1.1. http://docs.oasis-open.org/wsrm/2004/06/WS-Reliability-CD1.086.pdf, 2004.

[116] Paul, P., Raghavan, S.: Survey of QoS Routing. Proceedings of the 15th International Conference on Computer Communication, pp. 50–75, 2002.

[117] Phan, K.H, Tari, Z., Bertok, T.: eSMP: A Multicast Protocol to Minimize SOAP Network Traffic in Low Bandwidth Environments. Proceedings of the 32th Annual IEEE Conference on Local Computer Networks (LCN), 2007.

[118] Radha, V., Gulati V., Pujari, A.: Efficient Multicast E-Services Over APPCAST. Proceedings of the IEEE International Conference on Information Technology: Coding and Computing, 2:331–338, 2004.

[119] Rai, I.A., Keller, G.U., Biersack, E.W.: Analysis of LAS Scheduling for Job Size Distributions with High Variance. SIGMETRICS Performance Evaluation Review, 31(1):218-228, 2003.

[120] Righter, R., ShanthiKumar, J.G.: On External Service Disciplines in Single-Stage Queueing Systems. Journal of Applied Probability, 27:409-416, 1990.

[121] Rong, B., Khalil, I., Tari, Z.: Reliability Enhanced Large-Scale Application Layer Multicast. Proceedings of the Global Telecommunications Conference (GLOBECOM), 2006.

[122] Ross, K., Kurose, J.: Connectionless Transport: UDP. http://www-net.cs.umass.edu/kurose/transport/UDP.html, 2000.

[123] Roy, A.: OSPF Version 2. Internet Engineering Task Force (IETF), RFC 1247, 1991. http://www.ietf.org/rfc/rfc1247.txt.

[124] Salama, H., Reeves, D.: Evaluation of Multicast Routing Algorithms for Real-Time Communication on High-Speed Networks. IEEE Journal on Selected Areas of Communication, 15(3):332-345, 1997.

[125] Shah, R., Ramzan, Z., Dendukuri, R.: Efficient Dissemination of Personalized Information Using Content-Based Multicast. IEEE Transactions on Mobile Computing, 3(4):394–408, 2004.

[126] Schrage, L. E.: The Queue M/G/1 with Feedback to Lower Priority Queues. Journal of Management Science, 13(7):466-474, 1967.

[127] Silberschatz, A., Galvin, P.B., Gagne, G.: Applied Operating Systems Concepts. Addison-Wesley, 1998.

[128] Shaikh, A., Shin, K.: Destination-Driven Routing for Low-Cost Multicast. IEEE Journal of Selected Areas in Communications, 15(3):373–381, 1997.

[129] Shin, M.K., Kim, Y.J., Park, K.S., and Kim, S.H.: Explicit Multicast Extension (Xcast+) for Efficient Multicast Packet Delivery. ETRI Journal, 23(4): 202–204, 2001.

[130] Suzumura, T., Takase, T., Tatsubori, M.: Optimizing Web Services Performance by Differential Deserialization. Proceedings of the IEEE International Conference on Web Services, pp. 185–192, 2005.

[131] Terry, D.B, Ramasubramanian, V.: Caching XML Web Services for Mobility. ACM Queue Journal, 1(3):70-78, 2003.

[132] Sun Microsystems Inc.: Java 2 Platform, Micro Edition - J2ME. http://java.sun.com/javame/index.jsp, 2004.

[133] Sun Microsystems Inc.: J2ME Web Services APIs (WSA). http://java.sun.com/products/wsa/, 2004.

[134] Sun Microsystems Inc.: Mobile Information Device Profile (MIDP). http://java.sun.com/products/midp, 2007.

[135] Sun Microsystems Inc.: Performance Code Samples and Applications. http://java.sun.com/performance/reference/codesamples/, 2004.

[136] Takase, T., Miyashita, H., Suzumura, T., Tatsubori, M.: An adaptive, Fast, and Safe XML Parser based on Byte Sequences Memorization. Proceedings of the 14th International Conference on World Wide Web (WWW) pp. 692–701, 2005.

[137] Takase, T., Tatsubori, M.: Efficient Web Services Response Caching by Selecting Optimal Data Representation. Proceedings of the 24th International Conference on Distributed Computing Systems (ICDCS), pp. 188–197, 2004.

[138] Tari, Z. and Broberg, J., Zomaya, A. Y., Baldoni, R.: A Least Flow-Time First Load Sharing Approach for Distributed Server Farm. Elsevier Journal of Parallel Distributed Computing (JPDC), 65(7): 832-842, 2005.

[139] Tari, Z., Bukhress, O.: Fundamentals of Distributed Object Systems. John Wiley, 2001.

[140] Tian, M., Voigt, T., Naumowicz, T., Ritter, H., Schiller, J.: Performance Considerations for Mobile Web Services. Elsevier Journal on Computer Communications, 27(11):1097–1105, 2004.

[141] Waxman, B.M.: Routing of Multiple Connections. IEEE Journal on Selected Areas in Communications, 6(9):1617–1622,1986.

[142] Weber, R.R.: On the Optimal Assignment of Customers to Parallel Servers. Journal of Applied Probability, 15(2):406–413, 1978.

[143] Werner, C., Buschmann, C. Fischer, F.: WSDL-Driven SOAP Compression. International Journal of Web Services Research, 2(1):18–35, 2005.

[144] Werner, C., Buschmann, C., Fischer, S.: Compressing SOAP Messages by using Differential Encoding. Proceedings of the IEEE International Conference on Web Services, 540–547, 2004.

[145] Werner, C., Buschmann, C., Fischer, F: WSDL-Driven SOAP Compression. Proceedings of International Journal of Web Services Research, 2(1):18–35, 2005.

[146] Whittle, S.: Case Study: Amazon Web Services. `http://www.computing.co.uk/computing/analysis/2193374/case-study-amazon-web-services`, July 2007.

[147] Williamson, C.: Internet Traffic Measurement. IEEE Internet Computing, 5(6):70-74, 2001.

[148] World Wide Web Consortium (W3C): WAP Binary XML Content Format. `http://www.w3.org/TR/wbxml/`, 1999.

[149] World Wide Web Consortium (W3C): Extensible Markup Language (XML). May 2007. `http://www.w3.org/XML/`.

[150] World Wide Web Consortium (W3C): SOAP Version 1.2 Part 2: Adjuncts. April 2007. `http://www.w3.org/TR/soap12-part2/`.

[151] World Wide Web Consortium (W3C): Web Services Addressing (WS-Addressing. `http://www.w3.org/Submission/ws-addressing/`, August 2004.

[152] Yashkov, S.F.: Processor-sharing Queues: Some Progress in Analysis. Journal of Queueing Systems: Theory and Applications, 2(1):1-17, 1987.

[153] Yuan, X.: Heuristics Algorthims for Multiconstrained Quality-of-Service Routing. IEEE/ACM Transactions on Networking, 10(2):244–256, 2002.

[154] Zhang, B., Jamin, S., Zhang, L.: Host multicast – A Framework for Delivering Multicast to End Users. Proceedings of the 21st Annual Joint Conference of the IEEE Computer and Communications (INFOCOM), 3: 1366–1375, 2002.

[155] Zhang, N., Agrawal, S.K., Ozsu, T.: BlossomTree: Evaluating XPaths in FLWOR Expressions. Proceedings of the 21st International Conference on Data Engineering (ICDE), pp. 388–389, 2005.

[156] Zhang, Q., Riska, A., Sun, W., Smirni, E., Ciardo, G.: Workload-Aware Load Balancing for Clustered Web Servers. IEEE Transactions on Parallel Distributed Systems (TPDS), 16(3):219-233, 2005.

[157] Zeephongsekul, P., Bedford, A.: Waiting Time Analysis of the Multiple Priority Dual Queue with a Preemptive Priority Service Discipline. European Journal of Operational Research, 172(3):886-908, 2006.

[158] Zhu, Q., Parsa, M., Garcia-Luna-Aceves, J.: A Source-Based Algorithm for Delay-Constrained Minimum Cost Multicasting. Proceedings of the IEEE Conference on Computer Communications, pp. 377–385, 1995.

[159] Zipf, G.K.: Human Behaviour and the Principle of Least-Effort. Addison-Wesley, 1949.

Appendix A

Appendix A (WSDL Specification for the Stock Quote Service)

```xml
<?xml version="1.0" encoding="UTF-8"?>
<wsdl:definitionsxmlns:http="http://schemas.xmlsoap.org/wsdl/http/"
        xmlns:soap="http://schemas.xmlsoap.org/wsdl/soap/"
        xmlns:s="http://www.w3.org/2001/XMLSchema"
        xmlns:soapenc="http://schemas.xmlsoap.org/soap/encoding/"
        xmlns:tns="http://localhost/"
        targetNamespace="http://localhost/"
        xmlns:wsdl="http://localhost/schema/wsdl/">
  <wsdl:types>
    <s:schema elementFormDefault="qualified"
            targetNamespace="http://localhost/">
      <s:element name="GetStockQuote" id="GSQ">
        <s:complexType>
          <s:sequence>
            <s:element minOccurs="0" maxOccurs="1"
              name="Symbol" type="s:string"/>
          </s:sequence>
        </s:complexType>
      </s:element>
      <s:element name="StockQuoteResponse" id="SQR">
        <s:complexType>
          <s:sequence>
            <s:element  minOccurs="0" maxOccurs="1"
              name="ArrayOfStockQuote"
              type="tns:ArrayOfStockQuote"/>
          </s:sequence>
        </s:complexType>
      </s:element>
  <s:element name="GetQuoteAndStatistic" id="GQAS">
        <s:complexType>
          <s:sequence>
            <s:element minOccurs="0" maxOccurs="1"
              name="Symbol" type="s:string"/>
          </s:sequence>
        </s:complexType>
      </s:element>
      <s:element name="QuoteAndStatisticResponse" id="QASR">
```

```
      <s:complexType>
        <s:sequence>
          <s:element minOccurs="0" maxOccurs="1"
            name="ArrayOfQuoteAndStatistic"
            type="tns:ArrayOfQuoteAndStatistic"/>
        </s:sequence>
      </s:complexType>
    </s:element>
<s:element name="GetFullQuote" id="GFQ">
      <s:complexType>
        <s:sequence>
          <s:element minOccurs="0" maxOccurs="1"
            name="Symbol" type="s:string"/>
        </s:sequence>
      </s:complexType>
    </s:element>
    <s:element name="FullQuoteResponse" id="GFQR">
      <s:complexType>
        <s:sequence>
          <s:element  minOccurs="0" maxOccurs="1"
            name="ArrayOfFullQuote"
            type="tns:ArrayOfFullQuote"/>
        </s:sequence>
      </s:complexType>
    </s:element>
   <s:element name="GetCompanyInfo" id="GCI">
      <s:complexType>
        <s:sequence>
          <s:element minOccurs="0" maxOccurs="1"
            name="Symbol" type="s:string"/>
        </s:sequence>
      </s:complexType>
    </s:element>
    <s:element name="CompanyInfoResponse" id="CIR">
      <s:complexType>
        <s:sequence>
          <s:element minOccurs="0" maxOccurs="1"
            name="ArrayOfCompanyInfo"
            type="tns:ArrayOfCompanyInfo"/>
        </s:sequence>
      </s:complexType>
    </s:element>
<s:element name="GetMarketInfo" id="GMI">
      <s:complexType>
        <s:sequence>
          <s:element minOccurs="0" maxOccurs="1"
            name="Symbol" type="s:string"/>
        </s:sequence>
      </s:complexType>
    </s:element>
    <s:element name="MarketInfoResponse" id="MIR">
      <s:complexType>
        <s:sequence>
          <s:element minOccurs="0" maxOccurs="1"
```

```
               name="ArrayOfMarketInfo"
               type="tns:ArrayOfMarketInfo"/>
        </s:sequence>
      </s:complexType>
    </s:element>
<s:simpleType name="Symbol" id ="Sbl">
    <s:restriction base="string">
     <s:length value="3"/>
    </s:restriction>
    </s:simpleType>
  <s:simpleType name="Price" id="P">
    <s:restriction base="string">
    </s:restriction>
    </s:simpleType>
<s:simpleType name="LastUpdated" id="LU">
    <s:restriction base="string">
    </s:restriction>
    </s:simpleType>
    <s:simpleType name="Change"  id ="Chg">
    <s:restriction base="string">
    </s:restriction>
    </s:simpleType>
<s:simpleType name="OpenPrice"  id ="OP">
    <s:restriction base="string">
    </s:restriction>
    </s:simpleType>
   <s:simpleType name="CompanyName" id ="CN">
    <s:restriction base="string">
    </s:restriction>
    </s:simpleType>
   <s:simpleType name="ExDividendDate"  id ="EDD">
    <s:restriction base="string">
    </s:restriction>
    </s:simpleType>
<s:simpleType name="DividendYield"  id ="DY">
    <s:restriction base="string">
    </s:restriction>
    </s:simpleType>
<s:simpleType name="Volume"  id ="Vol">
    <s:restriction base="string">
    </s:restriction>
    </s:simpleType>
   <s:simpleType name="DayHighPrice"  id ="DHP">
    <s:restriction base="string">
    </s:restriction>
    </s:simpleType>
<s:simpleType name="DayLowPrice"  id ="DLP">
    <s:restriction base="string">
    </s:restriction>
    </s:simpleType>
    <s:complexType name="ArrayOfStockQuote" id="AOSQ">
     <s:sequence>
       <s:element minOccurs="0" maxOccurs="unbounded"
            name="StockQuote"
```

```
            type="tns:StockQuote"/>
      </s:sequence>
  </s:complexType>
  <s:complexType name="ArrayOfQuoteAndStatistic" id="AOQS">
    <s:sequence>
      <s:element minOccurs="0" maxOccurs="unbounded"
          name="QuoteAndStatistic"
          type="tns:QuoteAndStatistic"/>
    </s:sequence>
  </s:complexType>
  <s:complexType name="ArrayOfFullQuote" id="AOFQ">
    <s:sequence>
      <s:element minOccurs="0" maxOccurs="unbounded"
          name="FullQuote"
          type="tns:FullQuote"/>
    </s:sequence>
  </s:complexType>
  <s:complexType name="ArrayOfCompanyInfo" id="AOCI">
    <s:sequence>
      <s:element minOccurs="0" maxOccurs="unbounded"
          name="ComapnyInfo"
          type="tns:ComapnyInfo"/>
    </s:sequence>
  </s:complexType>
  <s:complexType name="ArrayOfMarketInfo" id="AOMI">
    <s:sequence>
      <s:element minOccurs="0" maxOccurs="unbounded"
          name="MarketInfo"
          type="tns:MarketInfo"/>
    </s:sequence>
  </s:complexType>
  <s:complexType name="StockQuote" id="SQ">
    <s:sequence>
      <s:element minOccurs="0" maxOccurs="1"
          name="Symbol" type="tns:Symbol"/>
      <s:element minOccurs="0" maxOccurs="1"
          name="QuoteInfo" type="tns:QuoteInfo"/>
    </s:sequence>
  </s:complexType>
  <s:complexType name="QuoteAndStatistic" id="QAS">
    <s:sequence>
      <s:element minOccurs="0" maxOccurs="1"
          name="Symbol" type="tns:Symbol"/>
      <s:element minOccurs="0" maxOccurs="1"
          name="QuoteInfo" type="tns:QuoteInfo"/>
      <s:element minOccurs="0" maxOccurs="1"
          name="Statistic" type="tns:Statistic"/>
    </s:sequence>
  </s:complexType>
  <s:complexType name="FullQuote" id="FQ">
    <s:sequence>
      <s:element minOccurs="0" maxOccurs="1"
          name="Symbol" type="tns:Symbol"/>
      <s:element minOccurs="0" maxOccurs="1"
```

```
                name="QuoteInfo" type="tns:QuoteInfo"/>
        <s:element minOccurs="0" maxOccurs="1"
            name="Statistic" type="tns:Statistic"/>
        <s:element minOccurs="0" maxOccurs="1"
            name="CompanyInfo" type="tns:CompanyInfo"/>
      </s:sequence>
    </s:complexType>
    <s:complexType name="QuoteInfo" id="QI">
      <s:sequence>
        <s:element minOccurs="0" maxOccurs="1"
            name="Price" type="tns:Price"/>
        <s:element minOccurs="0" maxOccurs="1"
            name="LastUpdated" type="tns:LastUpdated"/>
      </s:sequence>
    </s:complexType>
    <s:complexType name="Statistic" id="Stt">
      <s:sequence>
        <s:element minOccurs="0" maxOccurs="1"
            name="Change" type="tns:Change"/>
        <s:element minOccurs="0" maxOccurs="1"
            name="OpenPrice" type="tns:OpenPrice"/>
      </s:sequence>
    </s:complexType>
    <s:complexType name="CompanyInfo" id="CI">
      <s:sequence>
        <s:element minOccurs="0" maxOccurs="1"
            name="Symbol" type="tns:Symbol"/>
        <s:element minOccurs="0" maxOccurs="1"
            name="CompanyName" type="tns:CompanyName"/>
        <s:element minOccurs="0" maxOccurs="1"
            name="ExDividendDate"
            type="tns:ExDividendDate"/>
        <s:element minOccurs="0" maxOccurs="1"
            name="DividendYield"
            type="tns:DividendYield"/>
      </s:sequence>
    </s:complexType>
    <s:complexType name="MarketInfo" id="MI">
      <s:sequence>
        <s:element minOccurs="0" maxOccurs="1"
            name="Symbol" type="tns:Symbol"/>
        <s:element minOccurs="0" maxOccurs="1"
            name="Volume" type="tns:Volume"/>
        <s:element minOccurs="0" maxOccurs="1"
            name="DayHighPrice"
            type="tns:DayHighPrice"/>
        <s:element minOccurs="0" maxOccurs="1"
            name="DayLowPrice" type="tns:DayLowPrice"/>
      </s:sequence>
    </s:complexType>
    <s:element name="ArrayOfStockQuote"
            nillable="true" type="tns:ArrayOfStockQuote"/>
<s:element name="ArrayOfQuoteAndStatistic"
            nillable="true"
```

```
                    type="tns:ArrayOfQuoteAndStatistic"/>
  <s:element name="ArrayOfFullQuote"
                    nillable="true" type="tns:ArrayOfFullQuote"/>
   <s:element name="ArrayOfCompanyInfo"
                    nillable="true" type="tns:ArrayOfCompanyInfo"/>
    <s:element name="ArrayOfMarketInfo"
                    nillable="true" type="tns:ArrayOfMarketInfo"/>
   </s:schema>
 </wsdl:types>
 <wsdl:message name="GetStockQuoteSoapIn">
   <wsdl:part name="parameters" element="tns:GetStockQuote"/>
 </wsdl:message>
 <wsdl:message name="GetStockQuoteSoapOut">
   <wsdl:part name="parameters"
                   element="tns:StockQuotesResponse"/>
 </wsdl:message>
 <wsdl:message name="GetStockQuoteHttpGetIn">
   <wsdl:part name="Symbol" type="s:string"/>
 </wsdl:message>
 <wsdl:message name="GetStockQuoteHttpGetOut">
   <wsdl:part name="Body" element="tns:ArrayOfStockQuote"/>
 </wsdl:message>
 <wsdl:message name="GetStockQuotesHttpPostIn">
   <wsdl:part name="Symbol" type="s:string"/>
 </wsdl:message>
 <wsdl:message name="GetStockQuotesHttpPostOut">
   <wsdl:part name="Body" element="tns:ArrayOfStockQuote"/>
 </wsdl:message>
 <wsdl:portType name="StockQuoteSoap">
   <wsdl:operation name="GetStockQuote">
     <wsdl:input name="GetStockQuote"
                message="tns:GetStockQuoteSoapIn"/>
     <wsdl:output name="GetStockQuote"
                message="tns:GetStockQuoteSoapOut"/>
   </wsdl:operation>
 </wsdl:portType>
 <wsdl:binding name="StockQuoteSoap"
                type="tns:StockQuoteSoap">
   <soap:bindingtransport="http://schemas.xmlsoap.org/soap/http"
                style="document"/>
   <wsdl:operation name="GetStockQuote">
     <soap:operation soapAction="http://localhost/StockQuote"
                style="document"/>
     <wsdl:input name="GetStockQuote">
       <soap:body use="literal"/>
     </wsdl:input>
     <wsdl:output name="GetQuotes">
       <soap:body use="literal"/>
     </wsdl:output>
   </wsdl:operation>
 </wsdl:binding>
 <wsdl:service name="StockQuote">
   <wsdl:port name="StockQuoteSoap"
                binding="tns:StockQuoteSoap">
```

```
        <soap:address location="http://localhost/StockQuote"/>
      </wsdl:port>
    </wsdl:service>
</wsdl:definitions>
```

Appendix B
Appendix B (SMP Message Schema)

```
<xs:schema
 xmlns:xs="http://www.w3.org/2001/XMLSchema">
 <xs:element name="SMP:Header" type="SMPHeaderType"/>
 <xs:element name="SMP:Body" type="SMPBodyType"/>
 <xs:complexType name="SMPHeaderType">
  <xs:sequence>
   <!-- indexing the address of a client -->
   <xs:element name="c" type="cType"/>
  </xs:sequence>
 </xs:complexType>
 <xs:complexType name="cType">
  <!-- the index id of the client-->
  <xs:attribute name="id" type="xs:unsignedInt" use="required"/>
   <!-- the actual address of the client in the network -->
  <xs:attribute name="uri" type="xs:string" use="required"/>
 </xs:complexType>
 <xs:complexType name="SMPBodyType">
  <xs:sequence>
   <xs:element name="Common" type="CommonType"/>
   <xs:element name="Distinctive" type="DistType"/>
  </xs:sequence>
 </xs:complexType>
 <xs:complexType name="CommonType">
  <xs:sequence>
   <xs:element name="part" type="partType"
                     maxOccurs="unbounded"/>
  </xs:sequence>
 </xs:complexType>
 <xs:complexType name="partType">
   <xs:attribute name="id" type="xs:string" use="optional"/>
   <!-- refer to another part defined elsewhere -->
   <xs:attribute name="refer" type="xs:string" use="optional"/>
   <xs:sequence>
   <!-- This element stores the tag value -->
   <xs:element name="v" type="vType" minOccurs="0"
                     maxOccurs="unbounded"/>
   </xs:sequence>
```

```xml
</xs:complexType>
<xs:complexType name="vType">
  <!-- refer to an element id defined in the WSDL -->
  <xs:attribute name="eRef" type="xs:string" use="required"/>
  <!-- actual value of a tag, which can be empty-->
  <xs:attribute name="val" type="xs:string" use="optional"/>
</xs:complexType>
<xs:complexType name="DistType">
 <xs:sequence>
  <xs:element name="DPart" type="DPartType" minOccurs="0"
                       maxOccurs="unbounded"/>
 </xs:sequence>
</xs:complexType>
<xs:complexType name="DPartType">
 <xs:sequence>
  <!-- the node position for specified clients-->
  <xs:element name="cPos" type="cPosType"
                       maxOccurs="unbounded"/>
 </xs:sequence>
</xs:complexType>
<xs:complexType name="cPosType">
 <!-- the list of client indices-->
 <xs:attribute name="Ids" type="xs:string" use="required"/>
  <!-- the position of a node in messages addressed to the clients -->
 <xs:attribute name="pos" type="xs:string" use="required"/>
</xs:complexType></xs:schema>
```

Appendix C
Appendix C (A Sample SMP Message)

An SMP Message, called SMP_2, which aggregates $Soap_1$, $Soap_3$ and $Soap_4$ messages, is shown below.

```
<soap:Envelope>
 <soap:Header>
  Next-hop router's address
 </soap:Header>
 <soap:Body>
  <SMP:Header>
   <c id='1', uri='URI1'/>
   <c id='2', uri='URI2'/>
   <c id='3', uri='URI3'/>
  </SMP:Header>
  <SMP:Body>
   <Distinctive>
    <DPart>
      <cPos cIds ='1,2' pos='0'/>
      <part refer='p1'/>
    </DPart>
    <DPart>
      <cPos cIds ='1' pos='1'/>
      <part>
       <v eRef= 'AOSQ' val='2'/>
      <part/>
    </DPart>
    <DPart>
      <cPos cIds ='2' pos='1'/>
      <part>
       <v eRef= 'AOSQ' val='3'/>
      <part/>
    </DPart>
    <DPart>
      <cPos cIds ='1,2' pos='2.1'/>
      <part refer='p2'/>
    </DPart>
    <DPart>
      <cPos cIds ='1' pos='2.2'>
```

```
        <cPos cIds ='2' pos='2.3'>
        <part refer='p3'>
     </DPart>
     <DPart>
      <cPos cIds ='1' pos='2.2'>
      <cPos cIds ='2' pos='2.3'>
      <part Id='p3'>
        <v eRef='SQ' val=''/>
        <v eRef='Sbl' val='BHP'/>
        <v eRef='QI' val=''/>
        <v eRef='P' val='24.52'/>
        <v eRef='LU' val='24/01/2007 10:45am'/>
      </part>
     </DPart>
     <DPart>
       <cPos cIds ='2' pos='2.2'>
       <part Id='p4'>
        <v eRef='SQ' val=''/>
        <v eRef='Sbl' val='WIL'/>
        <v eRef='QI' val=''/>
        <v eRef='P' val='1.29'/>
        <v eRef='LU' val='24/01/2007 10:45am'/>
       </part>
     </DPart>
    </Distinctive>
  <Common>
      <part Id='p1'>
        <v  eRef= 'SQR' val=''/>
      </part>
      <part Id='p2'>
        <v  eRef= 'SQ' val=''/>
        <v  eRef= 'Sbl'  val='NAB'/>
        <v eRef='QI' val=''/>
        <v  eRef='P' val='28.56'/>
        <v eRef='LU' val='24/01/2007 10:15am'/>
      </part>
   </Common>
  </SMP:Body>
 </soap:Body>
</soap:Envelope>
```

.

CPSIA information can be obtained at www.ICGtesting.com
Printed in the USA
LVOW090234150212

268752LV00004B/75/P